BACKPACKING: One Step at a Time

BACKPACKING
One Step at a Time

By HARVEY MANNING

Foreword by Jim Whittaker
Cartoons by Bob Cram
Photos by Keith Gunnar

VINTAGE BOOKS

A Division of Random House • New York

VINTAGE BOOKS EDITION, MAY 1973, REVISED 1975
Copyright © 1972, 1975 by Recreational Equipment Inc.,
1525 11th Avenue, Seattle, Washington 98122

Library of Congress Cataloging in Publication Data

Manning, Harvey.
  Backpacking, one step at a time.

  Bibliography: p.
  1. Backpacking. I. Title.
GV199.6.M36 1975   796.5   75–8528
ISBN 0–394–72033–4

FOREWORD

BACKPACKING, camping, and mountaineering have grown tremendously in popularity since I came to Recreational Equipment in 1955, especially during the past 5 years. As one measure, REI's 1971 *increase* in sales over the previous year was more than its *total* sales in 1967, which could be interpreted to mean that more *new* people got out on the trails and into the mountains in 1971 than *all* the people who were there in 1967.

For another example, my brother and I operated the guide service on Mount Rainier from 1949 to 1952. In 1951, 291 persons reached the summit. In 1971, 2,149 climbers made the top! In our era the garbage at 10,000-foot Camp Muir amounted to so little it was jettisoned without qualms in the nearest crevasse, and the single privy precariously overhanging the Cowlitz Glacier handled every visitor. Now the guides backpack 60-pound loads of garbage down from Muir twice a week and at least once every 3 weeks helicopters haul away the remainder, plus the 50-gallon containers that support the four latrines.

The population explosion on Rainier's high rock and ice, which obviously can stand a lot of punishment, has been more than matched in meadows and valleys which are nowhere near as tough, in fact are

v

very fragile, and are in danger of being crushed by masses of backpackers and campers. Generally speaking, the forests of America have abundant capacity to absorb more hikers. However, the delicate ecosystems of alpine parklands, desert oases, ocean dunes, lakeshores, marshes, riverbanks, and the like are everywhere threatened.

We must lessen the impact of the human animal on the trail country, the wilderness. One way is by education. We must teach people to be as unobtrusive as possible. Use small backpacking stoves instead of building fires from the natural wood, dip the water out of lakes and streams to wash in rather than using soap in those lakes or streams, locate in established campsites, stay on man-made or game trails, pack out all garbage, take only pictures and leave only footprints. An alternative is to limit the number of people who walk the trails, climb the mountains — a last resort, in my opinion, believing as I do with Thoreau that "in wildness is the preservation of the world." Personally, I could not discourage anyone from backpacking, camping, climbing; the experiences thus gained meet too basic a need, and for evidence we must simply look at the youths of today who have rejected the philosophy of materialism and have gone back to nature.

I think the need exists even where it is not recognized or expressed. Throughout our nation there are children of the inner city who never have known any "valleys" but avenues with paved floors and concrete walls, any "mountains" but skyscrapers of glass and aluminum. If we can lead them into natural valleys and mountains and teach them how to be comfortable there, so they can grow and expand in an environment which even when hostile is fair, so they can feel the freedom of wild places, high places, then I think they will learn to enjoy, perhaps love, and surely respect nature, and realize all things natural — including themselves — are beautiful. With John Muir I say: "Climb the mountains and get their good tidings; Nature's peace will flow into you as sunshine into flowers; The winds will blow their freshness into you and the storms their energy, and cares will drop off like autumn leaves."

I will never forget a moment on Mount Everest in 1963. On May 22 we began our long descent from the basecamp established on March 21, having been more than 60 days above 17,500 feet, entirely in the realm of snow, ice, and rock. Coming down the Khumbu Glacier we left the ice at last, walked onto moraine, then down to Gorak Shep. Nine years later, one of my most vivid recollections of Everest is that startling vision of small green plants, and that incredible odor of warm, musty earth. Several days on Rainier or any other peak rising far above timberline gives a similar sensation. I wish everyone could know the feeling.

I feel we must teach the new climbers, campers, and backpackers to travel carefully and considerately, to fit unobtrusively into the landscape, to remember they are part of nature and any damage they do is — in the end — to themselves.

JIM WHITTAKER

CERTAIN of my lonesomeness-loving old companions of the trails, hearing this book was contemplated, expressed the opinion that with an estimated 20,000,000 Americans already having tried backpacking the real need was not another invitation to the sport but a lot more grizzly bears, mosquitoes, and blowdowns. The back country is being mangled by humanity, they complained, and many a sylvan scene we once enjoyed in solitude now offers all the amenities of the Black Hole of Calcutta.

True enough, I replied, but that is precisely the most compelling reason for the book. First off, the worst mangling is by machines, the bulldozers of mindless exploiters and the trailbikes and snowmobiles and all-terrain-vehicles of idiot recreationists whose souls are in their buttocks. The nation needs more footpower to turn back the advance of motorpower. Second, the hikers we seek to recruit as neo-Luddites, as friends of the Earth, must themselves reduce their impact by renouncing the ways of the wily woodcrafter, by walking lightly, respectfully, by subscribing wholeheartedly and passionately to the "new ethic."

But to do so, I continued, hikers must know the land-saving potential of modern equipment, and that is the other reason for the book, which gives rather short shrift to lore and helpful hints and concentrates on how to assemble an outfit that makes backpacking ridiculously simple *and* allows a good environmental conscience.

Sounds fine, said my misanthropic friends, but the message never will reach the ax-wielders and can-tossers because they don't read PACK IT OUT signs at trailheads, much less books, and even literate veterans look into hiking manuals only to sneer at the blunders. Granted, said I. Though there is much here of value to oldtimers who haven't realized the need for the new ethic and haven't kept up with rapid advances in equipment design, the primary audience is beginners. The old generation probably is irretrievably corrupt and damned anyway. The future must be built by the new.

A final objection — wildland travel can't be learned from a book! Agreed, said I. Our humble intent is to inculcate an attitude. The trails must do the real teaching — but preferably supplemented by human tutors, and thus the beginner is urged to join a hiking-camping-mountaineering-conservation organization.

The reasons for the book having been explained, a little should be said about its credentials.

After years of camping trips with my folks starting before I can remember, in 1938, as a Boy Scout, I hoisted pack on back and was introduced to the wilderness of brandnew Olympic National Park. In 1948 the Climbing Course of The Mountaineers led me to seasons of bagging peaks — mostly in the Cascades and Olympics, a few in the Canadian Rockies and Selkirks and Coast Range. My bookmaking began as chairman of the editorial committee which in 1960 produced the first edition of *Mountaineering: The Freedom of the Hills.*

The annual bag of tough summits dwindled as children arrived and grew, but trail-tramping and cross-country rambling continue, in the company of little kids and eccentric old friends.

Except for a childhood year in New England woods, some weeks in the High Sierra, and a scattering of brief visits elsewhere my personal pedestrianism has been entirely in the Northwest — ocean beaches and alpine gardens, coastal jungles and rainshadow semi-deserts, low valleys and high ridges, glaciers and tall heaps of rock.

If my qualifications and limitations as a provincial, opinionated, freaky veteran of rain-forest, alder-tangle, misty-meadow wilderness are judged unsatisfactory it doesn't matter. The unique credentials of the book come from the men and women of REI who since the founding of the "Co-op" in 1938 have hiked, backpacked, and climbed throughout the American West, from Alaska and Canada to Mexico and Peru, in Europe from the Alps to the Soviet Union, and to the summit of Mount Everest, and who in the course of serving hundreds of thousands of REI customers have absorbed their experience as well.

The following members of the REI staff participated in the planning sessions, seminars, and manuscript critiques that extended over the best part of a year: Bill Alma, Miriam Bishop, Bill Bourgault, George Brown, Alice Calloway, Del Carlino, Dave Chantler, John Collum, Vern Farmer, Joe Ganz, Steve Harder, Steve Hempelmann, Greg Houston, Walt Huber, Toly Kojev, Rick Kube, Dale Lanz, Gary Rose, Mike Ryan, Wally Smith, Bob Stadshaug, John Waldrop, Jim Wall, Ted Wolfrum, and Jim Wood. John Hartsfield and George Trager of THAW Corporation were most helpful on the subject of sleeping bags. Steve Hempelmann acted as manuscript coordinator, attending to a host of details necessary to keep things moving. Mike Reddy assisted in many ways, as did Ken Blaker and dozens of other people around the shop whose enthusiasm and encouragement made me feel like one of the family during the months I lived among and harassed them. Jim Whittaker conceived the idea of the book, reviewed the manuscript at every stage, and provided the constant support essential to maintain momentum.

In writing the text I mined not only the thousands of hiker-years of REI experience but that of some 35 other American retailers and manufacturers, from whose catalogs I freely appropriated useful data and expert opinion. I hope backpacker suppliers who approve of the book (or don't) will comment on the present text so future editions can be improved.

The contributions of Keith Gunnar as photographer, Bob Cram as cartoonist, and Bill James as designer speak eloquently for themselves; cross-fertilization of ideas enlivened our happy working relationship.

In conclusion I wish to thank all my freaky, creaky companions in hillwalking, but most especially Tom Miller, Pat and Ira Spring, Peggy Ferber, and goodwife Betty Manning for reading the manuscript and adding through their comments (counting families) another 200-odd man-years, woman-years, and children-years of wildland wisdom, or whatever. And again Peggy Ferber, who for 16 years has been taking the swamps of my manuscripts and typing them up neat and tidy.

From all of us to all of you: walk in joy, friends. Take only pictures, leave only footprints.

HARVEY MANNING

Time having passed and much of what I wrote 3 years ago having been rendered obsolete by the incessant tinkering of backpacking equipment designers, once more I descended upon the REI staff to badger their wisdom out of them. A dozen veterans of the first effort (named above) again participated in the brainstorming, joined for this second round by Mike Dwyer, Pat Egan, Greg Fuller, Dan Graves, Diana Jagersky, Scott Jouppi, Cal Magnusson, Bill Marts, and others. Mysteries of sleeping bags and insulated clothing were further unraveled for me by Dan Newman of Farwest Garments and Steve Kline of THAW, of bags and packs and tents by John Pollock of Jan Sport, of boots by Dave Page.

As before, I studied mountain shop catalogs from around the nation, plus articles in the backpacker-mountaineer magazines noted in the Appendix.

Finally I would like to thank the hundreds of readers from Maine to Florida, Michigan to Texas, Arizona to Alaska, who wrote letters pointing to my errors and offering the benefit of their experience on the trails. Keep those cards and letters coming, folks.

H.M.

CONTENTS

Contents

Part One

OFF AND AWAY ONTO THE TRAIL

<table>
<tr>
<td>

1:

</td>
<td>

HOW TO WALK

</td>
</tr>
</table>

PEOPLE not so very old can remember when nearly every American was an expert walker, traveling by foot to work and school, taking morning constitutionals and evening strolls, idling away Sunday afternoons on park paths or country lanes.

Nowadays, however, few urban and suburban folk know more than rudiments of the technique and their skills tend to deteriorate after childhood as they grow progressively more dependent on motorized transport. To be sure, just about everyone moves about by leg power to some extent, but generally awkwardly and unhappily. City walking is too disjointed—from one stoplight to another, from parking lot into supermarket—to develop a decent rhythm. Further, concrete is so punishing to feet and legs that pain quickly overwhelms pleasure. And in our squeaky-clean culture the prejudice against sweat gives pedestrianism the reputation of being nasty and brutish —not to forget that in some areas the mere fact of being afoot is considered prima facie evidence of un-Americanism and criminal intent.

Nevertheless, any person not physically disabled can readily master the refinements even if his longest previous foot journey has been from subway station to office-building elevator. No instruction is necessary, nor any patronizing manual stuffed with technical nonsense on how to point the feet and bend the knees; to learn to walk well one simply goes walking.

The major obstacles are mental. The beginner may be alarmed by a new awareness of heart, lungs, and muscles and imagine he is at the point of death. Also, after years of swift motion the slow passage of the landscape may lead to a sense of futility.

The following discussion, therefore, contains little about mechanics and for the most part concentrates on attitude; the intent is to help the beginner overcome superstitions and enjoy an easy and pleasant transition from enslavement by machines to the freedom of the trails.

PACE

How fast a pace is too fast? Too slow? Just right?

Manuals often declare 2 miles an hour is the proper rate for such-and-such circumstances and 3 mph or 4 for others, and that 1000 feet of elevation gain per hour is socially respectable if not quite

admirable. All such wise pronouncements by the masters should be ignored; there are too many variations among individuals, and among trails, for any rules to be meaningful. A small child may do well to toddle half a mile an hour while a troop of competitive boys are running 5 miles. Gaining 500 feet of elevation an hour may destroy a hiker wheezing after a long winter at a desk; athletes may climb 3000 feet an hour with neither huff nor puff.

Travel times given by guidebooks must be viewed with suspicion. One widely-distributed guide has been published by an egomaniac whose clear intent is to humiliate all who follow in his path. Another was written by two hill-hardened geologists whose legs separate just below the neck. At best a guide inevitably is hung up on the elusive "average." Average *what?* A hiker must test each book individually, comparing his own times on sample trips with those stipulated, and in this manner find a personal conversion factor.

How fast a hiker *can* go is one thing; how fast he *wants* to go is another. Some find joy whizzing through wildlands, jotting in their journals: "Made it from Bug Bog to Blister Pass in 3 hours 7 minutes flat—18½ minutes better than my previous best and possibly a new record." To each his own. Racers don't hurt anyone except competitors gnashing teeth because their best time from Bug to Blister is 3½ hours.

Most hikers, though, aren't out to set records but rather to enjoy

the full walk, admiring trees and flowers and birds and waterfalls along the way. The most pleasurable pace thus is somewhat or considerably slower than the maximum. (Of course, when darkness is near and the goal distant, or black clouds of flies gather for the kill, the rule is to say the heck with fun and *run*. Or at least stagger as rapidly as possible.)

Part One: Off and Away Onto the Trail

SETTING THE PACE

The beginner must realize that contrary to what he may have heard the aim of the sport is not to expiate sins by self-flagellation. If trails were unrelieved ordeals few would object to abandoning them to motorcycle gangs — and many are objecting most strenuously to this contemporary plague.

Legs and lungs and heart are the instruments for setting the proper pace. When legs feel leaden—slow down. When lungs seem about to burst into flame—slow down. When the heart is battering the ribs — slow down. When a chipmunk by the path dispels all consciousness of legs and lungs and heart the pace is just right.

Comfort is important not merely for its own sake but because only a tolerable pace can be sustained. The erratic dash-and-drop tactics characteristic of novices — going at top speed until completely breathless, stumbling to a gasping halt, then returning to all-out attack — are a constant misery and over the long haul slower than a steady plod.

The first stretch of trail should be taken at a deliberate loiter; the body, slothful from sleeping bag or car, complains less if introduced gradually to the task at hand. Speed automatically increases to the individual optimum as muscles loosen and juices begin to flow free and easy; often there is a sensation of "second wind," indicating the system has gotten it all together.

HOW LONG A WALK?

The beginner, while experimenting to see how fast he can walk comfortably, must also find how far he can walk, taking into account not only mileage but elevation gain — 5 miles with a rise of 5000 feet ordinarily demand more energy than 15 miles on the flat.

Each hiker must learn his own potential and adjust ambitions to match. One may cover 20 miles a day, or gain 6000 feet, with ease; another may struggle to make 5 miles or 1500 feet, or 2 miles or 500 feet. When personal abilities are defined future trips can be planned accordingly, keeping in mind the beauty part — that the more one walks, the farther and faster one can walk.

Some hikers love traversing great distances in a grand rush, rambling a dozen or two miles in a day to experience a wildland unity — "the One that remains while the Many change and pass." Others are content with several miles a day, lingering over fine details of rocks and springs and mosses. Both ways are good; the choice is up to the individual.

A related matter is how many *hours* a hiker can travel in a day, regardless of pace. Fresh from a city desk a person may not be able to stand erect, much less move, more than 4 or 5 hours; a trail-toughened veteran may lift 'em up and lay 'em down 10 or 12 consecutive hours with no pain, or 16 or 20 when seized by the mood.

WATER, FOOD, AND SALT

Water is as essential to life as air; at rest the normal adult may require 2 quarts a day, more when working hard. In desert travel 4 quarts a day is a commonly recommended ration. Except in deserts death by dehydration is a rare threat, but not debilitation — the average body is reduced in efficiency 25 percent by losing 1½ quarts of water, and during strenuous activity in hot weather this much can be sweated out in an hour.

The old Puritan formula was to suck prune pits or pebbles, on the theory that excessive drinking endangers the soul. With booze maybe, but not water. Except in areas where pollution is a problem the hiker should sample every tempting spring and creek and even in wet country carry a loaded canteen in case the dry spells are long. To be sure, moderation is the rule: gulping too much cold water can shock the stomach; also, dumping pounds of liquid into the body at one fill-up may require an extended rest while the bloated tank empties into the bloodstream.

Similarly, nibbling a snowball while walking a high, hot ridge — slowly, of course, to avoid "ice cream headache" — can prevent a blazing sun from shriveling the brain.

During hard hiking lunch should be an all-day meal, consumed in small, frequent installments to provide a steady flow of fuel without overloading the stomach. Weariness tends to kill the appetite, leading to a vicious cycle of deeper weariness, less appetite. Though the thought of food may be loathesome, the tired hiker should take a bit of candy, a sip of fruit juice; the shot of quick calories often miraculously revitalizes a depleted system by almost instantly raising the level of blood sugar. (However, a sudden *excess* of sweets can in some people trigger a complex physiological reaction in which the blood-sugar level is actually lowered.)

When sweating heavily a person should swallow a salt tablet or two every several hours to avoid symptoms of salt deficiency; these may be sudden and disastrous, such as severe headache, nausea, or disabling leg cramps; they may also be subtle and unnoticed, such as generalized weakness. The salt should be taken with water and preferably food. However, for older people especially, too much salt may pose other dangers; when in doubt a physician should be consulted.

UPHILL

Rambling happily along the flat is easy enough — when the trail turns upward, that's the beginning of the time of testing.

Physically speaking the secret of success is meeting steepness with slowness, constantly adjusting the pace to maintain uniformly-com-

fortable energy output, heeding signals from legs and lungs and heart. For very steep grades and weary hours the *rest step* combines mental discipline with robot regularity: (1) one foot advances; (2) motion halts momentarily while the forward leg rests, unweighted, knee bent, the body entirely supported by the rear leg with knee locked; (3) the rear foot advances to rest. Occasionally as low as 7000 feet and commonly above 9000 feet, oxygen shortage may cause *mountain sickness,* the symptoms including lack of appetite, nausea, and generalized debilitation and despair. The cure is to breathe more, using the rest step and at each pause taking a deep breath or two.

Deterioration of the spirit often is the major uphill hazard. Hope dwindles as the ridge crest seems to remain as far above in afternoon as it was in morning, impossibly remote. Panic may lead to assault tactics, but as each dash ends in gasping collapse the apparent certainty of final defeat erodes the will. Despair is intensified by boredom; one may grow terribly sick of any single tree which mocks the sluggish pace by its continued presence. The answer is to forget the impossible ridge, ignore the mocking tree, and retreat into an inner revery about the complexities of world politics, the problem of good and evil, how to defend against a knight's attack when two pawns down.

At last the best energies are spent and still the path relentlessly climbs and the sun falls. What now? Cry a little perhaps, but better shift gears further down, grind out a step at a time, and sink deeper

into thoughts of other times, other places.

In the extremity think no farther ahead than some easily achievable objective. Decide, for example, "I will walk exactly 20 minutes and sit down," and be sustained by anticipation of a chunk of candy and a swallow of water. Or, "I will take exactly 200 steps and stop for a breather." Or, "I will go to that boulder, then decide if I can continue or must lay my bones down, nevermore to rise again."

DOWNHILL

Downhill travel is simpler than uphill, as witness a falling rock. However, though some muscles and organs can pretty much relax, on a steep and rough trail other parts of the body take their lumps.

One alternative, typical of the young, is a semi-run, letting gravity have its way; but the jolt of each hard landing may reverberate up the spine and hit the head like a club.

The other method, favored by older folk, is patient restraint; but the knees, in holding back body weight, may become as loose as a rag doll.

And it is on the downhill that blisters blossom. Before beginning a sustained drop, boots should be laced tight, perhaps a pair of socks added. The first sensation of hot spots on soles or toes demands an instant halt for repairs (see Chapter 8).

REST STOPS

Walking is two separate and equally important actions—moving and not moving. Rest stops do not in themselves advance a party toward its destination but are an integral part of the long day's journey—and at least half the fun.

Manuals are full of rules: one expert declares a stop is mandatory every 40 minutes, lasting precisely 2 minutes—he also forbids hikers to sit down! Rules are fine and resting by the clock and marching by the whistle is appropriate en route to battle; civilians generally prefer walking in a less well-organized fashion.

Particularly with a party of any size a halt usually is necessary in the first half-hour for relacing boots, shedding sweaters, adjusting pack straps, and taking private trips in the woods.

Beyond that there is no formula for the frequency of rests. At the start, while fresh, many hikers like to charge forward an hour or two without pause to get a few miles under the boots in a hurry. An interval of 30-40 minutes is more typical, and near the end of a hard day, 15-20 minutes. A person who must stop every 5-10 minutes should try a slower pace. But when time is plentiful each waterfall, overlook, and boulder-perched marmot demands its due—these, after all, are what the hike is about.

Neither is there any formula for duration of rests. A party on a tight schedule must be content mainly with efficiency stops of several minutes and resume walking before muscles cool and blood slows. Another party, under no pressure, may pause a half-hour or more in scenes so enchanting they permit no shorter stay.

In early hours, with the entire day's task yet to be done, hikers tend to rest briefly. In late hours of a tough slog they commonly go down like falling trees and lie inert as logs until moss begins to grow on their boots. At any hour a standing breather lets legs and lungs and heart catch up with past over-exertion in preparation for resuming the journey at a more respectful pace.

Morning, noon, or evening, after a very long rest hikers should go gently a bit, just as at the start of the trip, while muscles re-loosen and the heart works back up to speed.

Stops are so important a part of the trip they should, whenever possible, be selected carefully. That is, if a rest will be wanted some-time soon, it is well not to collapse in a swamp but totter on to a bubbling creek, a splendid view, a field of flowers, a patch of cool shade, or whatever delights the way offers.

SOCIAL PROBLEMS

The complexity of walking increases geometrically with the size of the party, as Napoleon realized on the retreat from Moscow. Just as he finally abandoned the Grand Army, many problems can be avoided by traveling in small groups.

The lone hiker, of course, has no social difficulties at all, but lacks companionship and significantly increases his exposure to danger.

The etiquette of social hiking reduces to simply thinking about the other fellow. For example, a swift walker who crowds the heels ahead may lose a friend—or on a brushy trail suffer the retaliating dis-courtesy of willow whips released in his face without warning. By the same token a slow walker should not frustrate friends by hogging the centerline but step graciously aside and wave them on with a smile. The dozens more rules that could be stated are adequately covered by the Golden Rule.

Strangers met on the trail deserve the same consideration—unless they are riding motorbikes, in which case the proper response is every manner of hostility short of lynching.

Marching in a crowd is far more exhausting and nervewracking than tramping alone or with several companions. The pace of a bunch in close formation is always too slow for some, too fast for others, a pain for all. The garrulous walker also is disruptive, constantly forcing conversation; the big mouth has plenty of spare breath but the gasper may be prevented by politeness (which develops into hatred) from settling into an efficient breathing rhythm. Thus, unless individual paces are nearly identical, an experienced party generally strings out on the trail, regathering for sociability at rest stops—which are longer for the swifties than the plodders.

However, if the route is obscure or the party green, safety takes precedence and the rule is: *stay together.* The inconvenience is nothing compared to that of organizing a search.

A WORD TO WOMEN (AND THEIR MALE COMPANIONS)

Nowadays all but the hopelessly brainwashed (females as well as males) realize that as far as hiking is concerned a woman is just like a man—just as fast (or slow), just as strong (or weak), just as tough (or delicate), just as brave (or cowardly), just as smart (or dumb). If short-legged or small she perhaps can't hold the same pace as a long-legged man or haul the same load as a broad-shouldered man, but these are consequences of size, not sex.

However, one sexual characteristic has occasional significance, and novice hikers (both women and their male companions) should be aware of the possibility. In a few women the exertions of hiking or the effects of high altitude sometimes upset the menstrual cycle; the period may come earlier than usual and/or with an exceptionally heavy flow. Therefore, until a woman learns by experience how backpacking affects her, she must on every trip be prepared for the unexpected with a sufficient supply of tampons or napkins—plus plastic bags to carry them out of the wilderness if they cannot be *completely* burned in a wood fire.

Moreover, such common accompaniments of the period as cramps, nausea, weakness, dizziness, irritability, and headache may be intensified. Modifications of the planned schedule may be necessary, perhaps not hiking as far as intended or laying over in camp a day.

Finally, some evidence suggests that the odor of a woman having her period attracts bears, aggravating danger to the party's foodstuffs, and that it angers bears—a fact especially to be kept in mind when venturing into grizzly country.

It should be noted that pregnancy need not be a deterrent to hiking. Many women continue backpacking virtually until they're ready for the delivery room and are off on the trails again within a matter of weeks after the baby is born.

GETTING IN CONDITION

Most American hikers earn their daily bread in sedentary occupations and through dependence on labor-saving machines become soft and sloppy and physically miserable. Partly this is why they go walking—to toughen the flesh and gain the smug self-satisfaction of healthy animals.

However, to go directly from city to trail can be humiliating, depressing. Legs wobble, heart pounds, lungs heave—is it worth it? Why not buy a motorbike and exploit the only part of the body in top condition after years of freeway and desk?

No hiker of spirit is so tempted but many despair of ever achieving good enough form to get a mile from the parking lot without having to call a stretcher to get back. It is wrong, though, to accept defeat before the battle.

If trail country is far from home, strictly for vacations, city-bound folk can round gradually into shape through sidewalk strolls (in thick-soled shoes to avoid pounding feet to putty on pavement), jogging in the park, swimming, handball, calisthenics, or any exercise that expands lungs and toughens feet and legs and guts.

However, the best conditioning for the trail is on trails—starting the season with short trips on easy paths, gradually increasing the length and difficulty. On such trips the novice quickly learns there is nothing complicated about becoming as good a walker as his great-grandparents—all it takes is walking, walking, walking.

2: HOISTING PACK ON BACK

MANY and varied are the pleasures of a day on the trail and a hiker may enjoy a rich wildland life never carrying a load heavier than fits conveniently in a small rucksack. Especially in the Alps, where huts are closely spaced, and parts of America where an abundance of trail country lies near cities, a person can walk miles and years and always eat supper at a table and sleep in a bed under a roof.

But the day is only half the trail world. The act of hoisting pack on back has great symbolic importance, signifying acceptance of the other half, the night.

Day is simple by comparison; with a commitment to night come sleeping bag and tent or tarp, cookstove and pots, suppers and breakfasts—and the pack.

Backpackers grow sentimental about the "stone," which holds all necessities and amenities, is bedroom and kitchen and wardrobe complete in one bundle, and delight in the renunciation it expresses of the appliance-cluttered house in the city, the pollution-producer parked at the road, and all the frenetic complications of a society up to its neck in material possessions. To be sure the renunciation is temporary, but the brief escapes into sanity—and the anticipation beforehand and the memories afterward—do much to settle nervous stomachs and calm trembling hands.

However, though the veteran feels a sense of freedom in hoisting the load, the beginner may find the initiation traumatic. There is, first of all, an inbred fear of the night engendered by millenia of hiding from it in the tightest available cave, hut, castle, house, or apartment. And second, there is the lingering suspicion the sport is nothing more than the ultimate expression of masochism. In a world full of pain, who needs to go looking for it?

EASING IN GRADUALLY

Very sad cases are on record of disastrous introductions to backpacking, even when the equipment was ideal and the country beautiful and the weather superb. Such as, the honeymoon couple setting out for a week in the wilds, the longtime-hiker husband gently helping his never-having-hiked bride into the packstraps, and her toppling to the ground and lying there sobbing.

Generally it is best to learn to walk before attempting a backpack. On afternoon strolls, unloaded, then day hikes with rucksack, the use of lungs and legs is mastered, irrational fears allayed.

Having grown familiar with wildland days and accustomed to 10 or 15 pounds, the time arrives to try the "complete home" pack of 20 pounds or so and penetrate mysteries of the night.

Wisdom and nonsense have been written about how heavy a load a human can haul. Again, each hiker must experiment to discover his capacity. A rule with more basis in reality than most is that a person of average strength can carry about one-third of body weight, or 60 pounds for a 180-pound man, 40 pounds for a 120-pound woman; of course, these figures are above the pure comfort range—the man surely will be happier with 40 pounds, the woman with 25. They also assume the body is not overweight and thus substantially burdened even without a pack. The body-weight rule does not apply to growing children; however, the average girl at 14 and boy at 16 have adult capacities.

The rule perhaps has as many exceptions as applications. Tiny porters employed by expeditions often carry half or more their body weight, as do American backwoodsmen and climbers. ("It's not the stove that bothers me," says the legendary iron man to the awe-struck stranger met on the trail. "It's the darn sack of flour in the oven shifting around and throwing me off my stride.") A frail person, even after attaining top condition, may stagger under a quarter or fifth of body weight.

Then, how far can the stone be toted in a day? Some may never manage more than 5 miles with 25 pounds, while others may easily do 15 miles with 60 pounds.

Finally, how heavy *must* the load be? Certainly with moderately careful planning 20-25 pounds can easily cope with every eventuality of an overnight or 3-day trip. Some experts regularly go for a week in mild-climate, gentle country carrying only 30-35 pounds. Travelers of rough and stormy wilderness, perhaps not quite so attentive to ounces, eating somewhat better and including gear essential for foul weather and emergencies, find 40 or 50 pounds more common for a 9-day trip—and that therefore 9 days is close to the limit for a hike in reasonable comfort, though a bit of suffering can extend the length to 2 weeks.

In summary, the beginner must test his own back, starting with modest loads and short hikes, and rather gradually increase the pack weight and the length and duration of trips; this cautious progress is also important when an experienced backpacker is initiating a novice. Maybe that honeymoon would be better spent day-hiking and car-camping, with an occasional night in a mosquito-less motel.

ORGANIZING THE PACK

In olden days the typical pack consisted of a single large bag or a tarp-wrapped bundle lashed to the frame and the entire contents had to be dumped out whenever any article was wanted. The modern pack eliminates the bother, specifically designed as it is for efficient organization.

Still, the hiker must give some thought to stowing gear; any system will work so long as he remembers what it is. Obviously things used only in camp, such as supper food and cooking pots, belong inside the bag, and those required on the trail or for emergencies in the outer pockets. Aggravation can be saved by always putting each item in the same place to avoid, for example, unzipping every pocket, every time, to find the matches.

Chapters 7-15 discuss what should be carried; a preliminary word needs to be said about what shouldn't. Will that third sweater really be necessary to keep warm? Will anybody be hungry enough to eat

all those canned peaches? Will any possible storm be long enough to get through the *Cambridge Medieval History?*

Considered individually each item may be small and weigh only ounces and "come in mighty handy once in a while." But a dozen superfluous articles add up to the pounds that can turn the final miles of the day into an ordeal.

When assembling gear the hiker should give every piece of equipment a hard-eyed scrutiny. The Ten Essentials (see Chapter 15) must be exempted but all else demands careful consideration, remembering that mile by mile, hour by hour, the stone grows heavier.

LIVING WITH THE STONE

Walking with a pack is the same as walking without one, only more so. The pace is slower, the day's range shorter; rests are needed not only for the sake of legs and lungs but the aching back.

There are two basic ways to get into a pack: (1) Grab it by the shoulder straps and lift to the knee, slip one arm through a strap, swing the load onto the back, and slip in the other arm. (2) With pack on the ground, sit against it, slip on the straps, then turn onto the knees and stand up. To get out of the pack, reverse. When the load is very heavy rest spots should be chosen, if possible, so the latter method can be used. In any event the hiker must never, no matter how weary, drop the pack hard—that's how frames are broken and bag-seams split.

Brief breather rests give more benefit if a boulder or log is available upon which the pack may be set while still on the back, the weight thus momentarily removed from the body.

When the pack is taken off on steep terrain it should be placed with care; nothing is more depressing than watching bed and board bound down the meadows, over a cliff, into a river.

The backpacker has options in scheduling not open to the day-hiker. For example, when the planned camp lies thousands of feet up a sun-blasted slope, the party may prefer to spend the brutal afternoon sacked out by a river, cook supper there, and make the climb in the cool of evening. Similarly, desert walkers frequently take a "lunch" break of 4-6 hours.

And when the moon is full and a broad trail leads along a high ridge, the party may wish to sleep away the day in order to hike by night, seeing the world anew, answering coyotes barking and howling all around.

By hoisting pack on back the hiker accepts new responsibilities, but gains new freedoms too.

3:

SLEEPING

THE day's journey ends, packs are dropped, the hikers are home. If the weather is mild and night not urgently close and bugs no threat to sanity, the first order of business is mixing a pot of punch, loosening boots, and sprawling at ease to admire the parlor—ocean beach or lakeshore, forest and stream or high meadow, glacier moraine or desert oasis.

Eventually (immediately in storm or impending darkness) the time comes to construct other rooms of the house—the bedroom, kitchen (subject of the following chapter), and toilet. But gently!

Sorry to say, the old age of woodcraft lingers and even is formally taught by organizations which should know better. A platoon of woodsmen descend on a sylvan scene, unlimber weaponry, and commence the chopping and the digging, the tinkering and tampering and destroying. For what? A night's sleep!

Woodcraft is dead—dead because the modern equipment described in Chapters 11 and 12 makes pioneer-style engineering unnecessary. Dead because nature-sensitive hikers have deeper, subtler pleasures than slashing and gouging. Dead because there are too many of us and too little undisturbed wildland for every would-be son of the frontier to be allowed full freedom to play with his toys.

20

The ideal of the new hiker is not to construct a miniature Fort Ticonderoga as an exercise in ingenuity but rather to camp so simply that following parties must minutely inspect the site to find evidence of his stay.

Here, then, the subject of camping, to which thick books have been

devoted in the past, is given a mere several pages — and these concerned less with suggesting what the beginner should do than what he should *not*.

CHOOSING A CAMPSITE

More and more, in heavily-hiked regions, choice of camps is restricted. The kindest sleeping unavoidably damages fragile ecosystems a bit, and many bits make too much; to localize the impact instead of

letting every meadow and glade be sterilized, administrators are being forced to specify approved sites, banning overnight stays elsewhere. Trail-camping permits now are required in most National Parks and some Wilderness Areas and will be before long in nearly all. An itinerary thus should not be planned solely from maps and guidebooks, which may not be up to date; the land-managing agency, National Park Service, U.S. Forest Service, or other, must be consulted to learn current regulations.

Where restrictions do not yet exist ethical hikers nevertheless stop at established camps, usually slums from generations of woodcraft and plain slobbery, denying themselves the delights of unspoiled sites nearby. They compensate for the lesser esthetic pleasure by cleaning up garbage and enjoying the glow of virtue.

When there is no option but a virgin site beauty is secondary to toughness. The conscientious camper sleeps in woods rather than flower gardens, on dirt rather than heather; he observes the new regulations adopted by National Parks and National Forests which discourage—or specifically forbid—camping within 100 feet of lakes and streams. He takes pride in knowing the first rain will wash away every sign of his stay, that his home for a night soon again will seem virgin.

Preservation of ecosystems has absolute priority but comfort and convenience also influence choice of camps; the great thing about modern equipment is permitting a good sleep with a clear conscience.

The old woodcrafter rule was that a camp must offer wood, water, and shelter. But the new hiker carries shelter and fuel and when need be water and thus can build cozy homes in spots that would have appalled Daniel Boone—a salt flat, a gale-swept moraine, a wintry glacier.

A camp with water still is better than one without. Aside from that the main considerations are ground reasonably level (though not necessarily flat), reasonably dry (though ground sheet and/or tent floor plus sleeping pad allow sleeping in snow or a semi-marsh), and reasonably free of large rocks that can't be temporarily displaced (to be later replaced) or slept around.

During rainy weather it is wise to avoid dips or swales that may become ponds or creeks; knolls and slopes are less likely to be flooded.

During windy weather the lee of a hillock or clump of trees may be sought; in buggy weather the wind may be preferred.

The study of microclimates—why ridges and knolls often are warmer in summer than valleys and basins, why passes frequently are cold and windy while meadows a few yards away are warm and calm, and so on—intrigues a hiker as he gains experience.

When the ecological conscience permits, a party obviously chooses a camp with a view of valley, peaks, waterfall, lake, garden, or whatever may be the local attractions.

MAKING CAMP

In the woodcrafter era preparing for night was nearly as complex and lengthy a process as proving up on a 160-acre homestead. The hiker with modern equipment can do the whole job in a few minutes.

The only possible exception is shelter. Any tent is self-explanatory and the typical tarp rigs illustrated in Chapter 12 are simple enough, but the techniques should be mastered in the back yard or during a car-camping trip or short hike rather than, say, midnight on the tundra in a blizzard.

The first step in making camp, of course, is to set up tent or tarp on ground suitable for sleeping, removing prominent stones and logs (for later replacement) but avoiding major regrade projects which tear up the landscape.

Contrary to the prescription of woodcraft manuals the tent or tarp should *not* be ditched in advance of proven need. Whenever possible a site should be chosen which has natural drainage away from the sleeping area. Otherwise the new rule is to wait until the floods come and then scratch the very minimum channels required, carefully filling them when breaking camp.

Again to deny the woodcrafter past, *do not build a soft bed by cutting boughs;* even where the practice is not yet forbidden it is reprehensible and in any event boughs are unnecessary with the self-contained "sleeping system" described in Chapter 11.

The final steps in preparing for bed—spreading ground sheet, pad, and bag—scarcely need instruction. One controversy may be noted

which has nothing to do with ecology, and that is whether to sleep fully clothed or semi-nude. Some prefer the former for the supposed extra warmth and the ease of going to bed and getting up. Others say they sleep warmer near-naked and place clothes underneath the bag to pad hard spots or insulate cold spots. It's up to the individual to select the method he finds best.

SANITATION

Another facility of the wildland home, the toilet, requires brief mention—mainly because it's disgusting how many hikers don't have the manners of a cat.

Increasingly, heavily-used back-country camps are provided with privies and that takes care of that. However, in most places hikers still are on their own. Three rules must be observed: (1) avoid watercourses, whether or not water is currently running—go up on a hill in the woods or off amid morainal debris; (2) either scoop a small hole and fill it afterward or cover the evidence with loose dirt, stones, dead bark—consider the sensibilities of the next person who wanders into this particular patch of brush or pile of rocks; (3) don't foul potential campsites.

If the party is large more formal arrangements are needed, such as designating a certain crevice in a boulder field or perhaps digging a hole, informing the entire group of the location, and making sure everyone sticks to the designated spot—or spots, if segregation by sex seems desirable. Upon leaving, of course, holes are filled and ground-cover reconstructed.

COURTESY

Particularly where choice of camps is restricted by administrative regulations, but also in any much-traveled area, hikers must learn to get along with strangers. It is quite possible for dozens or scores of courteous campers to live close together and congenially on an acre or two. However, a single thoughtless bunch can ruin the neighborhood.

A major stimulus to the popularity of backpacking is the bedlam of car-camping. See the dark and silent campground. At midnight, the new arrivals. They drive around and around, shining headlights at every site, occupied or not. At last they park—motor running and headlights on. For half-an-hour they perform the door-slamming ritual, then spread out and begin yelling back and forth. At 2:30 a.m. they go to bed—and an hour later are chopping wood, banging pots and pans, slamming doors, waking up the birds. Shortly they will be thrashing about the lake in motorboats or razzing the trails on motorcycles.

Backpacking does not offer total escape from noisemakers. For the moment forget (impossible, but try) the trailbike invasion. See the troop of boisterous children swarm into camp, and *hear* them—none going more than 10 seconds without a shriek, whistle blast, or bugle call. The adults in charge smile benignly, drink covertly from flasks. Other campers who have been contemplating the solemnity and mystery of wilderness either grit teeth and begin suffering the nervous symptoms they took this trip to cure, or unrig camp and move on, seeking the peace and quiet of a snakepit or avalanche slope.

Noise is not the only pollution. Satan said, "Let there be light!" And lo, the gasoline lantern! Those who illuminate a camp invariably consider themselves benefactors and hang the lantern high so neighbors can enjoy the spill-over. But the neighbors may wish to become one with the night; when philosophy is lost they may sit in the harsh glare and make plans to buy noiseless, darkness-creating air pistols.

Certainly the sublime appeal of wilderness travel is the freedom to howl with the coyotes, to sweat and break wind, to be a natural animal unconstrained by stifling conventions. But whenever the population of a trail camp is considerable and a degree of crowding unavoidable each hiker should do his utmost not to pollute the quiet or the darkness, should strive to be more feline than simian.

In enjoying freedom do not invade the freedoms of neighbors. Impinge not upon their rights and privileges lest they, in maddened retaliation, impinge upon yours and a lousy vacation be had by all.

4:

BEDROOM is rigged and toilet designated. One room remains to complete the trail home—the kitchen. And in this aspect of architecture as in others the woodcrafter has left his mark throughout the back country, and again the new hiker examines the elaborate constructions of generations past and wonders what all the fuss was about.

To be fair to oldtimers, eating was a complicated business in years gone by; many a veteran, still exercising hard-won skills, refuses to admit they are obsolete, that he is wasting hours better spent contemplating the scenery—which he, in displaying his ingenuity and energy, is mucking up. The new hiker ought to be patient with the veteran; he may be somebody's grandfather.

The modern backpacker neither wants to nor must manhandle the land for the sake of a dinner. Using equipment and foods described in Chapters 13 and 14 meals are absurdly easy and quick to prepare and in a very short while the beginner becomes an expert.

This chapter, therefore, has little to say about cooking and eating and is almost entirely concerned with lightening the pressure of the camp kitchen on tender terrain.

KITCHEN ORGANIZATION

An overnight hike requires no fancier advance organization than dumping cooking and eating utensils and food in packs—only making quite sure to do so. Discouraging words to be heard 10 miles from the road are: "But I thought *you* had the pots!"

For trips lasting several days or more an hour of city preparation reduces time spent ransacking packs in camp. Complete meals may be packaged in poly bags (which also help keep foods dry) labeled Bean Supper, Oatmeal and Prune Breakfast, and so on. Considerable weight is saved in the process by shucking cardboard and paper containers—but not the cooking directions! A simpler method is grouping foods at the trailhead into, say, Soup Bag, Candy Bag, and whatever. Cocoa and sugar and the like should be double-bagged to avoid sticky sweaters and similar unpleasantness.

Meal preparation can be organized any number of ways. In a party of experienced hikers typically someone rigs tent or tarp while another assembles pots and food and others start the fire (with wood or stove) and haul water—all this done wordlessly and automatically by individual initiative. Generally each meal should have a single boss; too many cooks kick over too many pots and in the confusion forget to stir the macaroni. Except in the presence of an acknowledged master chef the job usually is best rotated from meal to meal.

An inexperienced party, especially with a number of children along, ordinarily needs a self-appointed leader or two (such as father and mother) to assign chores—by mild request or suggestion rather than shouted command to avoid resemblance to a military operation.

FIRE

The backpacker stove (see Chapter 13) has become an indispensable part of the hiker's outfit because that prime symbol of the wilderness home, the wood fire, is obsolescent, for a number of reasons: Heavily-camped areas are virtually wall-to-wall charcoal, firepits replacing the natural groundcover. In popular campsites all the easy wood was burned years ago and gathering fuel is a pain in the neck. Where the wood is gone but fires still allowed, idiot hatchetmen cut green trees—to no avail since they won't burn, but in the process logging parklands. In high meadows the only wood may be silver snags and logs, bleached bones of trees long dead; in a single evening a

party may consume portions of the scenery that otherwise would have delighted hikers for years to come. Finally, it is disappointing to travel far from city smog seeking the taste of clean air and be forced to camp in an acrid cloud, coughing and crying from the smoke of a dozen fires.

Use of native fuels has been officially banned in a number of American wildlands and will be in more as time goes on; the hiker should not wait for the compulsion of law but heed his conscience.

COOKING WITH WOOD

Still, the wood fire is not completely a memory. A stove always is less bother and gives more leisure for sunsets but seldom inspires philosophical reflections and except in a tent is worthless for warming cold bones. In forests which annually yield a large crop of dead branches and high valleys regularly receiving a fresh fuel supply from slope-pruning avalanches and on ocean beaches replenished with driftwood by each high tide—*and where campers are few*—fires are not yet criminal or immoral.

Even the hiker who always cooks on a stove should have some notion of how to start a fire in emergencies. (The lifesaving value may be over-rated, however—rarely can an exhausted person succeed in kindling soaking-wet wood; carrying proper clothing and a light bivouac tarp is more dependable.) As Smokey the Bear keeps warning, no technique is required when dry wood is plentiful. In hard rain and wind the wiliest veteran may be defeated without supernatural assistance.

A few hints may help the beginner; for thousands more consult the woodcraft literature. First gather a substantial supply of the driest wood available; in rainy weather look under large logs and break dead underlimbs from living trees. No ax or hatchet is needed nor should one be carried; if finger-picking fuel ("squaw wood") cannot be found a fire should not be built and probably can't be anyway. Some woods burn better than others; this must be learned through experience with local species.

Begin by igniting food-package paper, moss, twigs, or knife sliverings; the emergency firestarter from the Ten Essentials (or a splash of stove gas) may be employed if kindling is damp and wind disruptive. Proceed from small wood to large, never smothering the fire with excess fuel, helping as required by putting the mouth at the

critical point and blowing sparks into flames, tiny flames to big. An enclosure of rocks—the traditional "fire ring"—increases efficiency by reflecting heat inward.

The kitchen fire should be small; if conscience permits it may be enlarged later for a social or warming fire. Pots are best suspended on

a light metal grate (see Chapter 13), infinitely simpler and quicker to use than the dinglesticks and crossbars dear to the hearts of woodcrafters.

MINIMIZING FIRE DAMAGE

Smog in the wilderness? Yes—the exhalations of Los Angeles are killing highland forests and those of Puget Sound City often invade the Cascades. Perhaps more disillusioning are the blue clouds over tent towns far from industrial stacks and freeways. In a crowded camp the ethical hiker does well to hold down the number of polluters by politely asking to share an existing fire or hospitably offering his own to a new arrival. Better, of course, is to cook on a stove.

Whenever possible an established fire ring should be used to avoid killing yet another patch of plants, leaving still another heap of charcoal. If a virgin site must be used, virtually every trace of a fire built on bare dirt or gravel can be obliterated when breaking camp by returning fire-ring rocks to exact original positions and widely scattering the ashes and leftover wood. A further step, if the fire was on living soil, is to restore a semblance of virginity and speed regrowth by mulching the spot with duff or humus.

The rules for putting out a fire are rigid and mandatory. Drown the ashes with water or snow and stir until all are cool to the touch. Drench fire-ring rocks (watch out—if very hot they may explode) until none can possibly harbor a living ember. Make sure no underground hot spots are overlooked; a fire supposedly out may creep beneath the surface in forest duff or along dead roots or buried sticks and long after the hikers are gone erupt to the surface and sweep through grass, touch off forests.

The more talk about wood fires the more reasons for carrying a stove.

GARBAGE

Four backpackers, recently emerging from wilderness at the end of an 80-mile, 10-day trip during which they ate the sort of foods discussed in Chapter 14, put their double-poly garbage bag on a scales. Total weight: *1 pound, 14 ounces.* For a burden of ¾ ounce per man-day they (we) had the satisfaction of strictly observing the new PACK IT OUT law and leaving not a single kitchen scrap to mar the pleasure of hikers to come.

The rule of "Burn, bash, and bury" promulgated by reformers of half-a-century ago was an advance beyond frontier habits of drop-or-toss and blithely forget. However, studies have shown steel ("tin") cans ordinarily do not reduce to soil components in less than 20-40 years, or in some areas 100 years or more; in the process, iron salts often leach into and "rust" springs, creeks, lakes, and damp meadows. Plastic may not decompose entirely for 200 years, aluminum for 500 years, glass for 1,000,000 years. Digging pits to bury garbage dis-

The total nonburnable garbage of four backpackers from a 10-day hike. Weight including carrying bag, 1 pound, 14 ounces. It's no strain to PACK IT OUT.

turbs the ground and frequently destroys plant life. And when the pit is deep enough? Lo! Old garbage! Or maybe fresh.

Thus the new law. And PACK IT OUT means PACK IT *ALL* OUT. On the trail, stuff into pockets every gum wrapper and orange peel. In camp, if cooking on a stove, perhaps hold a discreet little paper fire to burn food packages—but don't bother on any hike up to 5 or 6 days; paper doesn't weigh that much. If a wood fire is built, paper and plastic may be burned—*but not aluminum foil,* some of which will oxidize but never all; inevitably the ashes glitter. Food packages of foil and paper or plastic are best given a quick burn in a hot flame and the naked metal then fished out before it starts disintegrating into a mess. Some hikers still like to scorch cans to remove food residues before stamping them flat for the garbage bag; others now wash the cans along with the cooking pots.

The final nicety is for a party to spend a half-hour or more meticulously removing tiny bits of foil and unburned paper, orange peels and egg shells, while drowning and stirring the ashes—and meanwhile policing the camp for oddments of debris. Into the bag it all goes for hauling to the road, glorying in the name of garbagemen.

Garbage left by miners, trappers, and other wildlanders of 50 or 100 or 150 years ago is now picturesque, fascinating to archaeologists, and as a matter of public policy might conceivably be preserved for the historical value—even in dedicated Wilderness Areas. But the garbage from last summer and last week is just plain garbage. Land-managing agencies and volunteers from outdoor clubs are cleaning up the trails and camps of America, many of which are now neater than they have been in living memory.

Pioneers (in the modern setting they are called "slobs") still walk and ride the trails, but as garbage vanishes many will mend their manners, if only to avoid being glared at by travelers who PACK IT OUT, PACK IT *ALL* OUT.

WATER POLLUTION

Hikers in settled areas and in wildlands fouled by sheep, cattle, and thoughtless horsemen long have suspected the water and on occasion treated it either by boiling or adding chlorinating tablets. Now pollution is becoming a problem even in regions where hikers once trusted every spring, confident that except for occasional indelicacies of wild beasts the purity was absolute. Therefore, on thickly-populated trails the creeks and especially the lakes, no matter how cold and crystal-clear, should be inspected carefully, and when dubious, the water treated before use.

As with garbage, water pollution easily can be eliminated from most of the back country if every traveler follows several simple rules.

First, as discussed in the previous chapter, take care of toilet needs far from watercourses.

Second, locate camps at least 100 feet from the shores of lakes, banks of small creeks, and the sources of springs; consider the immediate vicinity of the water supply as a semi-closed watershed and minimize human presence there.

Third, rather than washing dishes in lake or creek, loosing food particles and detergent, carry buckets of water into the woods or onto a moraine knoll and do the scrubbing and rinsing there.

Finally, when other travelers are observed polluting the water, calmly and politely lead them into the paths of righteousness.

KEEPING ANIMALS HONEST

Nearly all the relatively few dangers from wild animals (discussed in the following chapter) come directly from sloppy kitchens.

Any much-used camp develops a resident population of scavengers. There are "camprobbers"—juncos, jays, and nutcrackers—and wee,

timorous beasties that nibble and brazen snafflehounds that gobble. There are porcupines and skunks that methodically investigate the scene by night, oblivious to threats. And deer and mountain goats that seek salt and packrats that devour the armpits of well-used parkas. On ocean beaches there are clouds of crows and seagulls waiting for picnickers to leave the lunch unguarded. And there are bears, too.

The measures necessary to protect groceries depend on the numbers and determination of invaders. Local inquiry is desirable; rangers usually know what camps are under heavy attack. Stowing vulnerable (uncanned) foods in a closed pack or tightly-wrapped tarp may suffice—but usually not, what with quiet burglars chewing holes in tarp or packbag, resulting in loss of provisions plus destruction of equipment. The night is much more restful when the commissary is completely safe. The ideal method, where possible, is to place foods in a sack (perhaps large poly bags, doubled) which then is hung from a tree limb or a line strung between two trees, suspended higher from the ground than a bear can reach and far enough below the limb to discourage rats and mice from dropping onto the sack.

What does a party do, by day or night, if a bear arrives to inventory the gifts brought by his human pack train? If the bear is just entering a life of crime he may be repelled by loud shouts, flashlights, and banging pots and pans. And if not? *Don't argue!* He may have learned he can lick any dozen men with one paw tied behind his back.

In country known to be patrolled regularly by bears, and especially if they are grizzlies, food must *not* be kept overnight in or near tent or tarp, but rather stored some distance away.

People who visit wildlands generally like animals and enjoy doing them little favors—offering snacks, setting out saltlicks. Thus the evolution of the campground deer, that sick and sorry beggar, and the National Park bear, led astray by tourists.

Nor are hikers innocent. It began with the practice of burying partially-burned garbage, throwing bacon grease and fish guts in the bushes, and leaving leftover food for the next party. Certain bears, in certain places, came to consider human camps their pantries and stopped by regularly for lunch as soon as the people departed.

Then the camps grew crowded and as one bunch of hikers left another arrived and the bears couldn't wait for privacy and began taking their meals when they pleased, meeting objections with such gestures of annoyance as were appropriate and necessary, and learning the only retaliation was a lot of harmless yelling and pot-banging.

More and more frequently nowadays a grumpy bear meets a brave and stupid man and the man gets mauled and later the bear gets executed. Sometimes along with innocent bystanders guilty only of being bears.

To save the bears—and the hikers—it is essential *never, deliberately or otherwise, to feed the animals.* Keep foodstuffs tightly locked up in double and triple layering of packages and poly bags. Carry out all garbage and leftover food, including bacon grease; do not create an attractive nuisance.

The animals will feel better, not being tempted to depend on unnatural cuisine. Hikers will feel better, not being annoyed by nibblers and gulpers, menaced by manglers and slashers. And the rangers will feel better, not having to execute wildland natives whose only crime is becoming too human.

Keep the animals wild and honest and healthy. And keep the trails safe for hiking.

5:   BUGS AND BEASTS AND SERPENTS

MAN is not alone in the wilderness. Innumerable creatures large and small were there first, are there now, and hopefully will remain. A visitor must learn to live with them and respect their prior rights—enjoying hawks in the sky, deer in the meadows, and others that make interesting neighbors and mind their own business, doing his best to get along with the hostiles and the all-too-companionables.

A few trail-country inhabitants are an occasional danger to human life and limb. Some, notably certain insects and arachnids (or "bugs" as they are inaccurately lumped together in common usage and in this book), are mainly a menace to sanity. Far more for good reason are frightened by man, the most dangerous predator ever to molest the Earth.

The beginner doubtless has heard horror stories about encounters between man and beast, man and serpent, man and bug. However, he takes vastly greater risks of being maimed or murdered or mentally unhinged on highways leading from the cities (and in the cities) than along the trails. If hikers take the trouble to learn a little about the habits of the natives the two can share wildlands with minimum discomfort and terror for both.

SERPENTS

"Watch out for snakes," says the guidebook, and so hikers from such poison-free lands as Ireland and Puget Sound walk foreign trails a-tremble, leaping high at the sight of every lizard, and lie sleepless in bags, imagining every nocturnal rustle of bushes to be the approach of evil personified.

Certainly venomous snakes demand respect, but not panic. Some 1000-1500 persons are bitten in the United States each year—a small number, really, considering that millions of rural folk daily live and work amid potentially dangerous snakes. About one in a hundred dies

—a large proportion of the fatalities being among tiny children. Very few hikers are bitten and fewer still suffer serious illness, much less death.

Of the scores of snakes common in American trail country only four carry venom. The coral snake occurs in a portion of the South and Southwest and the water moccasin (cottonmouth) in wetlands of the South. The copperhead ranges rather widely through the East and various members of the rattlesnake family are found across the entire nation.

Residents of snake country, though they love to scare dudes with tall tales, are quite casual about the hazard, for good reason; in the memory of the oldest inhabitants of the Stehekin Valley of the North Cascades, going back 70-odd years, no human ever has been bitten there; dogs have been, some repeatedly, but only one, a pup, is remembered as dying.

Snakes fear man and given a chance will flee his presence; knowing this, the hiker can reduce confrontations by taking elementary precautions: Be a noisy walker to give ample advance notice of your approach. Watch the path ahead to avoid stepping on a snake or coming near one sunning on a boulder or cooling in a cave; listen for the rattle that often warns a rattlesnake is close by, scared, and thus dangerous. (However, since even a coiled snake can strike less than the length of its body the surveillance need not be extended any great distance.) Do not plunge blindly into thickets or run through boulder fields or scramble incautiously up rocks. For peace of mind if nothing else, perhaps wear long pants rather than shorts.

Authorities generally advise carrying a snake-bite kit, but in unpracticed hands of semi-hysterical first-aiders the kit can be more dangerous than the bite; the rule is to seek instruction before entering an area where it may be needed.

Enough, here, about timid creatures too much maligned and dreaded. In many parts of the continent, including most alpine regions, poisonous snakes are totally absent; the relatively few hikers who spend a good deal of time in lands of the serpents will want to study their habits thoroughly (see the Appendix), not only to learn to live among them without fear but also for the pleasure of getting to know fellow travelers. When visiting new areas guidebooks should be consulted to find if venom-carriers are present, and where.

BEASTS

Urbanites nourished on fairy tales and frontier lies frequently are acutely uncomfortable in forests, imagining every thicket conceals a beast ready to pounce. The night, they suspect, does indeed have a thousand eyes—and jaws, and fangs, and claws. Though this may be so in city parks, the wildlands of America contain few animals that threaten man; the menace is the other way around from extermination campaigns conducted with guns, traps, poisons, and the fallout from contaminated skies. Several creatures may be cited to suggest how little there is to fear.

Cougars and other cats do not attack man unless cornered, a distinctly avoidable situation; only the rare hiker ever is privileged even to hear, much less see one.

The same is true of wolves, now tragically scarce, and proven by modern research to be totally innocent of the slanders perpetrated by Little Red Riding Hood and paranoid shepherds and droll frontiersmen who delighted in seeing how big a lie they could get city folk to swallow. What substance there is for legends of lupine viciousness probably comes from attacks stimulated by the madness of rabies, incidents extremely rare but lingering long in memory and expanding enormously in myth. Rabies afflicts small beasts as well as large and is not restricted to wilderness; a fellow quietly besotting himself at a Manhattan Island bar once was bitten by a rabid bat that flew in from the street. On trail or in city no animal that seems ill or behaves oddly ever should be picked up, touched, or approached; it may be dying of rabies, plague, or some other disease that can be transmitted by a bite or by infected fleas. Be sure to tell the children.

Elk and moose should be shunned in the fall rutting season, when passion-mad bulls may mistake hikers for competitors and run them out of the country. In spring and summer the cows—and any mother with young—should be given a wide berth not to stir maternal hostility.

Skunks? Don't frighten them! Porcupines? An inexperienced dog may require hours of painful surgery pulling quills from jaws. Coyotes? Scary-sounding under the moon but harmless. Eagles? Occasionally they attack airplanes and nest-robbing ornithologists.

A word about the horse. First, pedestrians always should yield the right of way to equestrians, who often are unstable in the saddle and have scant control of their huge, clumsy steeds. Second, when stepping from the path a hiker should continue making normal gestures and above all *speak* to the poor, dumb beast so it will know it has met an ordinary human, not an alien monster.

SAVE OUR BEARS

Every summer the same story. A camper is mauled, perhaps killed, and a lynch mob cries for vengeance. Liquidate bears! It's *our* National Park, not theirs! Make the trails safe for man!

What price safety? Eliminate the most interesting large animal the ordinary person has a reasonable chance to see, eliminate bear stories, and wilderness would be lessened. However, bison and Indians and other nuisances were removed for the convenience of the conqueror; whether bears can survive remains to be determined. Surely it can only be so if hikers want them, and help them.

The first rule, discussed in the previous chapter, is to keep food locked up tight and leave no tempting scraps or grease or garbage; the scavenger is the greatest danger to campers—and its own race.

Second, do not fraternize. Forget Disney cartoons and Gentle Ben and cuddly Teddy bears—real-life bears are not cute. Forget Smokey the Bear—bears are nothing like dogs, they never really become at all humanized, at best tolerate and usually hate people. Enjoy them— but from a distance. Stay away from cubs! Though unseen, the deadliest of the species, the mother, is near, ready to take out after overeager photographers.

There are bears and bears. Before entering the realms of the Alaska brown and the polar bear a hiker must obtain expert local advice. The grizzly, driven from nearly all its former range and everywhere endangered, is notably a "problem" on certain trails of National Parks in and near Canada; the hiker should rigidly follow rules of behavior suggested by rangers; the novice would do well to skip *ursus horribilis* country entirely. The black bear, smallest and least belligerent of the family, is so only by comparison; being most common it presents the most frequent peril.

The major menace, the scrounger, has been covered already. On little-traveled trails where bears have not learned to exploit man and hold him in contempt the hiker may avoid unwelcome surprises by making normal noise as he walks, perhaps supplemented by bells on the pack or boots and occasional bursts of nervous laughter. Most completely-wild bears, even grizzlies, will give room if warned of a stranger's approach.

When the bear—whatever the species—holds its ground the hiker should stand still or slowly back away, and say a few words in a soft and friendly voice. If pursued, throw down the pack; the bear may spend enough time ripping it apart for a tree to be climbed. If caught, go limp and quiet, not resisting, not screaming, covering the head with the arms, and pray the lord or lady of the land is content with a few swipes and bites.

Can hikers and bears live together in wildlands? The question is open. Remember, the bears were there first.

BUGS

Every long-time hiker has a lurid repertoire of bug stories—the air thick with flailing wings, loud with snapping jaws—infants wailing, wives weeping, strong men teetering on the brink of madness. Wilderness veterans who face tempest and jungle with fortitude quail at the prospect of venturing into the domain of the Lord of the Flies.

However, formidable as are the insect legions, rarely can they totally defeat the hiker who learns their habits and employs proper defenses.

In camp a bugproof tent (see Chapter 12) provides a nearly perfect haven. While hiking or doing chores true peace is never possible, but recourses are available to preserve sanity. The target area can be minimized by covering up with clothing and donning a head net, though perhaps at the risk of heat prostration and/or claustrophobia.

Insect repellent (see Chapter 15) generally prevents bugs from drilling and biting but does not keep them at a respectful distance. The attentive cloud hovers close, landing on untreated clothing and glasses and flying into eyes, nostrils, and open mouth. Chemicals thus do not eliminate the harassment which often is the worst part of the whole business.

Frequently the only salvation lies in a resolute stoicism. Those who yield to paranoia have lost the battle and are not long for the trails. It is necessary to realize that bugs *belong* on Earth, that if the Architect had intended wildlands to be perfectly comfortable and convenient for man He would have designed them more like Disneyland.

In extremities some hikers find tranquilizers useful in gaining the proper mental composure; others prefer a shot of rum.

THE CAST OF VILLAINS

By learning to enjoy "bugs" (that is, insects and arachnids and other arthropods) a person enlarges his circle of trail companions; only a very few ever are a bother. Admire the gorgeous butterfly, the spectacular dragon fly, the patient spider, the graceful water skate, the glistening beetle. But probably it is too much to ask charity for the fly. And people with a phobia about creepy-crawlies do well to sleep in floored tents.

Ants trouble only the hiker who unwarily spreads his sleeping bag atop a colony—a typical location being the remains of a rotten log—and is wakened in the night by the pricking of myriad tiny needles.

Bee-type bugs (honey bees, bumblebees, yellowjackets, hornets, wasps, etc.) normally let people alone, except to briefly investigate bright-colored clothing they mistake for huge flowers; together with flies and mosquitoes, they are attracted and thoroughly confused by damsels who go forth wearing perfume. Accidentally stepping on a yellowjacket nest in the middle of a trail can be unpleasant, since a single warrior can deliver numerous stabs, but the spectacle can be entertaining to dirty old men when several get inside the blouse of a well-built girl. Individuals vary in their physical reactions to bee stings: some find them no worse than nettles; others puff up dramatically; in rare cases of extreme allergy the victim may go into severe, even fatal shock—the proper medication should always be carried by people who suspect they have such a problem.

Midges or gnats often fill the summer evening air in the vicinity of lowland marshes and lakes.

The chigger, found mainly in the East, is a mite that lives in grass, digs into the skin, and causes an itch.

Annoying these bugs may sometimes be, but none is dreaded by veteran hikers as are the next characters in this sordid chapter.

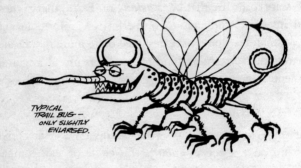

TYPICAL
TRAIL BUG--
ONLY SLIGHTLY
ENLARGED.

Ticks

The tick does not hurt, does not harass, but nevertheless is loathed. First because it is nasty, burrowing into flesh and engorging with blood. Second because at some times and places (but rarely) it carries Rocky Mountain Spotted Fever, formerly a much-feared disease with a very high mortality rate but now easily cured by antibiotics. As with the rattlesnake a mythology of terror has developed and folklore is full of nonsense about the creatures parachuting from trees and screwing into the skin.

The tick rarely ventures more than 18 inches from the ground; typically it anchors to brush and grass along routes used by animals, extends hooks, and waits for a host to come within reach; the hooks then clamp tight and the tick climbs aboard and begins to prospect.

Ticks are most plentiful in the springtime of dry lands, when fresh, green grass is sprouting and tender leaves are budding and browsers are enjoying the salads. Hiker-tick encounters mainly occur in May and June on low-valley trails leading into alpine regions of Western mountains.

When passing through tick-thick terrain it is wise to wear long pants treated with repellent. When sleeping in tick country repellent may be applied to all clothing, to sleeping bags, and perhaps tent entries. In the absence of sufficient repellent for thorough application hikers may wish to pair off morning and evening to completely inspect each other's bodies. (Please, no giggling.) By this means the danger of disease (which actually is not all that common) can be largely avoided since a tick normally explores several hours before choosing a drill site and even if infected cannot transmit germs for several hours more.

In the early stages of drilling the entire tick can be gently pulled straight out (not "unscrewed"); then or later, it possibly may be induced to withdraw by touching its rear with a drop of repellent, kerosene, or gas. Once partly imbedded, the only remedy is to pull the body off, halting the creature's operations by killing it. Perhaps later the patient should visit a doctor to have the body cut out. If localized infection develops, or a fever, medical treatment should be sought—in the latter case, urgently.

Ticks can roam clothing and sleeping bags and gear several days and thus must be watched for after the party has ascended into high mountains or returned to the city.

Mosquitoes

Except perhaps in parts of the South, the mosquitoes of America so far do not transmit malaria or yellow fever and the only region where they potentially are a mortal peril is in the far North, where by one estimate an unprotected person could lose half his blood in a half-hour. The needle is relatively painless and the itching usually minor and temporary. The central hazard is mental—the maddening whine, the constant cloud, the dumb penetration of ears, eyes, nose—moderated but not eliminated by repellent. Mosquitoes probably have stimulated the buying of more tents than rain and driven more hikers into fits and off the trails than all other causes combined.

In lowlands mosquitoes may be met in every season except winter —one or two, a few, or many, depending on the local climate. In alpine meadows and Arctic tundras they achieve the continental climax of mind-boggling when the ground is moist from snowmelt and the air is calm and warm; as pools and humus dry their numbers diminish; with the first frosts of fall they vanish. Through miserable experience a hiker learns the intolerable times and places and thereafter can schedule trips to notorious hell-holes for the off-season.

Mosquitoes have a limited temperature range. In high mountains they ordinarily go instantly to bed with the evening chill, probably to arise at dawn, thin out during the heat of day, and return in force as the afternoon cools. In warm lowlands they may appear at dusk and work all through the night.

A wind keeps them from clustering and thus a camp may be placed on a knoll for the breezes in preference to a sheltered nook nearby. Similarly, a dry hillock may be quieter than a lush vale a stone's-throw distant.

Flies

Scores of members of the fly family infest the trail country. Several may be described as representative examples of the range in size and habitat.

The tiny, silent *no-see-um,* mistaken for a speck of dust until it grabs hold, able to pass through netting as if it weren't there, often gets off an incredibly painful chew but mainly is felt as an overall prickle and itch. No-see-ums generally are confined to lowlands, such as dank river bottoms, which they may on occasion render uninhabitable.

The chief threat is the medium-sized category, represented in some areas by the *black fly,* in others by the *deer fly,* which in a typical manifestation resembles the house fly. In "fly time" every square yard of trail may harbor hundreds of sharp-eyed, sharp-toothed, loud-buzzing, wicked-minded villains and to calculate the numbers in an entire valley is to submerge sanity in a vision of infinity—an infinity of evil. Trails much-used by horses may be quite literally impassable. Driven by heat to fiendish hyperactivity, flies attack most furiously precisely on those sweaty, gasping uphill drags when the hiker moves slowest. Now and then a kamikaze plunges into ear, nose, eye, or wide-open mouth—to feel wings and legs scrambling around in the throat, to gag and retch, this is the ultimate initiation.

But all is not lost. The unbearable fly time usually lasts only a few weeks of summer, ending with the first heavy frosts, and the fly empire, though extending from low valleys to meadows, usually is impossibly crowded only in the upper forests. Moreover, flies vanish in the wind and evening chill; even the cool microclimate next to a waterfall may allow a peaceful lunch when the forest world all around is pure Hell. Finally, since flies patrol at random in search of a victim, the interior of a lean-to (or a tent with one closed end) has

only ¼ the number of the surrounding woods, since from three directions they bump into walls. Even an open-ended tarp cuts the population in half and a closed tent is perfectly secure.

Deer flies ordinarily diminish or disappear in parkland and meadows, which apparently by family agreement are the domain of the *elk fly,* which ranges upward into snow and rocks but luckily occurs in dozens rather than thousands. These enormous beasts, which take such big bites they seem to be slicing off steaks, can be slapped with relative ease—though for final destruction one may have to take a club and beat them to death.

6:

DANGER!

BEFORE this invitation to the pleasures of wildland walking proceeds a word must be heard from the Devil's Advocate.

There is misery on the trail, and pain, and death. Questions for the potential-but-not-yet hiker and backpacker: *Do you know what you're getting into?* Are you aware of the risks? Are you willing to accept those you cannot invariably avoid? If so, welcome to the wild bunch. If not, think about it, please.

A number of discomforts and dangers are discussed in other chapters; they will not be repeated here, nor an exhaustive catalog of perils presented in the tradition of seeking to scare the innocent half to death. However, conscience demands that a germ of fear be implanted, hopefully to grow into a mature respect.

BEGINNER-KILLERS

If a person brooded incessantly on all the ways there are to be maimed or killed he never would get out of bed—until he began to worry about murderous burglars, earthquakes, and bed sores. Certainly no one ever would stride blithely along a trail if at each step he were watching for snakes and bears, falling trees and mountains, flash floods and lightning bolts.

Paraphrasing the last journal entry of Scott of the Antarctic, made at the death camp on the return from the Pole, "we take risks, we know we take them. Therefore, when things come out against us, we have no cause for complaint." To live is to be insecure. But to die stupidly, from ignorance, is a damn shame.

Over the years a hiker encounters numerous hazards, common and uncommon. Certain of these, though, seem to have a particular affinity for the inexperienced, and several are especially notorious among rescue experts as beginner-killers.

WEATHER: HYPOTHERMIA

Except in desert country, where sunstroke and dehydration are the killers, the vast majority of weather-caused fatalities—among veterans as well as novices—result from hypothermia, where the body loses more heat than it can generate. (Older names were "exposure" and "freezing to death.")

A hiker needs only get rain-drenched and wind-blasted a few times to start paying close attention to the forecast before leaving on a trip and constantly watching the sky while in wildlands. Eventually he learns the characteristic weather patterns of home hills, develops some skill at interpreting clouds and winds, and can guess with better-than-random accuracy the prospects for coming hours.

But every summer, somewhere, a beginner sets out in morning sun so warm only a fanatic would carry an extra sweater or parka. He admires the pretty billow on the horizon—too far away, surely, to be a threat. But in afternoon the cloud arrives, and he wishes for that sweater and parka, yet still no need to worry, the car is just a couple hours distant. Then begins rain (or snow), driven by a gale. Muscles quickly become clumsy, thinking tangled. He stumbles and sprains an ankle, or misses the path and is lost in mist. Unless rescuers find him in time, the rest is silence.

A common misconception is that hypothermia is a danger only at below-freezing temperatures. The accompanying table shows a wind of 20 miles per hour at $40°$F cools the body as effectively as still air at $18°$F. *Wind chill* can cause hypothermia at temperatures far above freezing.

WIND CHILL

To find the approximate effective temperature (cooling power) of wind-driven air compared to that of still air, read downward from the still-air thermometer readings of the top line to intersect the wind speed in the left column.

Skin-Effective Temperature
(degrees Fahrenheit)

Wind		50	40	30	20	10	0	-10	-20
Speed	0 (still air)	50	40	30	20	10	0	-10	-20
(miles	10	40	28	16	4	-9	-21	-33	-46
per	20	32	18	4	-10	-25	-39	-53	-69
hour)	30	28	13	-2	-18	-33	-48	-63	-79
	40	26	10	-6	-21	-37	-53	-69	-85

Moisture cools somewhat by wetting the skin but mainly by reducing the insulation value of clothing; the thermal conductivity of water is 240 times greater than that of still air. Hypothermia is not confined to high ridges but can occur in low forests from *water chill.* The combination of wind and rain is particularly lethal.

Well-equipped hikers, faithfully carrying the Ten Essentials (see Chapter 15) rarely die from hypothermia; when they do, usually it is because they ignore the sky, their inner voices, and rigidly push forward rather than flexibly retreating or holing-up.

GRAVITY: FALLING AND BEING FALLEN UPON

Chapter 17 discusses rough-country travel and warns against attempting cliffs and snowfields properly left to trained climbers. Such ill-advised adventures by daring beginners fill pages and pages of the annual reports of rescue groups. The reports also devote considerable space to falls from trails; in steep terrain the tread often is wide and safe yet inches away is a cliff and to stumble over the edge perhaps is to tumble dozens or hundreds of feet.

How do hikers fall off trails? By rushing when they should be creeping. By fainting from heat exhaustion. By not carrying a flashlight and staying too long on sunset-colored ridges and while blindly descending dark woods missing a switchback.

Another danger of gravity is that piece by piece, year by year, mountains are steadily disintegrating. Far more common than spontaneous rockfall, though, is the peril of heavily-traveled trails where carefree and careless hikers kick rocks loose to plunge catastrophically onto people below.

GETTING LOST

Hikers who know the techniques of finding and keeping the route, as introduced in Chapter 16, rarely are lost longer than overnight. Moreover, those who carry the Ten Essentials have a survival rate of virtually 100 percent.

Even ill-trained, ill-equipped novices generally do not become seriously lost if the party always remains together in confusing terrain. They are, for one thing, less likely to miss the way, and if they do, reinforce each other physically and spiritually. It is the lone traveler who succumbs to panic, the prelude to tragedy.

If lost, what then? Rescue experts emphasize the problem is not being lost but staying alive long enough to be found.

First, as soon as confused, *stop;* don't plunge onward, getting more thoroughly lost. Sit down, rest, have a bite to eat. Think calmly. Do not let fear lead to panic. If two or more persons are lost together, discuss the situation—and do not henceforth become separated! The records are full of incidents where every member of a lost party was eventually found except the one who went for help.

Second, mark the location. Chances are the trail is not far away. Conduct short sorties in all directions—returning to the marked spot if unsuccessful.

Third, shout—and listen for answering shouts. Or blow a whistle if one is in the emergency kit—an excellent idea—whistling can be sustained much longer than shouting. (Three blasts at a time, three of anything being the universal signal of distress.) Friends or strangers may answer, their shouts guiding the way back to the trail.

Fourth, prepare for night well in advance. Conserve strength for the cold, dark hours. In bad weather look for the snuggest available shelter under trees or overhanging rocks. Build a fire if possible, not only for warmth but because someone may see the flame or smoke.

The hiker without considerable experience in cross-country navigation should, if first efforts fail, concentrate not on finding the way but on letting rescuers *find him*. Above all this means staying in one place. The hard cases are those who go and go as long as legs work, leaving the area being combed by the rescue party, eluding searchers as if by conscious intent, at last from injury, hypothermia, starvation, or a combination, dying alone.

GOING FOR HELP

Most provinces of North American trail country now are served by rescue systems coordinating land administrators, regional and local police, military and naval forces, news media, helicopters, and unpaid volunteers from outdoor clubs, Explorer Scouts, and/or units of the Mountain Rescue Association.

Though the average hiker ordinarily is never asked to join a rescue (for which only the most-experienced wildlanders available are wanted) he must always be prepared to undertake the very important task of summoning experts. Thus, before setting out on any trail, he must know how to activate the local system—usually by contacting the nearest ranger or policeman.

When a member of the party has been lost, injured, or become ill, what's to be done? It depends. How large is the party?

A lone hiker, disabled, at most can shout and wait and pray. Something for soloists to think about. (In empty country a broken leg or an inflamed appendix can be fatal.)

In a two-man group the victim—perhaps unconscious or delirious and requiring constant attention—must be left alone by his companion seeking help. Something for two-pal, girl-boy, and daddy-son parties to think about. (In rough terrain, walk as if on eggs.)

With three in the party the victim can be constantly tended while a messenger runs for the ranger. With four, two messengers can go to avoid the one becoming lost or hurt and compounding the problem.

Before leaving the scene of the accident (or illness or loss) the messenger should gather (preferably write down) data the rescuers will want: nature and location of the accident, extent of injuries, the number of people on the scene and their resources of equipment and experience, names of party members and phone numbers of next of kin.

Wherever they exist hikers should scrupulously observe sign-in/ sign-out regulations which in effect make the rangers back-up members of the party who will automatically come looking if the return is delayed. Elsewhere the schedule and route should be left with relatives or friends so rescuers can be alerted if the party is late getting home. Such precautions have sustained the life of more than one walker lying helpless, alone, but not without hope.

RESPECT

Probably no long-time rough-country wanderer can look back on his travels without wondering how he survived. He recalls the time he tripped on a root and his pack flew over his head and he teetered on the trail-edge looking straight down into a boiling river. And the time he was strolling a ridge under a fantastic cloud and suddenly hail pelted and rocks buzzed and lightning blinded. And the time he waded into a meltwater flood and in an instant the torrent threw him against a boulder a hundred feet downstream. And the time he swam to the middle of a cold mountain tarn and found his legs and arms going limp from hypothermia and only while sinking for good was able to crawl ashore. And the time he was walking a broad trail through forest and a mild breeze arose and with that final delicate push a huge snag killed in a fire 50 years ago crashed to the ground right in his path. And the night of the big storm when he huddled in his tent while torrents pressed down the roof—and next morning he crawled out to find that a few feet from his bed the meadows were obliterated under tons of boulders and gravel.

And so on, and so on, over the campfires the tales are told, the memories renewed. At last one veteran asks old companions of the hills, "How the hell did we ever *make* it, this far?" And they all laugh, nervously, for they all should have died many times when they were young and raw and fearless. And maybe they are silent a moment, remembering the companions who didn't make it. Including those who missed this campfire only by months or days—because veterans, too, sometimes die.

All well and good for the surviving veterans—they have buried friends and now know fear is healthy and when scared say so loudly and proudly and not for years have given a damn about being called "chicken." They quote the maxim from the Alps: "When a climber (hiker) is injured, he apologizes to his friends. When a climber (hiker) is killed, his friends apologize for him."

But the beginners? They may be driven by social pressure to run when they know it would be wiser to walk, to continue toward the planned objective when they know it is time to retreat. Or they may be dumb slaves of internal compulsions—a fear of not measuring up to manhood (common among boys), of not meeting a husband's expectations (the bride syndrome), of becoming old (the middle-aged athlete syndrome).

A hiker, no matter how inexperienced, almost always realizes when he is in great danger. He *knows* when the terrain is so steep a fall could be mortal. He *knows* when the wind is so ominous a bad storm is building.

Beginners die on the trails because they do not have the guts to be cowards. They have been led to believe that man has conquered the Earth and that to quail when confronted by the naked force of amoral, uncaring nature is to break faith with the pioneers, to deviate from the American Way.

Hiking tends to build humility. And respect. Qualities that not only improve the soul but enhance chances to walk wildlands for years with only an occasional disaster.

Part Two
EQUIPMENT: EVERYTHING YOU ALWAYS WANTED TO KNOW AND THEN SOME

7: ASSEMBLING THE OUTFIT

IN THE olden days of 30-odd years ago it was easy to buy equipment for hiking and backpacking—there was so little to choose from. And with gear then available at prices ordinary folk could afford and weights they could haul there was a general resignation to shivering when it was cold, getting wet when it rained, eating purely from hunger, and developing back trouble after a certain number of years on the trail.

Nowadays? A whole new world. Carrying loads lighter and more comfortable than oldtimers believed awaited them in Heaven, the modern backpacker travels and sleeps warm and dry in all but the worst conditions, quickly prepares tasty meals, and walks proudly erect, every resemblance to the shambling, stooped apeman erased.

Yet as in so many other aspects of contemporary life in the super-consumer nations of Earth, with physical luxury has come mental confusion.

See the novice enter a large mountain shop. His heart leaps with joy at the gorgeous array and he wanders in a happy daze, visualizing himself already in a wilderness camp, wiggling toes in viciously hand-some boots, cooking a savory dinner on an ingenious little stove, easy-on-the-back pack beside lightweight, storm- and bug-proof tent,

BOOT DEPARTMENT

within which is spread comfy sleeping bag.

Getting down to cases, he tries to select a pair of boots and finds dozens of models, all brutal enough to delight Attila the Hun—but which do his feet genuinely desire? He moves to the packs and each is a masterpiece of engineering—but which will bring his back true happiness? He switches to sleeping bags, jerks to stoves, flips to parkas, dabbles at food, giggles at hats.

Desperate, he runs from the shop empty-handed, wild-eyed, and trembling, seeking the nearest bowling alley, swimming pool, or ping pong parlor. Or cracks wide open and compulsively fills a shopping cart, only later discovering he has equipped himself not for weekend walks in nearby woods but for an expedition to the Karakoram, and is now bankrupt.

Veterans, too, suffer from the Gear-Buying Syndrome. Many a creaky fanatic stubbornly defends his medieval torture rack because he secretly fears humiliation amid the mysteries of body-contoured aluminum packframes, and wears the same style boots he did in 1940 because he is ashamed to admit he doesn't know a storm welt from a scree collar.

The new is not necessarily better than the old, but invariably is more complicated. Let no beginner, no veteran, abandon hope. Read on and you may be saved.

GETTING ORGANIZED

Perhaps every reader of these pages has spent a little time on trails, even if only on strolls through city parks. However, the most difficult case will be assumed, that of a person who always has lived amid unrelieved concrete and plastic and now by some flash of inspiration abruptly has decided to go hiking, and is so ignorant as hardly to know the flowers from the birds. More experienced walkers have permission to skim.

The transition from sidewalks to trails can be organized in the following steps.

FIRST, DECIDE WHAT YOU WANT TO DO, AND WHERE AND WHEN

If day hikes on broad paths are the maximum ambition, that's one thing. If the goal is to penetrate deep into wilderness on week-long backpacks, that's another.

Will most trips be in lowland forests, or in high mountains? On ocean beaches, or in deserts? Cold and wet country, or hot and dry? Entirely in summer, or partly on the fringes of winter?

Each sort of hiking, each hiking area, and each season, requires more or less special tailoring of the basic outfit.

SECOND, SEEK ADVICE

A number of books, pamphlets and magazines are recommended in the Appendix as supplementing the information presented here and/or giving different viewpoints.

The catalogs of mountain shops are indispensable guides to currently-available equipment and the latest advances in design (and price); personal visits to such shops add the third dimension.

By joining an outdoor club a beginner can, among other benefits, be tutored by veterans in locally-favored gear. (With common sources of supply has come, in recent years, substantial continent-wide and Earth-wide uniformity, but there remain regional and national differences based partly on experience with a particular province of the trail country and partly on carefully-nourished tradition.)

A novice with a trail-wise friend quite naturally and simply receives counsel and absorbs prejudices and quirks.

One should not be bashful (but not overly bold) about striking up conversations with strangers met in wildlands; often they will be delighted to lecture at length on their equipment—and lecture, and lecture, and lecture.

THIRD, PREPARE A CHECKLIST

Starting with the very general checklist at the end of this chapter, and advice from anywhere and everywhere, prepare a specific list of personally-needed gear.

FOURTH, DRAW UP A SCHEDULE OF PURCHASES

But before spending a nickel, ransack the closet, basement, attic, and kitchen. Unless the immediate goal is to join the ranks of the beautiful people in the mountain shop catalogs, much clothing too shoddy for city wear (old trousers, shirts, sweaters) or acquired for other outdoor activities (shorts, windbreakers) serves adequately for hiking. A decent enough camp kitchen can be improvised from beaten-up home utensils and tin cans. Work shoes may suffice for the first hikes, or tennis shoes for any and all short hikes.

Don't buy anything until it's needed for the next trip. Such as, if planning a series of day trips before trying a backpack, delay purchasing a packframe and sleeping bag to the last minute and use the additional time to examine the options.

Some articles can be rented from mountain shops—another way to postpone decisions, as well as to experiment with various styles of boots, packs, tents, snowshoes, and so on.

Buy inexpensive items for temporary stopgaps while carefully considering large cash outlays. For example, make do with a tarp that costs a dollar or two while studying the intricacies of tents.

However, avoid false economy in major purchases. Don't pay $20 for a pack that looks sharp in the drugstore but falls apart on the first hike; instead spend $35 for one that will last many years. And don't waste $18 on a "down" sleeping bag that spits out chicken feathers every time a cock crows.

The schedule of purchases obviously depends on financial resources. With no trouble at all and in a matter of minutes a big spender can run through $1,000 acquiring a complete, first-class outfit. However, by scrounging around the house and charity-operated thrift shops, buying second-hand equipment and cheap fill-ins, renting and borrowing, a rough-and-ready basic outfit can be put together for less than $100, spent over several months; the ideal outfit can be assembled piece by piece, as the budget allows, in following hiking seasons. Families have more of a financial problem, but that's not news.

WHERE TO BUY

In the good-bad olden days the choices of places to buy were as few as the items offered for sale. Sports shops catering to anglers and shooters carried equipment more or less suitable for backpacking, as did "Alaska outfitters" and miners' and loggers' suppliers in western cities. The authorized distributors of official Boy Scout equipment offered much that was useful for heavy camping, less that was practical for long-distance hauling.

For a brief period after World War II, during the epic era of war-surplus stores, the trails of America seemed to have been conquered by a vaudeville version of the Mountain Troops. There were army boots and army pants, army sleeping bags and army tents, army canteens and parkas and sweaters and messkits and field rations. And from the South Pacific there were jungle hammocks, camouflaged ponchos, and bug juice so potent it shriveled the skin. And for combined operations, navy liferaft sails and air force goggles. From the standpoint of the backpacker, that really was the only war ever worth having, though some military surplus continues to dribble into the civilian market.

Mountain shops had their tentative beginnings in America immediately before and after the war; in the past dozen years they have grown fantastically in size and numbers and before long probably no population center reasonably close to hiking country will be without several.

Though this book is not intended to shill for mountain shops, they are by their nature as specialists the logical basic headquarters for hikers, particularly beginners. An excellent preparation for assembling an outfit is browsing in one, asking staff members for advice, or studying a catalog and requesting guidance by mail. Just as there are differences of opinion and taste among veterans of the trail, so there are differences among shops in the gear they stock and recommend; though the average person usually settles in with a single convenient or favorite supplier, finicky and price-conscious hikers check regularly with several, in person or by catalog.

It must be noted here for the public record that not all existing and potential mountain shops are owned, managed, and staffed exclusively by experienced, wise, dependable, enthusiastic "mountain bums," as was once the case. Indeed, that's partly why this book is being published—to give beginners the benefit of some genuine bum advice.

The popularity of hiking and backpacking has caught the attention of mass-merchandisers, many of whom have expanded car-camping and sports departments to include trail gear. Few generalizations can be made about this category of suppliers. Some have limited and ragtag stocks while others offer a variety and quality comparable to mountain shops, and in some cases at substantially lower prices. Some carry well-known and dependable equipment and some do not. The staffs of some know the trails and some do not.

Quick-turnover, fast-in/fast-out emporiums have taken to advertising hiking gear at incredibly low prices. The discerning hiker may find genuine bargains at these establishments—loss leaders, or low-cost and quite adequate fill-ins, or even genuine military surplus! But the novice should beware of being stuck with pure, plain, no-money-back trash.

Many small items required by the hiker are, of course, stocked by supermarkets, drugstores, hardware stores, etc.

The thrift shops run by charities offer outstanding buys in used clothing and kitchenware and the like. The beginner on a lean budget should tour the thrift shops immediately after ransacking the basement and before starting serious spending. Parents with fast-growing kids should spend a lot of time at thrift shops. So should conservationists-environmentalists seeking to "waste not, want not, despoil not."

Anyone with a sewing machine, knowledge of sewing basics, and spare time can save up to half the normal cost of such expensive articles as parka, pack, sleeping bag, and tent by assembling kits sold by Frostline, Carikit, and EMSKITS, all of which advertise frequently in hiking/mountaineering magazines.

Note: In following chapters prices are noted for many items of equipment. These are not exact, in most cases have been rounded, and are merely suggestive of the general range.

BASIC EQUIPMENT CHECKLIST

As noted above, the beginner should prepare a checklist of equipment to be purchased or otherwise assembled. The list, regularly revised to reflect accumulated experience, has continuing utility, perhaps being posted in whatever corner of the house serves as the "hiking center" and consulted when getting ready for trips to make sure nothing has been forgotten.

No hiker, not even a raw beginner, can be satisfied by someone else's checklist, no matter if it was drawn up by a 40-year veteran of thousands of miles of trails and published in a best-selling book. Each person must do his own, based on conditions in his regular hiking terrain and on his personal idiosyncrasies.

The following list is limited to basics and does not include the myriad nice little items like binoculars, candles, pliers, reading material, playing cards, booze, and the hundred other things individuals may come to consider indispensable for safety or pleasure.

For short afternoon walks in summer sunshine on broad trails, no equipment is really necessary—nor any clothing unless the local authorities are prudes.

For full-day hikes the items listed below for "Day Trips" are generally essential; those in parenthesis may be essential in some areas, under some conditions. (See Chapter 15 for a discussion of the "Ten Essentials.")

For backpacking, additional gear is listed under "Add for Overnight," and a few more things under "Add for Special Situations."

Day Trip	Chapter Reference
Boots	8
Socks	8
Underwear	9
Shirts and sweaters	9
Parka	9
Trousers or knickers	9
(Shorts)	9
Headwear	9
Rucksack	10
(Child carrier)	10
(Canteen)	13
Food	14
(Sunglasses)	15
Knife	15

Matches, firestarter	13
First aid kit	15
Flashlight	15
Map and compass	15
(Sunburn lotion)	15
(Insect repellent)	15

Add for Overnight

Packframe and bag	10
Sleeping bag	11
Sleeping pad	11
Ground sheet	11
(Air mattress)	11
Tarp or tent and accessories	12
(Grate)	13
Stove and accessories	13
Cooking pots and accessories	13
Eating utensils	13
Food containers	13
Repair kit	15
Toilet articles	15

Add for Special Situations

(Gaiters)	8
(Poncho)	9
(Down vest or sweater)	9
(Rain pants)	9
(Mittens)	9
(Ice ax)	17
(Hiking rope)	17
(Snowshoes)	19
(Cross-country skis)	19

8:   BOOTS

EVERYONE should go barefoot now and then. A meadow delightful
to the eye is equally so to the naked sole, feeling the grasses and
flowers and the cool-delicious dew of morning. And a stream is only
known with true intimacy when toes are probing swift, cold water
seeking a finger-like grip on pebbles and boulders. Glacier-polished
slabs, squishy black muck, powdery dust, beach sand, pine needles,
snow, all give joy to the sensual foot.

But if feet can bring pleasure, so too are they exquisitely sensitive
to pain. And since civilized folk lack the built-in leather normal
among closer-to-the land people and the sore-footed hiker is no hiker
at all, but a semi-invalid, the average back-country traveler limits
barefoot romps to special occasions and for the general run of the
trail armors his feet against buffets of the rough earth.

An amazing variety of armors will more or less do the job. On
paths near tourist centers millions of miles are walked annually in
oxfords, sandals, thongs, even high heels. And not a few hikers have
roasted their boots by a campfire and retreated to the road with feet
lashed up in sweaters.

None of the above footwear is recommended, but their use demonstrates the possibility of going a long way with very little. Thus,

the beginning walker needn't worry about foot protection overly much—at first. Tennis shoes are perfectly adequate for short walks on good paths and satisfactory for longer trips on rougher ground, though at increasing cost in sore soles and bruised or turned ankles.

But once a person decides hiking is his sport, it's time to think boots.

Ah, but *which* boots? A large mountain shop may have a quarter-acre (and a half-dozen catalog pages) of boots-boots-boots in what seem at first glance to be a thousand distinct styles with an infinite variety of special features. In such a shop one can see novices, and also oldtimers whose treasured companions of the trail finally wore out, wandering in dazed confusion. Meanwhile, in the hinterland, others are staring at catalogs, baffled.

Actually, despite the wealth of options, a choice can be made with minimal struggle, in person or by letter, by telling the staff of a mountain shop the kind of hiking contemplated, the desired price range; from their experience they can instantly narrow the choice to several models.

This method is probably best for the first boots. But feet are—to coin a phrase—so basic to walking, and so individualistic, sooner or later a hiker may want to know his boots inside and out.

Beginners should skip the next section of this chapter, which tells more about boots than they care or need to know. For hikers preparing to buy their second or third pair, following is an unravelment of the most significant—but by no means all—mysteries of the catalogs.

THE INS AND OUTS OF BOOT CONSTRUCTION

LEATHER

The skyrocketing cost of leather has stimulated experiments with synthetics and plastics. To date, however, they have proven unsatisfactory for hiking, since they lack leather's ability to conform to the foot.

Leather in the boot upper, where quality is of supreme importance, may be bragged up in catalogs and ads with laudatory terms such as "shoulder leather," or "Russia (heifer) leather," or "Galluser leather." Having no idea what they mean, the ordinary purchaser must take it on faith that if he's paying a pretty price he's getting a pretty good leather.

Leather of lesser merit is used for insoles and midsoles; it may even be "reconstituted"—that is, a cemented composition of ground-up leather.

For comfort, inner liners may be *calfskin* or super-soft *glove* (*glove-tanned* or *garment-tanned*) leather. The latter, and also *kangaroo* leather, commonly are used for the above-ankle portions of the high boots once standard on American trails but now virtually abandoned.

Tanning

Since the hide would quickly rot without treatment, it is put through as many as 19 mechanical and chemical operations while being cured, or tanned, into leather.

In *chrome tanning* or *dry tanning,* the most common process in America and most of Europe for making the leather in city shoes and also boots, the hide is tanned with soluble chromium salts, giving a hard finish with a dry look.

In *oil tanning* or *vegetable tanning,* favored by a number of Italian manufacturers and some American, the hide is tanned with vegetable material ("bark tannins") derived from plants and woods, giving a soft, supple finish with a wet, oily look.

In the relatively-uncommon (for boots) *combination,* or *vegetable-chrome* tanning, agents are combined.

The advantages of the methods are a matter of highly-technical industry debate. Excellent leathers are produced by all three and the main reason a hiker should know which sort his boots are made from is in order to give proper treatment for water-repellency and leather maintenance, as discussed below.

Double tanning, by whichever method, is just what it sounds like —a doubly good job.

How Is It Sliced?

As worn by the animal, the hide varies in thickness from one part of the body to another. In preparation for boot (or other) use, the hide may be sliced into as many as half a dozen layers of different thickness or *gauge.* Thin-gauge leather is characteristic of light-duty boots, heavy-gauge of heavy-duty.

Leather made from a layer including the outer surface of the hide (*grain side*) is called *top grain.* This is the best slice for boot uppers, for obvious reasons the toughest and most water-resistant. The inner surface of the hide is called the *flesh side.*

Any slice not including the outside of the cow is called a *split.* Splits are fine for insoles and midsoles but inferior for heavy-duty uppers, being hard to waterproof and very stretchable. When used for an upper a split leather is called *suede,* a poor choice for slogging wet trails but excellent for dry paths, especially in hot climates, because it is lightweight, porous, and easy-breathing.

Which Side Outside?

The cow wears its skin with the grain side outside, the flesh side inside. Hikers, when they appropriate the hide for their feet, may do the same, or may not.

In a boot upper, top-grain leather with the grain side outside, facing the "right" way, is called *smooth* or *smooth-finish* or *smooth-out* leather. Partisans say this tougher and more water-repellent surface is the proper one to confront the harsh wilderness. Critics say the tough outer layer is quite thin, readily breached in rough travel; once penetrated, it allows water to pour through the soft underlayer.

A top-grain leather with the flesh side outside is called *rough-out* or *flesh-out* or *reversed* or *reverse-tanned* or *rough-tanned* leather. (The term "suede-like," sometimes encountered, is misleading; to be sure, a flesh-out leather looks the same as suede, but the latter is a split.) Partisans say that to preserve its water-repellency, the tough outer layer of hide is best kept from contact with the brutal wilderness and that the flesh side, though it scuffs and abrades easily, is never weakened structurally and wears away only bit by bit.

Experts argue back and forth. They agree, though, that the quality of a hide is more significant than whether it is used rough-out or smooth-out; first-rate boots are made both ways. The important distinction is whether a leather is top-grain or split.

Natural or Prettified?

A bootmaker using a highest-quality hide frequently is so proud of it he retains as much as possible of the original appearance. In such *full grain* or *natural* leather no attempt has been made to conceal healed scratches or small pits caused by tick and fly bites. The natural look is not only considered the most beautiful by connoisseurs but maintains the full inherent strength, durability, and breathability. The color of boots made from full-grain leather usually is not uniform throughout due to variations from hide to hide.

A *corrected-grain* leather is not necessarily inferior in strength and may be of excellent quality. However, the manufacturer has chosen to hide blemishes to obtain a uniform appearance. For example, in a *pebble-grained* leather the surface has been stippled by tiny gouges.

A smooth or rough-out leather may be *dyed* lightly (or not at all) to retain the natural look. Most suedes and some other leathers are dyed black, gray, green, blue, red, brown, or whatever. The dye doesn't harm the leather and may have more appeal to style-conscious walkers than the color of a cow.

STRUCTURE OF THE BOOT

The complications of leather-making are nothing compared to those of boot-designing. Mathematically speaking there could be—and to the bewildered layman sometimes seems to be—an infinite number of combinations of features.

The maze may best be charted by systematically exploring each area of the boot in turn.

The Upper In General

One school of experts holds that the best way to build a boot upper is from a *single piece* of leather, thus keeping seams—lines of potential weakness and leakage—to a minimum. Another school defends *sectional* (from two or three pieces) construction, saying (1) the upper can more easily be made to conform to the foot, (2) smaller pieces of prime leather can be utilized and thus the total expense is less for the same quality, and (3) seam leakage isn't that much of a problem anyhow. Neutrals don't get very sweaty about the matter, admitting that most climbing boots have one-piece uppers, most hiking boots sectional, and that perhaps this means something, but insisting that either method will work fine for either purpose. Certainly, a lot of stitching on an upper by no means indicates a bad boot.

A *double-stitched* upper has two lines of stitching at every point, thus reducing chances of all stitches being cut at once. Triple-stitching gives that much more insurance.

The least complicated and costly design of an upper is found in a *shell* boot, unlined and unpadded, with a single layer of leather between foot and outside world. Many hikers like such a simple boot, preferring to add their own padding, as situations warrant, with insoles and socks; hot-country hikers particularly despise fully-padded boots, or "sweat boxes."

Most contemporary boots have some amount of lining, reinforcing, and padding. The more there is, the more the foot protection, insulation, comfort—and weight and expense. For light hiking, less is better; for hard pounding in cruel terrain, more is essential. Where lies the golden mean? In a different place for each use. One observation may be made: just as the average American tends to buy more automobile than he really needs, so does the average novice tend to buy more boot than he really needs; sexual symbolism apparently is involved.

The *lining* may be complete, partial, or nonexistent. Usually of pigskin, calfskin, or some other soft, supple leather, the lining lets the foot glide smoothly in and out and minimizes chafing.

Most boots have *padding* in the ankle area; others are padded elsewhere, perhaps throughout, though rarely to the toe. The padding material, inserted between the outer wall and the liner, may be foam, rubber, or felt. (To be avoided for ordinary hiking is the *insulated* boot designed for extreme cold.)

Reinforcing at heel and toe is discussed below. There may also be *side-reinforcements* of leatherboard or other material above the ball of the foot and from the ball backward toward the heel. Reinforcements where needed for foot support and protection, and wherever possible for softness and flexibility, are characteristic of the best boots. Cheaper boats may give protection and support with stiff materials, making them uncomfortable and difficult to break in. Quality boots with a good deal of reinforcement may have a *hinged instep,* a small cutout from the leather of the upper that allows the boot to flex.

The Upper Part of the Upper

Hiking boots come in overall heights, measured from the top to the welt, where the sole joins the upper, of from less than 6 inches, or barely covering the ankle, to 9 inches, or partway up the calf. A height—say 5½ inches—that protects and supports the ankle is the minimum for any extended walking and suffices for good trails. Where stream crossings, mud, and snow are expected, a height of about 7½ inches is preferable to keep moisture from coming over the top. Some hikers of well-watered mountains like to go even farther, up to 9 inches; this height is objected to by others as making the boot difficult to get in and out of and perhaps constricting the muscles of the calf, especially in uphill walking. The excess leather in high boots also tends to stretch out of shape and either bunch or buckle behind the ankle, sometimes pressing on the Achilles tendon.

Many boots have a gap-closing device at the top to prevent water or snow or pebbles from slipping down inside. Most common is an elastic fabric, perhaps padded, that fits snugly against the leg. Among the names for the device are *scree shield, scree collar, scree gaiter, snow protector,* and *cuff.* Half or less of all hikers find this feature effective; the others feel it doesn't work at all (though few think it detrimental) and prefer to do the job, when necessary, with a separate gaiter, discussed below.

The collar may include a roll of foam padding to comfort the Achilles tendon, which in some boots is further pampered by cutting the leather of the upper low in back and adding a soft panel of garment leather.

The Back of the Upper

Many climbing boots have a *hinged heel* (*flexible rear hinge*); a section of the upper is cut out and replaced by a softer leather that lets the boot flex slightly.

All heavy-duty and many medium-duty boots have a *heel counter* (*heel cup*), a piece of leather or rigid fiber inserted inside, cupping the heel to help anchor the foot to the boot sole, thus minimizing heel lift. Added protection is also given the heel.

A *heel cap* (sometimes called *outside heel counter*) is an extra piece of leather stitched to the boot exterior to guard against abrasion.

The Toe

Boots in the American pioneer tradition have a completely *soft* toe, easy on the foot—until it runs into or is fallen upon by a rock. So frequent are such foot-rock encounters that toes on nearly all modern hiking and climbing boots are more or less *hard,* ranging from being slightly stiffened by a piece of plastic inside to total bomb-proofing by counters of leather, leatherboard, or plastic. The result may be described as a *toe guard, hard toe, box toe,* or whatever. Rarely a boot may be found with a *toe cap,* the same thing as a heel cap but in a different place.

The *moccasin toe* still has fans. Because the structure is soft (and difficult to make hard), the hiker's toes are cosy. Moccasin toes and high-top uppers generally go together on boots of the old, old American design which still is beloved of woodsmen who tramp mainly soft, mucky forests.

Tongue and Closure

In the tongue-and-closure area the boot designer has three concerns: (1) preventing water from seeping or pouring through the gap, (2) providing the foot expeditious entry and exit, since donning and doffing wet or frozen boots can be an excruciating test of muscle and will, and (3) being kind to delicate flesh. In the upward progression from easy dry trails to rough sopping terrain, increasing attention must be paid the tongue and closure. The expedients adopted by designers are countless; they all, however, represent one of two basic approaches.

Tongue and closure. Left: *hiking boot with gusseted tongue (plus inner tongue)*. Center: *light climbing boot with overlapping split tongue (plus inner tongue)*. Right: *trail shoe with simple split tongue*

The *gusseted tongue* bars water by placing an unbroken barrier between foot and wet world. On simple boots the barrier may be nothing more than a small strip of soft leather attaching the tongue to the boot upper, the tongue being described as *sewn-in;* the barrier strip, and sewing, may extend to the top or only part of the way. On more complex boots the barrier is a considerable mass of flexible leather that opens out in a *bellows* to let the foot in and out, folds neatly when laced. In a variation, the boot has two tongues, a soft inner one for comfort and an outer gusseted tongue.

The *split tongue* permits the boot to be opened very wide so the foot can gain easy ingress when the leather is frozen rock-hard; it keeps out water (though perhaps never so absolutely as a gusseted tongue) by creating, with the help of laces, devious passageways that discourage inward-working moisture. Many a split-tongue design has two tongues, a soft inner (often partly sewn-in) and an outer which actually is the boot upper, split down the middle. The most elementary example of the split tongue is found on city oxfords and light trail shoes, where the halves of the upper are drawn together over the inner tongue by laces. On heavier-duty boots the split halves of the upper overlap. A few boots have a third tongue outside the split tongue for more complete baffling of water.

Having thus simplified (?) the tongue situation, it now is necessary to re-complicate it by saying there are many combinations of gusseting and splitting, resulting in a variety of hybrid designs.

On light-duty trail shoes the tongue proper may be a single thickness of leather. On heavier-duty boots that require tight lacing, the inner tongue is *padded* to cushion the foot against pressures of laces; it may also be *contoured* or *hinged* for easy flexing.

Lacing

Completing the closure is the lacing, which may be by eyelets, D rings (also called swivel eyelets), hooks, or a combination.

A few boots, including light trail shoes as well as some traditional American designs, have *all-eyelet* lacing, with the eyelets formed by grommets set directly into the upper. The advantage is that grommets

Lacing systems. Left: swivel eyelets and hooks (the leather is smooth-out). Middle: grommet eyelets and hooks (rough-out leather). Right: all-eyelet lacing (suede leather)

virtually never fail until the boot is ancient, and even then the holes seldom enlarge or split out, since before this can happen the metal pieces must break loose. The disadvantage is that lacing is tedious.

More common are boots having *eyelets partway up, then yielding to hooks*—the latter being much quicker to lace and unlace. An alternative to the grommet-type eyelet set into the upper is the *swivel eyelet,* in which a D ring is attached to a clip riveted to the upper; this design combines easy lacing with maximum water-repellency and insulation. *Speed lacing,* most common on older ski boots, employs closed hooks; a single quick pull tightens the laces all the way from bottom to top.

Incidentally, most hikers do not realize that hooks, rings, clips, and grommets can be quickly replaced in any shoe-repair shop and most mountain shops. There is no need to accept the loss of metal fixtures fatalistically and go about with half a lacing system, the boot only loosely lashed to the foot.

As for *laces,* leather retains a few adherents but stretches when wet and thus loosens. Nylon is more popular nowadays for its greater durability; soft-woven, unwaxed laces hold knots best.

A *built-in lace lock* is a common feature of rock-climbing shoes, where extremely tight fit is essential from instep to toe. It is mentioned here only because rock shoes look much like lightweight trail boots.

Some climbing boots have a lacing system that allows the boot to flex at the ankle, and/or *flush lace hooks,* where the metal is inset to avoid snagging during intricate rock-climbing moves.

A tip about lacing: The beginning walker, or any walker at the start of the season, may find his tender shin being abraded by the top of the boot, especially the knot. The remedy is to lace to the top, then lace back downward two or three rows and tie the knot there. This method gives support the full height of the boot but removes the knot from the tender spot, as well as from the knot-loosening activity of the ankle; it also reinforces the heel and helps keep the entire lace system secure.

Another tip: If toes feel cramped, lace the lower area of the boot loose, then tie a knot and lace the upper area tight. Or in a different situation, such as downhill walking, lace tight down low, especially at the toes, tie a knot, and lace loose up high. In summary: experiment.

One final tip: If you are having trouble lacing stiff boots tight enough, try the *cargo knot*. Bring the laces to the middle of the boot, wrap them over each other, and thus, when cinching, reverse the normal direction of pull and gain a mechanical advantage.

Insole

The bottom of the boot is where the hiker meets earth, thudding against the hard places, slithering on the slippery places, and thus where he seeks cushioning and traction. It also is the area of most complicated boot engineering because of the problems in attaching the upper to the soles and keeping them firmly together.

The sole has three parts: insole, midsole, and outsole.

The next-to-foot insole (inner sole) usually is leather, sometimes cellulose. Ordinarily it is covered by a thin synthetic *sock liner* that gives low-friction foot entry. Some boots have *cushion* insoles, foam rubber covered by lining leather.

On a *channel* insole, typical of better, stronger boots, the stitching of insole to midsole is done in a channel cut into the insole leather.

Midsole and Shank

Boots meant only for soft paths sometimes do not have a midsole; the insole is attached directly to the outsole. On bumpy ground such boots let every sharp pebble stab the foot. When foot collides with mean and nasty earth perhaps 10,000 or more times a day, midsoles are badly wanted for stiffness, support, and cushioning. The heavier the construction, the greater the number of midsoles: perhaps from a minimum of one in front increasing to three under the heel, to a maximum of three leather and one rubber throughout.

Many experts favor leather midsoles, saying they help shape boot to foot, absorb sweat, breathe, are flexible, and break in quickly. Others lean to rubber, stiffer but cheaper and giving a firmer bond to the outsole, plus more cushioning. Combinations of leather above and rubber below are common. In addition, some boots have a cork or foam *filler* between midsole and insole, again for cushioning.

All but the simplest boots have a *shank* to support the arch, protect the instep, and keep the foot straight. Since the softer the boot sole the more comfortable the foot movement, light-duty boots generally lack any kind of shank and are easily bent double in the hands. Medium-duty boots with a medium shank can be bent a little, and heavy-duty boots with a heavy shank cannot be bent at all.

The shank may be half-length or full-length, depending on the intended rigors of use. In descending degree of strength are shanks of tempered spring steel, plastic or fiberglass, reconstituted leather or stiffened nylon.

Boots with sturdy shanks and many midsoles, and thus nearly or completely rigid, always have a *rocker bottom,* shaped to curve up slightly or considerably at toe and heel to permit an approximation of the normal walking configuration of a naked foot.

Outsole

Until World War II just about every American hiker and climber gained traction on trail, footlog, meadow, and snow with nailed soles. For the hiker there were hobs, rosebuds, slivvers, and logger's calks (pronounced "corks") in the instep. For the scrambler and climber there were Swiss edge-nails liked by a scattering of oldtimers—but for the masses (all couple thousand or so) the tricouni nail or "trike."

Then the Mountain Troops came home from Italy wearing the "Bramani," a legendary boot that weighed a ton, sold for nickels and dimes at surplus stores—and was fitted not with an iron-studded bottom but with rubber lugs. A splendid, passionate debate began throughout North America. Trikes were attacked as "heat sinks," conducting the heat of the foot out of the boot. They were defended as infinitely superior to lugs on hard snow, footlogs, heather, steep grass—indeed, virtually every sort of terrain except rock and well-maintained trails.

A few mountain shops still carry tricounis to please the hard-core nailmen who vow the age of iron will return. And maybe it will, but the debate waned in the early 1960s and since then the lug has held almost universal dominion on American, as European, trails and peaks.

Left: *Vibram rubber-lug sole, Montagna style.* Right: *molded lug sole, all one piece.*

Virtually every current hiking and climbing boot has a rubber-lug (really a high-carbon neoprene, which is synthetic rubber) sole. Though Galibier, Pirelli, and several other brands are about the same, Vibram dominates the market. Vibram soles come in 12 different neoprene compounds of varying hardness and in several designs, ranging from the comparatively shallow, soft, and flexible Roccia typical of lightweight boots, to the Montagna with deeper tread and harder rubber.

Some very light boots and children's boots (and a few heavier boots) are of cemented construction (discussed below) and have a shallow *molded lug sole.* Unlike the Vibram-type sole, molded lugs are difficult to replace, but no matter—most such boots disintegrate or are outgrown long before the lugs erode away.

It must be noted that the longevity of lugs is determined not by the number of years the boot has been owned but by how many miles the hiker has walked and where. Lugs may last a decade in travel on soft humus, four or five years with a moderate admixture of rockslide, or one summer of bashing up and down raw moraines. Since the mid-1960s, when the "European climbing boot look" became a campus fad, Vibrams have been subjected to a punishment for which they never were designed; city sidewalks literally eat lugs alive. The novice hiker who wants to look sexy in the city but doesn't have a lot of money to spend on the costume should pick some cheaper modish footwear and save lugs for the wildlands.

Attaching Sole to Upper

The attachment of sole to upper is, for the layman, the most mysterious aspect of the boot; listening to violently dogmatic experts merely compounds confusion. For openers, then, let it be declared that every customary method of attachment, whether or not it involves *welting* (stitching of sole to upper) has distinctive virtues (and vices) and is good for a certain range of uses.

Cement construction is the least expensive. The upper is folded under a light insole and a one-piece rubber outsole cemented on. No midsole, no welting. The boot is very flexible, gives little support, and usually cannot be resoled. Many light-duty trail boots are cemented. The comfort on soft paths, and the economy, are attractive.

Somewhat similar is *injection molding,* familiar in modern ski boots and used on a few trail shoes and super-heavy mountaineering boots. Molten neoprene applied under pressure takes the place of welting or cementing.

With the *inside-stitching* method, also called *Littleway construction* (or *Littleway welt*), the upper is folded under and sandwiched between insole and midsole, the outsole is glued to the lower midsole, and the layers are fastened together by a double row of lock-stitching, concealed within the boot and thus protected from moisture and abrasion. (A boot so made can be recognized by the absence of exterior stitches.) Advantages of Littleway are that the sole can be closely cropped to be nearly flush with the upper, the boots are more waterproof than outside-stitched ones, and are less expensive to build and repair. Disadvantages are that the stitching of midsoles to insole makes the boot relatively stiff and that the *last* (the foot-shaped form of metal or plastic around which a boot is built) must be removed before final stitching, in which case the upper may not fit the boot so well and may require an extended break-in period. The better trail boots, an increasing number of hiking boots, and a few climbing boots are of Littleway construction.

The term "welting," though sometimes applied to Littleway, ordinarily is reserved for *outside-stitched* (*welted*) boots, of which two types are common.

With the *Norwegian welt* (*European welt*), presently used on nearly all climbing boots and many if not most heavy-duty hiking boots, one line of stitching angles inward, securing insole to upper, and a second line is vertical, securing midsole to the outward-turned upper. (A Norwegian-welted boot can be recognized by the two lines of stitching visible on the ledge atop the sole, though the inward-slanting line may be difficult to see.) Advantages are that, because the last remains in the boot until construction is complete, the insole conforms around the last without distortion, assuring a good fit; that replacing midsole and outsole is easier than with a Goodyear welt (though not as easy as with a Littleway); and that—according to proponents—it is the strongest and most durable way to build a boot. Disadvantages are the expense of manufacture and the vulnerability of the outside stitching to wear and leakage.

With the *Goodyear welt* (*U.S. welt, true welt*), found on most men's street shoes and many American-made boots, the upper is stitched directly to a raised rib on the insole and to a narrow piece of leather (called the *welt,* just to complicate terminology) which goes completely around the boot exterior at the junction of sole and upper. The welt is then stitched to midsoles. (A Goodyear-welted boot can be recognized by the single line of stitching on the ledge atop the sole.) Advantages are that the method permits rapid machine production and thus lower cost. Disadvantages are that when repairs are needed only the outsole can be easily replaced.

(To further foul up this welt business, some mountaineering boots have, in addition to the above, a *storm welt,* an all-around exterior piece of leather sewn to upper and midsole as an extra guard against leakage.)

In conclusion, price of a boot typically ascends in the progression from cemented to Littleway to Goodyear welt to Norwegian welt. Despite the quarreling among manufacturers, good boots—for their intended purposes—are made by all these methods.

VARIETIES OF BOOTS

The preceding section may be fascinating to the studious hiker buying his second or third pair of boots. The novice, however, if he has accepted our advice, has at most skimmed that section and begins here.

Making a checklist of desired features and then seeking a boot that has them is one way to make a selection, the way of some experienced hikers ("equipment freaks"). But the best procedure for the beginner—and for most hikers for all the boots they ever buy—is to choose from the standpoint of planned use. That is, a person decides what sort of hiking he wants to do and then restricts examination to models designed for his purpose; from among those models, he *picks a boot that feels good,* far and away the most important attribute of a boot and a matter extensively discussed later in this chapter.

Manufacturers and retailers gradually are moving toward a standard categorization. Though there is not complete uniformity, the scheme that seems to be gaining greatest favor is to describe boots of the kinds suitable for hikers as (1) trail shoes, (2) hiking boots, and (3) climbing boots. Two other categories, kletterschue or rock-climbing shoes, and mountaineering boots, are of no interest to hikers.

The categories partly are differentiated by *price,* which in the merchandising world at large reflects quality of materials and manufacture; but which at mountain shops, where all boots generally are of good quality, principally indicates the amount of foot protection. That is, every added midsole and stiffener and pad, every such feature as shank, heel cup, hinged instep, and so on, pushes up the price.

Every added feature also adds *weight,* which is an even more accurate indicator of boot category. Let the novice be warned: heavy-duty boots are really and truly heavy and carrying unnecessary loads on the feet is devoutly to be avoided; the U.S. Army Research Institute of Environmental Medicine has determined that carrying a pound on the feet demands as much energy as carrying 6 pounds on the back; what with a boot being lifted more than 1000 times a mile, after a while even toenails seem a painful burden.

Mountain shops find that the major error of novices is over-booting, wasting money buying a climbing boot for trail-walking and then wasting energy dragging it around. The word is: buy enough boot, but not too much.

TRAIL SHOE

In the department store and Super-Thrifty Drugs version called a "wafflestomper," and in mountain shop catalogs a "lightweight hik-

Representative boots. Above: trail shoes, weighing 3–4 pounds for an average-sized men's pair. Middle: hiking boots, 4–5 pounds. Below: climbing boots, 5–6 pounds

ing" or 'lightweight trail" boot, the trail shoe serves well for short hikes on well-maintained trails.

The leather is often suede, occasionally top grain, construction is cemented or Littleway, midsoles are nonexistent to few, padding and reinforcing and shanking are minimal. The boots are flexible and comfortable. Protection against buffeting by the terrain is minor— not much more than with a good tennis shoe or sneaker, a decent alternative for casual walking.

Trail shoes range in price from around $20 to $35, with a few as high as $50 and some very light wafflestompers as low as $15. Weight per pair in an average man's size is about 3–4 pounds; in an average woman's size, about 2½–3½ pounds.

HIKING BOOT

The hiking boot, called in catalogs "medium-weight hiking and climbing" or "lightweight climbing" boot, is the proper choice for people who travel rough trails with lots of water and muck and rock, now and then venturing off trails into moraines, scree, snow, brush, and steep flower fields.

Leather is top grain, construction sometimes Littleway but usually Norwegian or Goodyear welt, midsoles are thicker and shanks stiffer and the padding and reinforcing more extensive, making quite a rigid boot but giving a high degree of protection.

Hiking boots range in price from around $30 to $40, with some at $50. Weight per pair in an average man's size is about 4–5 pounds; in an average woman's size, 3½–4½ pounds.

CLIMBING BOOT

The hiker who does considerable off-trail bulldozing through brush, moraines, and snow has needs resembling those of the climber and thus may be interested in what catalogs typically describe as "medium-weight climbing" boots. The price range is $40 to $65. Weight per pair in an average man's size is about 5–6 pounds; in an average woman's size, 4½–5½ pounds.

Relatively few hikers want this much boot. None want the "heavy-duty" or "heavy-weight" "climbing or mountaineering" boots which weigh up to 7 pounds or more per pair and cost from $60 to $150.

CHILDREN'S BOOT

A major objection to children is that they grow (and grow, and *grow*) and *out*grow boots at a financially ruinous rate. Hard-pressed parents often outfit their offspring in cheap sandals that fit the budget, on the theory that kids can stand anything. In fact, little feet are at least as tender as big feet and need as much protection. Kinder parents buy proper boots to start and then, to stay out of bankruptcy court and on the trail, hand them down from one child to the next or pass them around a circle of friends in similar straits.

As with adults, tennis shoes suffice for light walking.

Stepping up to the trail-boot category, the "patrol boot" is found at department stores and the like in various brands, generally selling for about $10 or less. The customary ripple rubber sole is adequate for easy trails; avoid those with smooth soles.

A giant step up is the classic Bambino, a true hiking or climbing boot scaled down to serve from the cradle through early adolescence. Fully lined and padded, with molded lug sole, soft and flexible yet firm, sturdy, and rugged, Bambinos in the 11-year-old size weigh 1¾ pounds the pair. The price in various sizes runs around $20, give or take a dollar.

Bambinos may in the long run be less expensive for a family than patrol boots, wafflestompers, or whatever. Some mountain shops which carry the line give a generous trade-in if the boots have been treated carefully; parents thus can keep their kids in first-rate footwear after the initial blow by modest annual or biennial expenditures. (At such shops, of course, thrifty parents should first ask to see the *used* Bambinos.)

A boot very similar to the Bambino is the Lowa Junior Hiker; the lighter and less expensive Bambini, Scrambler, and Fabiano Child's Boot are in the trail-shoe category.

HANDMADE BOOT

A generation ago the goal of every hiker-climber was someday to achieve the ultimate in comfort, durability, and swank by having boots lovingly built by hand to fit his personal feet.

The demand for handmade boots has dwindled now that mountain shops offer so great a variety of ready-made models. However, hikers with exceptional foot problems may find that no ready-made boot, no where, no how, is anything but a bone-mangler, a blister factory, no matter how expertly modified by stretching or addition of insoles and arch supports.

Custom bootmakers remain active in most parts of America containing trail country and many mountain shops will, upon request, recommend a dependable nearby craftsman. The alternative is to try the yellow pages of the telephone book.

The cost may be $80, or $100, or $150, depending. However, custom boots often last, with periodic rebuilding, years and years. And if the choice is between hiking foot-happy and hiking footsore or not at all, any price is cheap.

BUYING BOOTS

The best way to buy, of course, is to visit a shop, browse around, consult the staff and try on boots, many boots, in the chosen category. The trying-on cannot be overemphasized, because boots are manufactured for that anatomical rarity, the "average" foot; actually, if people went around with faces veiled and feet bare, they would recognize each other as readily by individual peculiarities of feet as they do now by those of faces.

Some mountain shops rent boots, allowing a novice to go hiking while struggling over a decision on what to buy.

In selecting the proper *length,* it is important that the toes do not extend all the way to the front of the boot; if they do, they will bump, especially in downhill travel, and soon become sore and blistered; also, the toe nail will be jammed into the cuticle, causing pain and perhaps loss of the nail. As an approximate rule of thumb, with the boot unlaced and the toe pushed to the front, a person should be able to slide one finger down behind the heel. If the finger is snug the fit borders on too tight; if two fingers can be inserted the fit borders on too loose. When the boot is laced tight, a person should not be able to push the toes against the front (stand on the slope of the shoe-shop stool to test toe room).

Variations in feet are such that a boot that fits well from the ball of the foot forward may not fit rearward to the heel (the instep area), length of the arch (from ball to heel) can be more critical than length of the total foot.

In selecting the proper *width* for the ankle area a visual inspection should be made to ensure that there is, when laced tight, a gap of at least 1/4-3/8 inch between the tongue and hooks; otherwise the tongue will run against the hook posts and allow no space for tightening.

The width elsewhere must be judged by feel. The boot should be comfortably snug, allowing toes to move yet holding the ball of the foot firmly to the sole and permitting little if any lateral movement or "slop." Some slight up-and -down motion ("lift") of the heel is nearly unavoidable and does no harm in itself; however, with improperly adjusted socks the foot may rub back and forth and blister. Boots stretch in use, becoming somewhat wider (though not longer) and thus the width in the shop should be a bit on the tight side.

When trying on boots, wear two pairs of socks, one light and the other medium (so say some experts) or a single pair of heavy socks (so say others). Remember the stretch that will come with use; if a hiker plans to wear two pairs of heavy socks on the trail and does so in the shop, within a year he will have to wear three pairs to fill the cavity.

FITTING BOOTS TO ODD FEET

Many hikers, perhaps a majority, cannot find any boot that fits well precisely as it comes off the shelf. These are the people with narrow heels or flat arches, or long skinny feet or short fat feet.

For those with wide bridges or toes and narrow heels, the only hope may be handmade boots; an extra pair of socks may hold the heel securely and keep it from rising up and down at each step, but more often than not the solution creates a new problem—constriction of the toes.

Other foot peculiarities may also require custom boots, but various simpler alternatives suffice for most situations. For example, many hikers use a *heel cushion,* or *lift.* Others add one or more *insoles,* which not only remedy fitting problems but give extra cushioning. *Arch supports* are invaluable to some hikers. Another common device is the *tongue pad.* Finally, a boot can be stretched slightly at

critical points at any shoe-repair shop.

Adjusting the number and weight of socks is done by all hikers at various times on the trail as their feet swell or shrink.

BREAKING IN BOOTS

If a boot doesn't feel basically "right" in the store it never will feel good on the trail and therefore one should not put too much trust in the corrective action of breaking in the boot. If the boot is fundamentally incompatible with the foot, never the twain shall be happy together, and the boot is going to win all the arguments.

Leather forms around the foot to a certain extent as the body heats it. People with very average, very tough feet never have to worry about breaking in a boot—if they've chosen properly. The breaking in takes place in the first few miles of the first hike, with no pain, no blisters. However, the beginning hiker, especially, is well-advised to try his new purchase on a short walk or two before committing his feet to a long trip where disabling blisters could be a serious matter.

Some boots, constructed of cheap materials or designed for very heavy duty, are so stiff that two or three fairly long and strenuous hikes may be needed before they feel broken in. If they are still a misery, face it, they're a lost cause. Go back to the mountain shop and trade them in on a new pair.

Beware of the drastic measures recommended here and there as "safe" and ensuring a quick and perfect fit. Breaking in a recalcitrant boot by soaking it in warm water may, indeed, help shape it to the foot—but at the cost of weakening the inner structure, which is composed of various materials that dry at different rates, shrink differentially, and in the process pull apart. Water is not good for a boot. The cold water of the wilderness carries on a war of attrition; the hot water of the "instant break-in" hits like a blitzkrieg.

Still worse are such other methods as soaking the boots in alcohol, which is lethal.

ORDERING BOOTS BY MAIL

Many American hikers and climbers cannot conveniently visit a boot supplier and must order by mail. In such case one should first study a catalog or two carefully—and the information in this chapter. However, the novice buying his first or second boots ultimately must throw himself on the mercy of experts—either experienced friends or the supplier. Fortunately, there now are in America a number of suppliers who are skilled in selecting boots for distant feet.

The first thing the purchaser-by-mail must realize is the futility of trying to find an exact equivalence between his or her street shoe size (or the size of his current boot, if any) and that of the proper size in the desired style and brand. The boots stocked by mountain shops are made on several continents, in half a dozen nations. They are made on the American last, and on the very dissimilar European last, British last, and Italian last. Also, every manufacturer has his own sizing system and no two are exactly the same.

Suppliers rather uniformly give the following instructions for ordering by mail:

1. Send street-shoe size and width. These do not tell what boot size is right, but provide a starting point.

2. Do not order by boot size unless you have previously tried on the *exact* style and brand of boot you are ordering.

3. Using your larger foot (nobody has feet exactly the same size), put on the socks you intend to wear in the boots. Stand (with weight evenly distributed on both feet) on a piece of cardboard or stiff paper and trace a heavy line around the foot, making very sure to *hold the pencil absolutely vertical at all times*. (Some suppliers recommend that tracings be sent of both feet.)

4. Cut out the foot tracing, write your name on it, and enclose it with your order.

To this, suppliers generally add that a first choice of model should be stated plus one or two acceptable alternates. Most boots come from distant points and a supplier's stock of any given size or style may become depleted in periods of heavy purchasing, with no chance of quick replenishment.

When the boots arrive, they should be checked carefully for proper fit, following the methods described above. Wear them *around the house* until satisfied, and if not, return them; most suppliers accept returned boots that have not obviously been used. If the boots prove unsatisfactory after a hike or two, they will still be accepted as trade-ins on new boots by mountain shops which deal in used boots.

BEING KIND TO BOOTS

Being kind to boots is being kind to the feet and the pocketbook. Mistreated boots vent their spite on tender flesh. They may, if badly abused, die prematurely, thus taking revenge on the bank account.

The boot was once part of a cow; now it must be treated as part of the hiker. However, the boot cannot cry out in pain, as could the cow, and as can the hiker, and therefore one must watch over its health all the more solicitously.

HOW TO COOK A BOOT

Two classic ways to destroy boots are (1) "drying them out" by a campfire and (2) sitting around a campfire, boots on, "warming up the toes." Throughout the back country are shriveled corpses of boots so murdered; coming upon such relics, one wonders how their owner got home—barefoot, or with feet wrapped in sweaters and bits of tarp?

It must be kept in mind at all times that though the cow is long since dead and its hide has been tanned, it is still a skin and will be wrecked by any heat the living animal could not tolerate. The test is simple: while sitting by the campfire, put your fingers on the boot leather; if it is uncomfortably warm to the touch the leather is being cooked.

A less obvious but equally effective way to cook a boot is by putting it too close to the heater of a car on the way to or from a trip, or storing it close to a furnace or hot-air vent or atop a radiator at home.

The mud treatment is another very common method. If after a hike the boots are tossed in a corner with mud still on them, the mud dries and in so doing dries out the leather and the cement holding the boot together—especially around the sole, where the mud is usually caked. The leather crystallizes, the cement fails, and the boot falls apart, if not instantly, on a forthcoming hike.

Very wet but not muddy trails (all snow, or mostly creeks and puddles) automatically wash the boots; if not, messiness can be avoided by brushing them at hike's end with a whiskbroom kept in the car for the purpose.

Once home the boots should be immediately washed with a stiff brush and cool water, the interior sprayed with disinfectant to prevent mold and then stuffed with crumpled newspapers or paper towels which absorb the moisture exhaled by wet leather, help hold the boot in shape, and stop deep wrinkles from setting in. Placing the boots in a ski-boot rack or press while being dried and/or stored prevents curling. When the boot is dry it should be treated with a leather-conditioning and waterproofing compound—the next subject on the agenda.

CONDITIONING AND WATERPROOFING THE BOOT

The process that began when the cow hide was tanned into leather must be continued through the life of the boot. Since the cow no longer can circulate natural juices and oils into the skin, the hiker must take up the task with various substitutes. If he does not, the leather sooner or later lets water flow freely through. It also, in drying out, becomes stiff—an efficient blister machine. Eventually it cracks, the upper and sole separate, and the time has come to buy new boots —and vow to take better care of them.

As mentioned above, the hiker must know how the leather of his boot upper was tanned (if the clerk doesn't know, ask him to check) in order to apply the proper conditioning and waterproofing preparation; the wrong compound may actually do more harm than good.

Compounds come in liquid and paste and aerosol forms, but the critical characteristic is the active ingredient, the two most important of which are oil and silicone. The general rule is *oil on oil-tanned, silicone on chrome-tanned* leather.

Oil-Tanned (Vegetable-Tanned) Leather

Oil-tanned leather may be treated with liquids (Red Wing Shoe Oil, Huberd's Neatsfoot Oil) or greases, which are merely thick oils (Huberd's Shoe Grease, Red Wing Shoe Conditioner).

The compound should be applied liberally to the uppers, worked in vigorously, especially around the seams, and allowed to dry, preferably overnight, before use.

Oil should be kept away from the welt-sole area; it softens the natural-fiber stitching (synthetic-fiber stitching is used on uppers) and thus reduces resistance to abrasion.

Chrome-Tanned (Dry-Tanned) Leather

Chrome-tanned leather is best treated with Sno-Seal, a wax and silicone mixture; the wax holds the silicone in place and thus gives longer-lasting water-repellency than such liquid or spray preparations as Red Wing Silicone Dressing and Dow-Corning Silicone for Leather.

Chrome-tanned leather requires particularly tender care; the silicone should be applied as soon as the boots are purchased and very regularly thereafter. *Oil or grease must never be used;* they enter the pores, filling air spaces and reducing insulation. Plain wax can also be used; it remains on the surface, providing waterproofing, but is more difficult to apply than a silicone mixture.

Suede Leather

The best treatment for this thin, porous leather is very frequent application of a liquid or aerosol silicone compound.

Special Areas of the Boot

What's good for the upper may be bad for the cemented-together layers of the sole. Oil adversely affects the adhesive bond; the solvent which often is the vehicle for silicone (especially in sprays) may temporarily dissolve the cement and permanently weaken the bond. The recommended treatment for the sole area is shellac, a wax and shellac mixture (Leath-R-Seal), or wax (Kiwi Polish).

Areas particularly vulnerable to water intrusion, such as the welt and seams, also may be treated with Leath-R-Seal.

Rock climbers often coat the toes and seams of boots and rock shoes with epoxy to minimize abrasion.

SOCKS AND GAITERS

SOCKS

Socks provide insulation, padding, and skin comfort—they do, that is, if they are the proper socks, in the proper amount, for any given foot in any particular situation.

Hikers who wear knickers usually prefer knee-high knicker socks. For others, the socks should be high enough to come an inch or two above the boot top to avoid a creeping-down-in and bunching-up action.

Socks come in various weights and materials, and luckily so, because individual preferences are many and divergent. Generally speaking, most of the total mass of socks should be wool for greatest warmth and moisture absorption, but with some admixture of nylon for greater durability. Some socks have nylon reinforcing at heel and toe, the points of heaviest wear; some have a percentage of nylon throughout. Hikers whose skin is irritated by direct contact with wool ~~en~~ wear a light inner sock of cotton-nylon-wool, or even a nylon ~~k.~~

sock combination depends on the boots being worn— ~~nal~~ preference. One common choice is two pairs of medium-weight, dominantly wool, nylon-reinforced socks. Another is one pair of heavy socks and one light or medium weight. And so on. Some hikers always, or sometimes, wear three pairs. Some wear a single pair, perhaps filling out the boot with insoles.

Even for day trips a person may do well to carry an extra pair of socks in the rucksack; during the hike water literally may be squeezed from the foot, which thus shrinks enough to slide around in the boot. Many hikers, when beginning a long descent, automatically stop to add socks to tighten the fit and avoid downhill blisters. Contrarily, the feet may swell while hiking and feel crowded; it is then proper to remove socks or possibly substitute lighter ones.

On overnight and longer trips the hiker should have at least two extra pairs in the pack to provide adjustments of padding, for a change to dry socks, and to replace those that wear out. (On the other hand, a climber once wore only one pair of socks, and the same pair, for 45 straight days on Yukon glaciers. Eventually, seeing all his extras weren't needed, he threw them away to save weight.)

The choice of socks is a matter of personal taste, developed by learning to know one's feet. The only general rule is to have enough to meet any changing situation.

When socks get wet on a backpack trip the normal instinct is to dry them by a campfire; the mountain world thus is littered with masses of charred wool. If enough time is available, and care is taken, socks can be dried by a fire, but it's a lousy way to spend an evening. Many hikers dry socks by wearing them to bed, not recommended if they are soaking wet. An alternative is to spread them on bushes to dry in the sun, if any. Another is to tie them to the outside of the pack while traveling—a good method unless it's raining or the route lies through brush.

Hikers with tough feet often say the heck with it and wear the socks wet. Hikers with tender feet cannot afford to be so casual and must carry an abundance of spares; wet socks are especially productive of blisters.

Care should be taken to avoid wrinkling and bunching of socks in the boots, since lumps make blisters. For the same reason socks with holes should be discarded.

GAITERS

No matter how tightly constructed the boot, no matter how carefully treated with waterproofing compounds, always there is the gap at the top. In wading a creek, the stream may pour directly in. In traveling snow, crystals work down inside and melt. In walking through wet grass or brush, moisture soaks the top of the socks, which then wick water down to the feet.

The built-in snow or scree guard described earlier may close the gap adequately—or may not. For extra protection the gaiter is available in several designs of differing materials and weight.

The long gaiter, 16 to 18 inches, extending from the laced area of the boots to the upper calf, is for deep, soft snow.

The short gaiter, 6½ to 9 inches, also called an *anklet,* suffices for the average hiker (if, indeed, he cares all that much about keeping his feet dry).

BEING KIND TO FEET

The hiker blessed with naturally tough feet can break just about all the rules of boot selection and sock use and never suffer more than an occasional blister. Less fortunate souls can follow all the rules meticulously and spend much of their outdoor lives hobbling in pain. A brief experience of trails tells a person in which category he falls, and obviously those who find themselves afflicted with innately tender feet must pay very close attention to the rules at all times, and devote special effort to getting their feet, as well as the rest of the body, in condition for long hikes by first taking a number of shorter walks.

If boots are chosen properly for the kind of travel planned, and also the proper mix of insoles and socks, sore feet and blisters should be a rarity.

Unfortunately, people do make mistakes in choice of boots and socks, such as, for example, by using a wafflestomper for a 50-mile cross-country hike. Also they become careless, especially when tired. And finally, a beginner, or any hiker early in the season, may go through a period of developing calluses in the appropriate places—a blister being nature's way of saying here is where the foot needs a callus.

The most important rule in foot care is not to neglect warning signals. If a hot spot develops, stop instantly. Straighten crooked socks, switch socks from left foot to right, dump out pebbles, or perhaps pound down a nail which has punched through the insole. If the trouble stems from the foot sliding around in the boot, tighten laces or add another pair of socks. And while making whatever adjustment is called for, put a bit of adhesive tape or better, moleskin or molefoam, on the hot spot. Some hikers engage in preventive taping before they set out, protecting areas they know from experience always blister.

Another preventive measure especially favored by hot-country travelers (walking on a desert in summer sun is literally like walking on a frying pan) is stopping periodically to wash or air the feet and to apply talcum powder or medicated foot powder.

One more: clip toenails short before a hike.

If despite all adjustments and care (or because of the lack of them) a blister develops, first aid is required. If the blister is small, cover it with moleskin or molefoam or a band-aid and a layer of adhesive tape. If large and full of liquid, insert a needle (sterilized in a match flame) at the base, drain liquid by pressing the blister gently, apply antiseptic, band-aid, and tape and over this, moleskin or molefoam.

Never "tough it out" on the trail to avoid delaying companions. The party will not appreciate the consideration if it afterward finds itself immobilized in camp with an invalid. On occasion blistered hikers have had to be evacuated by helicopter or packhorse—even to medical care when the blisters have become infected.

Tramping long trails, picking up boots and laying them down thousands of times a day, is at best a brutal experience for citified feet. It therefore is very nice indeed to have dry socks for wearing around camp within boots laced loose and sloppy. Despite the extra weight, some hikers carry canoe moccasins or other lightweight footgear to give surcease from boots.

Nothing is more delightful than to stick hot, sore feet in a cold stream at the end of a hard day, hold them there to the point of numbness, then on withdrawal feel the tingling rush of new life. A further advantage is that the process cleans the feet, not a bad idea every few days on a long trip.

The hiker absolutely must have awaiting him in the car a pair of light shoes or moccasins plus clean, soft socks. No matter how deep an affection is developed for boots, trusty companions of the trail, the feet go into delirium when at last they escape from prison.

9:   CLOTHING

So THE story goes, a lone youth once hiked across the Olympic Mountains with no equipment or food and wearing nothing but tennis shoes and swimming trunks. He shivered a lot and was thoroughly scratched and bitten and sunburned, yet during the week spent little time wishing for more clothes—he was too busy looking for berries and grubs.

Though for reasons both of comfort and safety such naked adventuring cannot be recommended for the average hiker, who should settle for a less intimate contact with nature, the youth's journey underlines the fact that overdressing is among the most common errors made by beginning backpackers. Typically, for example, the Boy Scout's mother burdens him on his first overnight hike with three sweaters, a muffler, and a union suit, fearing as she does the lethal effects of a weekend unprotected by roof, walls, and central heating.

However, let it be noted that no Boy Scout was ever killed by extra sweaters. Overloaded surely and likely humiliated, but never drained of life, as many have been by wind and rain. Tennis shoes, shorts, and T-shirt are a fine, free costume for an afternoon stroll in sunshine, but if the rain comes down and the wind comes up, and the car is distant, misery is certain and tragedy possible. Every year rescue parties carry

103

back from high trails the bodies of hikers who set out from the parking lot in warm sun, unprepared to cope with the sudden storm that caught them unawares.

How much clothing is enough, and how much is too much? It depends on the trip—short afternoon, long day, overnight, full week; in forest, desert, alpine highland; winter, summer. It also depends on the person, since some people have metabolisms and built-in insulation (fat) that make them comfortable sitting in a snowbank in a blizzard while others have a trembling fit when a cloud momentarily covers the sun.

Specifying what hikers and backpackers should wear is like telling women how long their skirts should be, and men how wide their ties. Fads have an influence—some hikers are as fashion-conscious as lodge skiers. Individual tastes, based partly on learned personal needs and partly on personal quirks (and backpackers tend to be quirky, the more so the longer they're at it), are even more of an element.

However, the following summaries tell what a consensus of experienced hikers considers sufficient for the *average* person in typical *summer* conditions in country with some potential for *turning wet and cold* on short notice.

In each case the beginner is advised not to rush out and buy all new garments, but as much as possible to improvise from clothing already owned.

For a several-hour *afternoon walk in good weather,* wear shorts or any other pants; T-shirt or any other shirt; and perhaps wrap a wool shirt or sweater around the waist.

For a *full-day hike,* add to the above, to be carried in the rucksack if not worn: long pants, wool shirt or sweater, parka, extra socks, and some sort of hat or cap.

For an *overnight or longer hike,* add another wool shirt or sweater, for a total of two; and possibly mittens.

Now, having gone so far out on a limb, qualifications must be added. This much clothing suffices for *most* hiking country, for *most* people, in *summer conditions.* It is too much for desert country. It is not enough for climbing country, winter conditions, or cold people. Also, there are pants and pants, parkas and parkas, and a garment good for a walk in the desert may be lousy on a rain-blasted ridge, and vice versa. Thus it is necessary to examine each category of clothing and the various alternatives.

UNDERWEAR

The rule for both men and women is to use on the trail whatever underwear is preferred for casual, not dress-up, city life.

Cold people; and any people in wintry conditions, may be interested in *thermal action* underwear, tops or bottoms or both, made of an outer layer of wool, cotton, and nylon fabric, an inner layer entirely of cotton, and reaching far down the legs and arms. Most hikers, though, find this improved modern version of "long johns" a complicated way to keep warm and leave it to the skiers and expeditionary climbers.

Fishnet, and also *circular knit* underwear, of cotton or a wool-cotton mix, has a very open weave that lets the skin breathe easily but sops up perspiration; when used in combination with a shirt or parka it also traps dead air and creates a barrier against loss of body heat. Again, the advantages are appreciated mainly in cold conditions or by cold people, but wool-cotton fishnet is also excellent for comfort in soaking-wet weather.

For ordinary hiking enough warmth can be gained from outer layers of clothing which are less difficult to get in and out of than underwear. So the advice for most hikers is to forget the fancy stuff and use whatever feels good in city life. However, the underwear should be all or largely cotton, which absorbs sweat and thus does not get clammy, as do nylon undergarments commonly worn by women.

SHIRTS AND SWEATERS

At different times during a single day the hiker may have two opposite problems: (1) retaining warmth generated by his metabolism
when wind and rain and snow are striving to steal it away; (2) getting rid of excess body heat when all the world around is bathing him
in energy from the solar furnace. One minute too cold, the next too
hot, often the hiker is beset by extremes and must make frequent adjustments to stay in the narrow comfort zone between broiling and
shivering.

Second only to the head-and-neck area (discussed below), the
torso, especially the front, is the most critical portion of the body in
controlling the human thermostat. For complex physiological reasons, if this section can be kept properly warm (cool), the rest of the
body will tend to feel comfortably warm (cool).

Though applicable elsewhere on the body, here the *layer system*
has special value. The essence is to depend on several thin layers of
insulation, and the dead air they trap between them, in preference to
a single, massive layer, such as a logger's mackinaw or any other
heavy coat. With such materials as wool, cotton, polyester, and nylon
the layer system gives the most warmth for the least weight and also
allows fine tuning of the heat control, rather than a simple on-off,
totally hot or totally cold. (Insulated garments are another story, told
below.)

The hiker may set out on a chill morning with torso covered by
undershirt, a light cotton shirt, and a wool shirt. Once he is warmed
by walking, off comes the wool shirt. During a long rest, as sweat
cools, he may put the wool shirt back on. If the day turns cold he may
add a sweater, and if wind comes up or rain down, a parka. Thus, by
carrying several light garments, he can vary his torso coverage from
bare skin up to four or five layers.

Some hikers tinker too much and drive companions crazy by incessantly stopping for addition or subtraction. Veterans tend to enlarge their concept of the comfort zone; that is, they accept a certain
amount of excess warmth or chilliness for the moment, knowing that

a few minutes later the balance may shift the other way. Also, they depend as much as possible on varying a single garment—typically, a wool shirt (worn over a cotton undershirt). As ventilation is needed the sleeves are rolled up and the front unbuttoned. As warmth is wanted, down come the sleeves and the front is closed up. At a rest stop, when sweat turns icy, they start hiking again rather than putting on a sweater.

There should always be an inner layer of cotton—undershirt, T-shirt, old dress shirt, or light turtleneck shirt. Cotton is soft on the flesh and absorbs perspiration without feeling clammy, and is especially appreciated in warm weather.

For any hike beyond the shortest stroll a person should carry, if not wear, a medium-weight wool shirt. A full collar and a neck button keep the neck warm. The tails should extend well below the beltline to avoid goose bumps on the midriff.

The greatest warmth and durability and comfort are provided by 100 percent all-new (virgin) wool. Reprocessed wool, in which old garments have been chopped up, bleached, dyed, and recarded, has much shorter fibers and is not so soft. However, when the pocketbook is light, a reprocessed-wool shirt (with perhaps an admixture of other fibers) selling for less than $15 may be preferred to an all-new-wool shirt selling for $25 or so, and be quite sufficient.

For any long hike a person should have a medium-weight sweater or a second wool shirt large enough to fit over the first. A heavy sweater is to be avoided—if more warmth is desired, better to carry two light sweaters (or an insulated sweater). The sleeves should be wrist-length and the bottom should extend below the beltline. Though the pullover is most common, some prefer a buttoned-front coat style for the ease of getting in and out and of varying the warmth/ventilation. A turtleneck protects the neck but can become uncomfortable unless it has a partial front opening.

Beautiful and expensive sweaters of 100 percent virgin wool are warm, durable, and comfortable, as well as stylish. However, any castoff will do. Exceptional bargains in sweaters—and shirts too—often can be obtained at thrift shops operated by charities.

In cold but dry weather a light nylon *wind shirt,* weighing about

3 ounces and wadding up to fit in a pocket, adds as much warmth as an extra sweater.

PANTS

For first walks and any short walks a beginner can't go far wrong by wearing on the trail any old slacks or shorts or pants of any kind that happen to be around the house. The important thing is that they be cut full enough to allow easy action, not binding the hips or knees during long strides.

Since the main centers for controlling the human thermostat are the torso and head, pants often are worn less for warmth than protection from sunburn, nettle stings, poison ivy and oak, and mosquito bites; this, however, is not so in cold country, notably high mountains, where every part of the body must be insulated in a storm or a freezing night.

For long day hikes and backpacks the hiker must pay more attention to selection of pants. However, no single garment is best for all provinces of the backpacking world. What works fine on dry trails may not be suitable for rough travel through brush. And pants that are splendid for warm lowlands may be miserable for cold, wet mountains—and vice versa.

MATERIALS

Cotton is comfortable, warm when dry, and serves very well in good weather. Once wet, however, it provides virtually zero insulation. Cotton-nylon and polyester-cotton (Dacron is a common trade name for polyester) mixtures are light and strong, more durable than pure cotton, and breathe easily, but give less warmth.

Wool, though less comfortable next to the skin, is famous for being warm when wet, the reason being that only a little bit of the next-to-skin fuzziness needs to dry out, as it will from body heat, to give insulation. For travel in cold, wet conditions, wool (or largely wool) pants are essential.

Insulating almost as well as pure wool and more durable are the mixtures of wool and nylon characteristic of some of the highest-quality pants designed for the rugged use of climbing but equally good for hiking in rough conditions, such as brush.

STYLES

Shorts

A great many hikers, in all sorts of terrains and conditions, like the freedom and ventilation and easy action of shorts, whether those manufactured specifically for walking, such as "Bavarian" or "Sierra" designs, or an old pair of swimming shorts or cutoff jeans.

For any hike except the briefest in good weather, the hiker who wears shorts must carry long pants in his rucksack—for the cool nights, the sudden storms, and emergencies that prevent a quick return to civilization. Long pants also should be carried in sun-blasted country to prevent a massive and disabling burn.

Some backpackers wear shorts even in a hard rain, keeping trousers dry in the pack for putting on in camp. Indeed, they may actually

Clothing sufficient for a pleasant-day, several-hour walk not far from road or camp: shorts, light cotton shirt, and wool sweater in case of chilly moments

Hikers dressed for a day hike in cool weather: knickers and wool shirt, trousers and wool sweater. Storm clothing is in rucksacks

take off their pants when rain begins, or when starting a long passage through wet brush, or fording a stream, and substitute shorts.

Lederhosen are durable, very hot in hot weather, cold in cold weather, and cute on the right figure.

Knickers

Knickers, worn primarily by climbers, also are popular with hikers. They rarely bind at the knee and by opening the bottom strap and buckle and rolling down the knicker socks ordinarily worn in combination one can gain ventilation almost as good as shorts.

The best all-purpose knickers are wool or wool-nylon, with a hard finish and double seat, selling for about $30–$55. Cotton knickers are for dry, warm climates.

Trousers

Blue jeans were common on trails years before they were adopted as the uniform of the Now Generation. The price is generally a good bit less than $15. Being cotton, they are warm when dry, cold when wet.

The same is true of more elaborate trousers, such as "trail pants" or "mountain pants" of cotton-nylon, selling for around $5 in army surplus and $15 in civilian models. Pants going by these names may tempt the hiker because typically they are equipped with plenty of pockets, including "cargo carriers" on the thighs, very convenient for ready access to small items frequently used on the trail.

In country which can be wet and chilly, all-wool or wool-blend trousers are far and away the best. In coastal mountains an excellent combination is shorts for ordinary hiking, wool or largely wool pants for cold nights and storms.

Not particularly stylish but warm and inexpensive and deservedly popular are plain all-wool trousers. An excellent buy—usual price, $5-$8—is army surplus. Charity-operated thrift shops offer the real bargains. An old pair of men's suit pants may be obtained for $1-$2 and, perhaps with patches added at the knees and seat, give miles of service on the trail long after too crummy for civilization. Some hikers install 12-inch zippers on the legs for ease in taking off and putting on over boots; this can be an important safety measure, since if pants are hard to don one may not do so in emergency situations, precisely when they are essential.

Rain Pants

Hikers in well-watered country sometimes carry lightweight rain pants to keep trousers and socks dry; rain chaps, which slip individually onto the legs, have the same purpose. Both are made of materials discussed below in connection with parkas.

Very light plastic rain pants tear easily when snagged and self-destruct with the first long stride. Heavier plastic rain pants may be durable enough to go busting through brush.

Rain pants are totally waterproof, breathe not at all, and thus perspiration cannot escape except circuitously. Worn during steady walking they wet the legs from the inside as thoroughly as rain would from the outside; they therefore are best suited for camp use or loitering along an ocean beach in a winter storm.

However, when an overgrown trail is to be walked or a route punched through brush and rain has saturated the greenery, every step is a showerbath; in such relatively rare (for the average hiker) cases a complete *rain suit* of pants and parka is excellent.

The objection to rain pants is they are an extra item to carry for relatively infrequent use even in soaked country. As mentioned above, shorts are an alternative; they are, that is, when the rain is fairly warm and not driven by strong winds.

Rain pants also serve very well as *wind pants*; even a dry wind can be severely—potentially fatally—chilling in wintry conditions.

HEADWEAR

The most critical portion of the body for regulation of the thermostat is the area of the head and neck; the brain receives 20 percent of the body's blood supply, 25 percent of its oxygen, and the head, having little fatty insulation, may account for up to half the body's total heat radiation. If head and neck are cold the whole body will shiver, and if they are warm one may feel quite comfortable even with bare legs on a frosty night.

Similarly, in scorching sun an overheated head can lead to dizzy misery, even heat stroke.

*Typical **headwear** for various conditions. Above: sou'wester rain hat, mountain hat, glacier hat, and beret. Below: stocking cap, balaclava, and handkerchief hat.*

Finally, in hard rain, if head and neck can be kept dry, one does not feel totally drenched and blinded.

It is perfectly all right to choose headwear for style or personality so long as the choice gives the necessary protection. At least one climber has attained the summit of Mt. Rainier wearing an opera hat and causing a sensation, but he had a stocking cap in his pack.

For Rain

The *rain hat,* sou'wester style, though designed specifically for ocean conditions, such as walking beside the surf in winter or along a high ridge of the Cascades in a summertime 3-day blow, also provides sun protection, just as other headwear also provides rain protection.

For Sun

The natty *"mountain hat"* ordinarily worn by guides because tourists expect it of them guards the head against rain and hot sun, as do the *"crusher"* and the *"glacier hat,"* also known as the "Aussie tennis hat." These and others have a brim that shades the eyes from glare somewhat and when turned down keeps the sun off ears and nose.

For sun protection on deserts and scorched hills one may wear a *"handkerchief hat,"* knotting a large handkerchief or bandana at all four corners to fit comfortably on the head. It may be periodically dipped in streams, rubbed with snow, or saturated from the canteen for additional cooling.

A bandana may also be used to protect the neck, a particularly excruciating place to have a bad sunburn.

A *sweat band* on the forehead keeps sweat from running into the eyes.

For Warmth

The most complete protection against cold is provided by a wool *balaclava,* or *toque,* which covers the entire head and neck except the face.

Next best (and least expensive) is a wool *watch cap* or *stocking cap* which can cover the upper head only, be rolled down over the ears, or even down onto the back of the neck.

The *beret* is almost as good, perched jauntily atop the head or pulled down over the ears.

Any headwear that does not extend to the neck may need to be supplemented by a *scarf* (or bandana) or *neck band,* a simple wool collar.

Some hikers are content in all but the coldest weather with nothing more than an *ear band.*

MITTENS

Not many hikers and backpackers travel in the kind of weather where any greater hand protection is required than sticking them in pockets. However, those who spend much time in high mountains or in winter walking should carry a pair of wool or wool-nylon mittens. Gloves are almost mandatory for heavy brush liberally sprinkled with devils club and other stickery plants but are not recommended for most hiking, since by separating the fingers they provide nowhere near as much warmth for the weight as mittens, which let the fingers snuggle together.

PARKAS

Hikers whose travels are confined to dry climates and low elevations may never, or rarely, need a parka. Even in wet and chilly highlands many people wear parkas infrequently and some have roamed the hills from early youth to old age with no garments beyond shirts and sweaters. However, when the wind blows hard and cold and/or when the rain comes down in torrents, shirts and sweaters lose more or less of their insulating value unless covered by an outer shell resistant to water and wind; a parka may then be essential for even minimal comfort and in extreme conditions can be a lifesaver.

Still, the beginner should take care not to over-parka, buying a garment designed for climbing and beyond a hiker's needs. Except for those with insulating filler (discussed below) the primary function of a parka is wind and water protection, and only secondarily warmth (which comes mainly from shirts and sweaters); the backpacker's parka thus should be very light.

MATERIALS

The ideal material for a parka would be very light in weight yet very durable, completely rainproof yet allowing perspiration to escape, and inexpensive. Despite frequent claims to the contrary no such material has been invented so far and all those in current use represent compromises.

Plastic, more to be warned against than recommended, is light, inexpensive, and watertight. Parkas and ponchos made of it weigh from ⅜ to ¾ pound and sell for a dollar or two. No rain can come in—and no sweat can get out. They serve well for very occasional, very gentle use, such as standing around camp, but both in the pack and on the body must be carefully protected against tearing and puncturing, and in cold weather against cracking. Their life-expectancy while hiking is measured in hours, if not minutes. A plastic parka is not a "real" parka; that is, it cannot be relied upon in killer situations.

Cotton long has been the most common fabric for parkas, being relatively inexpensive, sturdy, and easy to clean. Since it is an organic fiber, cotton is highly absorbent; the threads swell as they soak up water (and/or water-repelling compounds), closing the gaps between them and making the fabric more water-resistant. Because it also absorbs moisture from the inside, cotton almost never has a clammy feel. At the same time it breathes well and lets much perspiration exhale through the pores. On the debit side, cotton parkas tend to be relatively heavy, up to 2 pounds or more, and once thoroughly soaked are a long time drying. Further, the cloth can mildew and rot if not dried and aired after each trip. Well-built cotton parkas sell from around $30 to $50 or more, depending on quality of the material, complexity of structure, and special features.

Ventile, an English trade name, is 100 percent cotton woven with an exceptionally high thread count, meaning it is very tight and strong and water-resistant; once damp it becomes nearly impenetrable to rain yet still breathes. In some opinion Ventile parkas continue to be best for all-around use, the chief objection being they are quite heavy.

For all the advantages, fabrics of pure cotton are used less and less nowadays.

Nylon is stronger than cotton for equivalent weights, abrasion-resistant, dries quickly, and usually wears out for other reasons long before it begins to rot. A major difficulty is the synthetic threads are completely impervious to penetration both by water and water-repelling compounds. In the first instance this means perspiration stays on the surface, causing clamminess. In the second it means the compounds do not unite with the fiber, as they do with cotton, but must be "painted" on to fill interstices between threads. Since the repellent is thus a separate layer, bending or twisting eventually causes it to pull loose. Nylon can be left untreated (uncoated) and fully breathable for wind-only protection, or coated to be made extremely water-repellent. The seams are most vulnerable to leakage; experiments are being conducted with a new-style "sewing" machine that welds rather than stitches nylon—if and when perfected it may permit construction of seamless parkas that are almost completely waterproof.

Some parkas of *coated nylon taffeta* weight as little as ½-¾ pound and sell for less than $25 to about $35. Others weigh more and cost $40 and up.

Ripstop nylon, a very light fabric with intermittent heavier threads which stop a rip from running, is used for a few ultra-light parkas. Since water-repelling compound reduces the stretch and thus nullifies the ripstop feature, such parkas generally are not coated and are mainly for wind.

In the quest for the ideal, various mixtures have been tried. Quite popular at present are *cotton-nylon* fabrics, 60-40 Cloth being a common trade name. Some advantages of both cotton (comfort, moisture and water-repellent absorbence) and nylon (strength, wind resistance) are combined, as well as some disadvantages (less water repellency than coated nylon). In most expert opinion cotton-nylon is the best material presently available for durable, dependable, all-weather parkas. Various models weigh 2–3 pounds and cost $35 to $55 and up.

Waterproofing

Neoprene, synthetic rubber, is employed in the *rubberized cloth* of some rain parkas and rain pants. The fabric is strong and water-tight—and heavy. It rapidly deteriorates and cracks when exposed to sunshine (ultraviolet light).

A *vinyl* (plastic) coating on cotton, also providing a strong and completely waterproof fabric, is used for more expensive raingear—which again is quite heavy and bulky.

The customary coating for nylon parkas is *urethane* or *polymer.* The more used the greater the water-resistance and weight. A very light coating restrains the cloth from stretching and makes it vulnerable to tearing. A heavy coating increases strength since the added layer itself is tough.

Cotton parkas ordinarily are not treated by the manufacturer with water-repellents, but as discussed below the hiker can add compounds himself as wanted.

STYLES

The materials of a parka determine many of its characteristics. The way the materials are assembled determines others. Obviously.

The completely-waterproof poncho, a portable tent, is mainly worn while puttering around camp in the rain, but sometimes also during downpours on the trail.

Poncho

The poncho, essentially a tent designed to be worn while walking, strictly speaking is not a parka but is employed for many of the same purposes, plus others, and often in preference to a parka. Many ponchos have grommets to allow use as emergency tarps. Most are big enough to be worn over a pack and give rain protection to the entire body except the lower legs. With care, all can serve as ground sheets. Depending on the fabric, ponchos weigh from less than 1 to nearly 3 pounds and range in price from $6–$8 for heavyweight army-surplus rubberized cotton to $15 or more for coated nylon.

A poncho is splendid when standing around or doing camp chores in a downpour; in strenuous hiking it becomes a portable sauna. The design is cumbersome and in anything but the simplest maneuvers fouls on brush, pack, cooking pots, feet, and other hikers. Comes a high wind and the poncho flaps and flies and tangles and obscures. All in all, the poncho is better in theory than practice—but has great virtues for some uses and many steadfast adherents.

Part Two: Equipment

Front-Opening or "Jacket" Parka

Of the two basic parka designs, the jacket style, with a complete front opening, is best for backpacking. A full-length zipper allows easy getting in and out and also good ventilation. In a warm, misty rain, for instance, one may wish to wear the parka to keep head and shoulders dry, but open the front to avoid sweat saturation.

Since zippers sometimes fail and a wide-open parka is worthless in a storm, for high-country (or winter-ocean) travel the front should have a *storm flap* with a back-up system of snaps. These reinforce the zipper and replace it in event of failure and can be used in its stead for more ventilation.

Pullover Parka, or Anorak

The second basic design, the anorak, has no front opening that might allow penetration of rain or wind. The price paid is that the garment must be donned and doffed over the head and ventilation is difficult. Such parkas are better for climbers than hikers.

The *cagoule* is a very full-cut, calf-length parka designed to be worn over bulky garments, as in bivouacking during high-altitude or winter climbing. Many stormy-country hikers like them for camp-standing-around.

Various Parka Features

As with boots, packs, and sleeping bags, the parkas sold by mountain shops exhibit a bewildering variety of features. Here, only a few of the most significant will be noted.

The lightest parkas are of a *single layer* throughout. Others have complete *double-body* construction, either of two layers of cotton; or coated nylon outside for water-repellency and cotton poplin inside for water absorption and thus comfort; or cotton outside and uncoated, breathable nylon inside for wind-resistance and for ease in putting on and taking off, the nylon being more slippery than cotton. Double-body construction gives a thermal barrier and thus more insulation—and weight. Some parkas are of double construction only in the upper half and the sleeves.

The *hood* may be an integral part of the parka or detachable.

The best hoods cover the lower face when tightened by the drawstring. Some fold into a back-of-the-neck pocket secured by drawstrings.

Cuffs may be elastic, to hold the garment to the wrists. Many have buttons, snaps, or Velcro ("sticky tape") for adjustment and a gusset in the sleeve for ease in pulling over gloves or mittens.

A *drawstring waist* is useful for cinching the parka around the midriff, holding it tight to the body in storm winds. Similarly, a *bottom drawstring* brings the skirts close to the hips.

There may be no *pockets,* or two slash pockets for handwarmers, or patch pockets, or any number of pockets inside and out, zippered or snapped or with Velcro closure, for carrying items to which convenient access is desired.

Some parkas have two overlapping layers of fabric in the upper back, the two not sewn together, to allow some ventilation through the gap.

Since seams and stitching are most likely to leak, and since the upper part of the parka takes the brunt of rain, the better parkas intended mainly for rain protection either have one-piece construction to avoid all seams and stitching at the shoulders or else place all seams on the sides and under the sleeves. In parkas not designed to be waterproof the seam location is of no consequence.

Whatever parka is chosen the skirts should come well below the waist. It should also be *full cut* to allow room inside for sweaters and to permit easy mobility. A tight parka steams up fast, tears easily with sudden movements, and causes claustrophobia.

CHOOSING A PARKA

The above details will interest the hiker more as he gains experience and seeks the ideal parka for his particular favorite province of the backpacking world, whether ocean beaches, low-elevation trails in forests or deserts, or misty, windswept meadows and moraines of high mountains. Each person must first identify his personal needs and then make his choice.

Hikers in warm, mild climates require no parka, no poncho. However, in most trail country and certainly in cold, wet regions the parka or poncho frequently is a comfort and occasionally a lifesaver.

For most, the best choice probably is very lightweight, very water-repellent, adequate for emergencies—say, a coated-nylon, front-opening, "shell" parka weighing ½–¾ pound, costing about $25–$35. Such a parka will not hold up in brush as well as heavier ones and when worn while hiking will soon soak the shirts and sweaters with sweat and feel clammy to boot. The answer is, the hiker doesn't wear it except while relatively immobile, such as in camp or during rest stops—the exception being when the wind is howling and the rain is driving sideways and the parka may give the margin needed for survival.

Representative front-opening (jacket) parkas. Left: 60-40 Cloth (cotton-nylon), nylon-lined in upper body, sleeves, and hood. Middle: coated nylon taffeta shell (with hood folded into back-of-the-neck pocket). Right: coated nylon, cotton-lined in upper body and sleeves

There are tragedy-saddened veterans who insist that no hiker should set out on any long walk in high, storm-prone mountains without a cotton-nylon parka weighing 2 pounds or so, selling for about $35—or perhaps an equivalent weighing somewhat more and costing up to $60.

REPRESENTATIVE PARKAS RECOMMENDED
FOR HIKERS
(All are front-opening, or jacket, style)

Material	Use	Approximate Weight (pounds)	Approximate Price
Plastic	Very gentle, infrequent use; not dependable in emergencies	⅜	$2
Coated nylon taffeta shell	Mainly around camp in the rain; emergency use during storms on good trails or in open, brushless country	½-¾	$25–$35
Coated nylon taffeta lined with cotton	Extended, strenuous activity in cold, wet country	2	$35–$55
Cotton-nylon (60-40 cloth)	Extended, strenuous activity in rough, brushy country in all sorts of bad weather	1½-2	$35–$55
Ventile cotton	Ditto the above	2½-3	$45–$60

CARING FOR THE PARKA

When not being worn a nylon parka, especially if coated, should be stowed in a plastic bag and guarded from excessive crumpling and crushing in the pack.

Particularly with light nylon parkas a roll of *ripstop repair tape* should be carried. Ordinary adhesive tape doesn't adhere well to nylon, or to any material when wet.

A cotton or cotton-nylon parka used largely for wet weather can be sprayed periodically with a water-repelling compound in aerosol form; mountain shops stock a number of brands. With pure nylon the treatment has negligible value; the compound is not absorbed by the fibers and soon rubs off.

INSULATED CLOTHING

Demanding a separate section all to itself is a category of clothing both very old and very new—old because inhabitants of cold climates long have stuffed double-wall coats and pants with straw, moss, lichen, dog hair, wool, cotton, or kapok; new because only with the adoption of down and polyester for the filler have such garments become practical for climbing, skiing, and hiking.

For travelers of mild climates insulated clothing is massive over-kill. However, hikers with poor inner furnaces may never otherwise be really cosy on the windy evenings of bleak tundra and moraine. The garments weigh enormously less than wool counterparts providing equal insulation. They also compress to tiny wads when stuffed in plastic bags and occupy little space in the pack.

The characteristics as fillers of down and second-generation poly-ester (Dacron fiberfill II and Fortrel PolarGuard), and their differing virtues, are discussed at length in Chapter 11, "Sleeping Bags." With clothing as with sleeping bags, the novice may ask, "Which is best?" The answer is, each is better for certain situations.

For equal weights, down is much the warmer of the two and thus the proper choice for backpackers who must frequently endure extreme cold, as at high altitude or in winter, but who rarely are bothered by prolonged rains. However, when wet, down loses virtually all insulation value; in damp country an additional rain parka is required to protect the down, which once soaked takes days of sunshine to dry.

Polyester retains most of its insulation value even when drenched, is quickly dried by body heat alone—never mind if the sun seems to have vanished permanently—and thus is the proper choice for backpackers whose roamings are largely in summer highlands relentlessly swept by gale-driven rains fresh from the ocean and, in the intervals between storms, steadily bathed by chill drizzles and fogs.

The shells of insulated garments are never waterproof, at most they are rain-repellent. They usually are made of taffeta or ripstop nylon; a high-thread-count taffeta is approximately as resistant to tearing and abrasion as ripstop and is more comfortable; ripstop is more rugged, better for strenuous activity in rough terrain. For the

Insulated garments popular among cold-country hikers. Left to right: sweater, vest, and parka.

heaviest-duty garments, 60–40 Cloth is the standard.

Sewn-through construction (see Chapter 11), giving a quilted look and permitting perspiration to exhale freely, is best for most clothing. Box, double-quilt, and overlapping constructions use more filler, add weight and cost, and are mainly for severe cold.

The simplest insulated garment is the *vest,* sleeveless, covering the trunk only, with snap- or zipper-closed front. Weight is about 1 pound, cost from $20 to $35.

A step up is the *sweater,* a zipper-front, mid-hip-length jacket with sleeves, weight about 1½ pounds, costing from $30 to $40. (Some hikers prefer the upper part of a set of *underwear,* rather similar and costing a bit less.)

Finally, the *parka,* similar to the sweater but with a flap over the zipper, extending farther down the hips, and ordinarily having a hood, weighs about 2 pounds and costs from $40 to $60 and up.

Heavier parkas, as well as socks, booties, mitts, pants, and underwear lowers, are principally for activities other than backpacking.

10:   PACKS

CANDY bar and apple in pockets, cup on belt, sweater around waist, camera over shoulder—off and away the happy hiker strides.

Good enough for an afternoon stroll. For a long trail day, though, or a short one if much lunch or children's clothing is to be hauled or mushrooms are to be gathered, stuffing pockets and draping the body interferes with free-action walking. The answer? A pack, of course.

At any distance from the road the hiker must carry the Ten Essentials (see Chapter 15), used infrequently but then because they are in dead earnest *essential*. The articles weigh little but won't fit conveniently in pockets. Again the answer is a pack—to avoid the dangerous temptation to leave the essentials behind and risk discomfort or disaster.

Borderline hikers seem to distrust and fear packs, perhaps because of their once-deserved evil reputation as back-manglers, or perhaps out of humility—who can say? Walk any popular trail near a tourist center and see people who are hikers at heart (or they wouldn't have left the parking lot) lugging picnic hampers or sacks of sandwiches by hand, loads of sweaters under arms, and cameras and canteens and binoculars strung from shoulders, bouncing and banging. And see more sophisticated others wearing spiffy "mountain pants" and hard-

ly able to lift their legs because of jamful "cargo carriers."

The borderline hiker is wise not to rush prematurely into purchase of a pack. He may never wish to take walks longer than a
couple hours on easy, safe trails. Or despite a first flurry of enthusiasm
may get bitten by one fly too many and take up sailing. However,
once he crosses the border and decides to go walking for good and real
and far, it is pack time.

Agreed. But *what* pack? No other item of equipment, not even
boots, presents so many complicated options. The bewildering assort-
ment available reflects the importance of the pack—which ranks
with boots and sleeping bag as one of the Big Three Decisions facing
a backpacker. It also reflects the continuing creative experimentation
by manufacturers, each questing the Ultimate.

Or rather, the Ultimates, since no one pack is ideal for every realm,
every activity of the wilderness world and since there is widespread
disagreement among manufacturers as to what constitutes the ideal.
The hiker can quickly rule out many (but not all) packs designed
specifically for skiing and climbing, but there still remain numerous
choices.

The starting point is: *What will the pack be used for?* Afternoon
strolls, full-day rambles, occasional overnights, every-weekend year-
after-year long-distance backpacks, 10-day heavy-loaded semi-expedi-
tions—the requirements differ.

And then, *how fares the bank account?* The affluent hiker can buy several packs for various purposes and in each case pick the highest-price model available. But poverty-stricken youths and parents impoverished by numerous offspring must spend carefully, seeking multi-purpose packs and the best possible combination of comfort, convenience, durability, and economy.

More will be said later about choosing a pack, or packs, but first the subject must be broken into digestible chunks. To sort things out, one major distinction is between the *rucksack,* mainly for day hikes but in

Rucksacks on the trail. Left: *small frameless bag with day-hike load.* Right: *frame bag with overnight load, sleeping bag carried under top flap*

the upper ranges of the category splendid for long backpacks, and the *packframe and bag,* which can do day duty quite well but is chiefly intended for overnight and longer trips.

If the novice keeps his head this chapter need not send him into a fugue of indecision. At least it will prepare him for the trauma of visiting a mountain shop, in person or by catalog.

RUCKSACKS

Lumping together all the transport devices traditionally labeled "rucksacks" is about as informative as calling all the passengers on Noah's ark, including Noah, "animals." Yes, the fanny pack and the Jensen monocoque are related; so are the chipmunk and the woolly mammoth. Scanning the hundreds of sizes and shapes offered by scores of manufacturers, the novice may well ask, "My gosh, who needs *this* aggravation? Why *bother* with a rucksack?"

Representative rucksacks. Left: *day pack for light loads.* Center: *day pack for medium loads.* Right: *pack with detachable pockets and exterior attachment points, suitable for heavy day loads and/or overnight loads*

Actually, many hikers don't, perfectly content on every occasion with the packframe-bag. However, those who ease gradually into trail country by taking a series of day walks before venturing overnight are wise to buy an inexpensive rucksack, delaying purchase of a packframe-bag until they've studied the choices. The rucksack has continuing utility when backpacking commences, such as for short explorations from a basecamp; to eliminate an extra item, it can do double duty as stuff bag for the sleeping bag. Moreover, rucksacks no longer are confined to trails but are put to good use in hitchhiking and cycling, in toting books around school and groceries home from the supermarket. Finally, the bigger designs so comfortably handle heavy and bulky loads that they are quite rational alternatives to a packframe-bag.

RUCKSACKS FOR SHORT DAYS AND LONG WEEKS

Rucksacks weigh from 1 to 5 pounds, cost from $10 or less to $75 or more, have capacities from several hundred to several thousand cubic inches. An eyeball inspection quickly separates those suitable for trips of various lengths—day, overnight, or longer.

Day Pack

Pouches that fasten to the belt with loops and *belt bags* (*waist packs, fanny packs*) that strap around the waist supplement pockets for short walks, holding from a few ounces to several pounds. Photographers like them for gadgetry.

The simplest true rucksacks, refined versions of the carriers peasants lugged up and down Alps for centuries, are cotton or nylon bags with one or two outside pockets, shoulder straps, and perhaps a waist strap (*belly band*) to control bouncing and flopping. The load hangs directly from the shoulders, painlessly enough if weight is under 10 or 15 pounds. As with all rucksacks, gear must be stowed thoughtfully to prevent sharp edges from stabbing the back; clothing or a sheet of foam rubber can provide padding. Such a pack weighs about 1 pound and sells for $10 to $20.

Day or Overnight

The hiker who can't spend a day on the trail without three flower-identification books and two cameras, a bundle of spare clothing for a child, or a nine-course lunch, should avoid a little, limp-cloth rucksack which when crammed full forms a hard round ball that beats a tattoo on the vertebrae. A better choice is one of the larger models weighing 2–2½ pounds, costing $20 to $45, and tolerable for 25–30 pounds—thus serving overnight as well as day jaunts.

Most packs in this size range have a flexible frame or internal stiffener to shape the bag and support the load. Rather than a simple belly band, there may be a *hip belt* (mesh or padded) that transfers weight from shoulders to hips.

Virtually all rucksacks of overnight capability are intended primarily for climbers and ski-mountaineers and thus have attachment points for ropes, ice axes, crampons, and skis. The humble hiker needn't be overawed; bereft of hero tools though he is, the points work just as nicely for strapping on sleeping bag, tent, watermelon, and whatever else won't fit inside the pack.

On Through the Week

The largest rucksacks have outgrown the name; *soft pack* seems to be emerging as the generic term distinguishing them from the pack-frame-bag. Weighing 3–5 pounds, costing $35 to $75, some of these packs are comfortable up to 40 pounds; others shift weight to the hips as efficiently as any packframe and handle burdens as heavy as a person can stand upright under.

One species of soft pack is merely a swollen brother of the smaller rucksacks, with a more elaborate suspension system and internal frame.

A second species, the famous Don Jensen design, is totally frameless and absolutely soft, though variations have a stiffener pad to guard the back against stoves and cans. The genius of the Jensen is that it is structured to form a tall, slim column or "monocoque" contoured to the horizontal and vertical curvatures of the human back; when stuffed properly full (as it must be for best effect) the "spine" of the pack becomes a "frame." Because of this feature, the pack must be selected to fit torso length precisely; most manufacturers offer several sizes. The Jensen is further characterized by a lower compartment with separate outside access; when filled by the soft mass of sleeping bag or clothing the compartment wraps halfway around the hips and even under a horrid tonnage the pack rides there with amazing cosiness.

Soft packs for hikes as long as a week. Left: completely soft Jensen-type packs, zippered main compartment front-opening, sleeping bag stowed in lower compartment. Right: rucksack with light, semi-flexible internal frame, detachable pockets, zippered main compartment back-opening

Soft packs are magnificent for the climber and ski-mountaineer who seeks the joys of a wildland dancer but, to perform his art, must also be a mule. The load rides snugger than with a packframe, not lurching and jouncing to disturb the delicate balance wanted when scrambling over frost-wedged boulders or swinging a turn in deep powder snow, and there are no awkward projections to embrace bushes and jutting rocks. The average hiker, however, is happier with a packframe-bag, which demands less fine-tuning.

RUCKSACK DETAILS

Nylon rucksacks perhaps best combine strength, lightness, and water-repellency. Those of *cotton* or *cotton canvas* are less waterproof and a bit heavier but are more durable, breathe more freely to minimize back sweatiness, hold shape better than limp nylon, and don't cost as much. *Leather* rucksacks are expensive, heavy, rugged, and quaint; they are especially picturesque with lederhosen.

Outside pockets, often omitted from climbers' rucksacks because they snag on rocks, are badly wanted by hikers. Some models have one pocket, others two, three, or four. Zipper closures are favored; straps and buckles are more foolproof but more trouble. *Detachable pockets* give versatility. *Inside pockets,* snagproof and weatherproof, are inconvenient.

The *main bag* may be divided into two vertical compartments to help distribute weight; large models may have a separate, outside-access bottom compartment. Most usually the bag is a *top-opener,* closed by zipper or drawstrings; in the latter case, a *toggle,* a spring-loaded clamp, is handy for locking the strings. A *top flap* tied with a single strap and buckle or with a pair increases rain protection; an extra sweater or parka, or the sleeping bag, can be carried under the flap. A few rucksacks have a *front-opener* bag, entry via a zipper next to the hiker's back. More common is the *back-opener,* with zippers permitting quick access to the entire interior; risk of zipper failure, a calamity beyond profanity and tears, is reduced on back-openers that have *cinch straps* to compress the load and remove strain from zippers, as well as serving to carry ice ax, skis, or tent poles.

Shoulder straps may be leather, canvas, or nylon. For heavy loads the straps should be padded; extra slide-on pads can be purchased if soft shoulders cry out for relief. Straps are adjustable for length at the bottom only or, on fussy models, at the top too.

The *frame,* where it exists, may be as elementary as a stiff pad of urethane foam or as complex as an assembly (semi-rigid or flexible) of tubing, staves, or rods; of aluminum, steel, or fiberglass; forming an H, X, U, Y, or ladder. (Where will ingenuity end?) The frame may be adjustable by means of mechanical fittings or by means of staves that bend to give a custom fit. It may be detachable when a totally soft pack is desired; for example, when stowing inside a pack-frame-bag.

In view of all the planet-gadding going on in these last-gasp days of the cheap-energy era, worth mentioning is the rucksack that swallows its straps and other exterior appurtenances into a zippered pocket, leaving a neat bundle which eliminates the hassling typically suffered by a backpacker when traveling by plane, train, or bus.

PACKFRAME AND BAG: MINUTE DETAILS OF CONSTRUCTION

Man really is not well-designed to walk on his hind legs at all and placing a heavy weight atop the precariously-erect skeleton definitely goes against nature. Yet for a very long time man has been doing so

and the history of packing would in itself make a book—the basket or pot carried on the head, the pole balanced on the shoulder by loads at either end, the blanket roll slung over one shoulder and tied on the opposite hip, these are only a few of the ways in which man has turned himself into a donkey (another poor beast never intended to carry burdens).

Over the centuries and over the miles, many a suffering soul has mused upon possible better alternatives. Among the designs that evolved in America before World War II the most widely accepted and acclaimed was the famous Trapper Nelson, with a wood frame somewhat contoured to the body in the horizontal dimension though not the vertical, a canvas back, and a canvas bag attached to the frame by steel wires running through eyelet screws in the frame and grommets in the bag. The Trapper Nelson, rugged and inexpensive (currently in the area of $20), lives on, as do various other relics of the past, but nowadays is carried mainly by sentimentalists.

The Bergan rucksack (actually a packframe) with a tubular steel frame, also from the pre-World War II era, perhaps started the trend to metal, especially when thousands of the army adaptation (the notorious "kidney-killer") were released onto American trails in the great age of war surplus. Frames of tubular aluminum began to appear, lighter than steel but still not compromising much with the human back and with a tendency to fall apart when sneezed at, as they frequently were. Then Kelty and other pioneers inaugurated modern

times and the continuing quest for the Ultimate Pack.

A time may come, perhaps 10 or 20 years from now, when field-testing by millions of hikers will have sorted out and simplified the options. At the moment, though, packframes and bags are in flux, and the backpacker may develop a hostility toward manufacturers and their incessant picky-picky tinkering with this fine detail and that. However, he should thank them even when they confuse him; they have provided a degree of comfort inconceivable to oldtimers bent over under the torture racks they accepted as just retribution for sinful lives.

The following quick and incomplete review of the alternative materials and constructions available in contemporary packframes and bags will not satisfy the serious student of the subject, who should read many (one or two won't do) catalogs of mountain shops and manufacturers and there listen in on a scholarly, gentlemanly, but passionate debate. The beginner, when his mind goes numb even with the following oversimplified and partial survey, should skip to the next section on how to choose a packframe and bag.

THE PACKFRAME
The Skeleton

Most frames are made of *aluminum alloy* tubes; a few are made of lighter and costlier *magnesium alloy*. Experiments with *plastic* so far have had debatable success.

The two commonest *frame outlines* are (1) an H in which the outside members are separate pieces and (2) an upright or inverted U formed by bending a single tube. In the vertical dimension the frame is contoured to the back, with either a moderate or an exaggerated bend; on some, the lower portion sweeps sharply forward to bring weight more directly over the body axis.

Three to five horizontal *crossbars* (in a U design the outside member itself makes one of the crossbars) are curved to fit back contours. They give rigidity yet permit enough flexibility to absorb shocks. Some models can be lengthened at the top with a *frame extension* for very tall loads.

The most-used method of joining the metal members is *welding* (heliarc, tungsten arc), generally considered the strongest method. *Brazed* frames are inexpensive and quite sturdy if carefully made. Several manufacturers use *epoxy* bonding, declaring it is stronger than welding, a claim not unanimously accepted. A number of designs dispense with permanent joints in favor of plastic or metal *couplings* (or *bolts* or *screws*), in theory not as rigid as welding but in practice just as satisfactory and offering advantages of adjustability. Indeed, two or three manufacturers dispute the conventional wisdom that rigidity equals strength; their coupled-together frames flex considerably, resisting stress dynamically. Of course, the more parts to a frame, the more the cost.

Some frames are *adjustable*, either by using the above-mentioned couplings that let the crossbars be moved or by telescoping the outside members; frame length and packbag position can be varied to suit bodies of different dimensions and loads of different weights. Manufacturers whose frames are non-adjustable ordinarily compensate by offering two to four sizes.

Above paragraphs describe the contemporary "standard" frame. However, the inventors are busy busy busy and boundaries of the "standard" relentlessly expand to encompass new ideas. To bring the load closer to the body, rucksack-style, the Cannondale Wilderness employs a rigid *internal frame*. Not so radical, that, compared to other inspirations. The Bal-Pak, dreamed up by a man whose back was a total wreck but who refused to abandon backpacking, is a sort

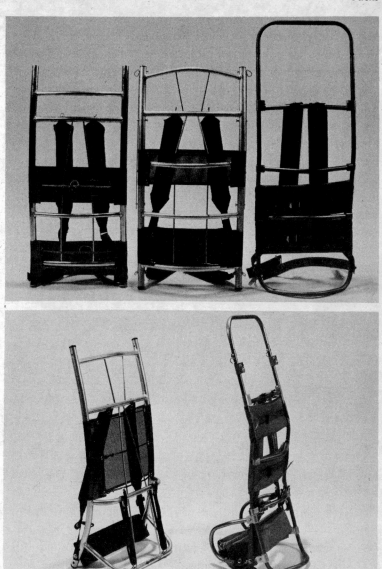

Representative packframes. Above: examples of "conventional" frames. Below: more "radical" frames. On the left, a frame swept sharply forward at the bottom to bring weight close to hips. On the right, a hip-hugger frame with arms that place weight snugly on hips.

137

of birdcage arching over the shoulders; half the load is carried in back, half in front. The Modular-Pak breaks into components which serve as tent poles, camp seat, stretcher, or ladder. Far out? Well, a generation ago the Trapper Nelson gang laughed at Dick Kelty.

Nobody is laughing (a good many are snarling) at the *hiploader frame* (*hiphugger, wraparound*), which has two padded arms jutting forward from the bottom and hugging the hips when drawn tight by a belt. Though deriving from a 19th century patent by Henry Merriam, only recently has the concept been explored in detail; half a dozen manufacturers now produce variants. Enthusiasts insist that the hiploader is the greatest advance since the Kelty, is the first *true* hip-carry pack. Critics foam at the mouth. Points of consensus seem to be: a hiploader is not for every body and decidedly not for the thick-waisted or pencil-skinny; it must be meticulously selected for perfect fit and kept in precise adjustment or every step is torture; except for versions with adjustable (or removable) arms, the comfort limit is about 40 pounds; nevertheless, if a person is slender yet has a definite hip platform he/she may find the hiploader supremely comfortable—there are hikers not of average build (narrow-backed, for example) who say no standard frame ever has given them peace, that the hiploader is the one pack they can carry without tears of pain.

Backbands

Attached to the frame and forming the bearing surfaces against the hiker's body are the backbands, usually nylon, occasionally cotton, fabric, webbing, or (for better ventilation) mesh. On several models the bands are padded.

Two is the typical number, though in some designs a padded hip belt (see below) replaces the lower one. Either or both bands may be adjustable up or down for personal fit; if bands are fixed particular attention should be devoted to buying the correct size of frame. Knotted cords or turnbuckles maintain tension in the bands, which must be kept taut to prevent crossbars from pressing the flesh.

For the ultimate in cool non-sweatiness, a few manufacturers dispense with backbands, providing instead a full-length or part-length panel of nylon mesh or a bearing surface of light cords strung horizontally. Whether the airiness is necessary, or worth the possibly lesser durability, is a question.

Shoulder Straps

The shoulder straps, attached to the frame bottom at the sides and to a crossbar at shoulder height, ordinarily are adjusted for length by a single pair of buckles; designs with two pairs permit the load to be carried high or low. Other niceties of adjustment displayed by various models are: two or more sets of attachment points on the crossbar so straps can be moved closer together or farther apart to suit shoulder width; as noted above, a crossbar that can be raised or lowered.

In the shoulder-bearing segments the straps usually are 2–3 inches wide with built-in padding of heavy, dense latex or urethane foam; soft-shouldered hikers may purchase extra slip-on pads. It is important the padding extend far enough downward so the lower nylon-webbing segments of the straps don't bite the tender underarms.

Hip Belt

The key component of the modern pack is the hip belt (waist belt, waist strap), hailed as the most revolutionary step in recorded history toward transforming humans into happy asses.

Olden-day packs (the Trapper Nelson) were "shoulder-carry" designs; when mangled shoulders sagged, the whimpering hiker leaned farther forward to shift weight directly onto the back; in the final extremity he cupped hands under the frame horns and lifted—until his arms went dead.

The design pioneered by Kelty and others lets shoulders and back do a decent share of the work but employs the hip belt to place much of the weight on the hips—60–75 percent claim the theoreticians, perhaps 30–50 percent say skeptics; certainly the percentage varies from one model to another and with different adjustments of belt and shoulder straps. The load is carried high, in a vertical line parallel to the body axis; weight is transmitted through the frame to the hip belt, from there to the strong muscles of the hip area, and thence to the sturdy legs. With this "hip-carry" system, strain is lessened on

Hip belts. Left: simple web belt. Center: padded half-belt combined with padded lower backband. Right: padded wraparound belt

shoulders and back and the hiker walks upright rather than in the old Trapper Nelson crouch.

The simplest belt consists of two straps of nylon or cotton webbing, about 2 inches wide, buckling in front.

More favored by hikers of slight build, wincing under pressure of frame on pelvis, and by all hikers laboring under very heavy loads, is a *padded hip belt* (*wraparound* or *full-circle belt*) 4–5 inches wide and extending all around the body, in the process replacing the lower backband. The belt may or may not be adjustable up or down for best positioning on the pelvis. An alternative is a *padded half-belt* which covers only the sides of the body but is combined with a padded lower backband to approximate a full wraparound. If a hiker buys a pack lacking a padded hip belt, he may add one bought separately.

A hiker who frequently travels rough terrain appreciates the convenience of a spring-loaded *quick-release buckle,* since for safety reasons the hip belt always must be completely unbuckled before fording streams, walking logs, or making similar maneuvers where it may be essential to jettison the pack in a hurry.

No dogma goes unchallenged by heretics. There are burly, broadshouldered hikers so strong-backed they don't need the hip belt, despise its confinement, and never use it, thus converting modern hip-carrier packs into old-style shoulder-carriers. However, most hikers fully exploit the belt by keeping it tight; if a pack is properly adjusted to put weight on hips, a thumb can easily be slid between shoulder strap and shoulder.

THE BAG

Inexpensive bags often are of durable *cotton duck,* rather heavy and water-absorbent. Most are of very strong and abrasion-resistant *nylon duck* or of *nylon Cordura cloth,* which looks tougher but isn't, actually just prettier and higher priced. Claims to the contrary, no bag is waterproof; in sopping weather the pack should be protected by a truly impervious *rain cover,* either an article made specifically for that purpose or a poncho or sheet of plastic.

A bag may have a *reinforced bottom,* perhaps of leather or heavy-coated nylon. The best bags are *reinforced at all stress points* and are *double- or triple-stitched* throughout with synthetic thread, the seams kept away from fabric edges to avoid fraying, and *lockstitched* (back-stitched, back-tacked, bar-tacked) at ends to prevent unraveling. Leather or nylon *lash points* may be provided for tying gear to the pack exterior.

The more *zippers* on a bag the more important that they be rugged and dependable, of a non-locking type and with large, easy-to-operate pulls, and covered by *rain flaps* to shed water. Most used are nylon zippers, either with molded teeth or interlocking coils. The best metal zippers have die-cast teeth, smoother-running than punched teeth.

Various devices connect bags to frames. In an older but still-used design, *pockets* or *sleeves* integral to the bag slip over the upper horns of the frame; the bag is suspended from these and held to the lower frame by straps. A few bags snap onto *frame-mounted studs* or have bag-attached *bolts which screw into nut plates* set in the frame. In greatest current favor are *clevis pins.* (The clevis pin is a stud that goes through a grommet in the bag, then through a hole in the frame, and is held in place by a split lock ring or key wire. Taping the rings or wires keeps them from falling out, which they tend to do when damaged; the smart hiker has spare sets of pins and rings in his repair kit.)

An *expedition* bag extending the *full length of the frame* is pre-

Representative packbags for very bulky loads. Left: full-length, undivided "expedition" bag. Gear also can be carried under the top flap. Right: two-thirds-length bag with extension frame (hidden) added for top load, exterior attachment points for lashing on gear

ferred by alpine heroes lugging massive loads and sloppy hikers whose method of "planning" gear and food is to throw stuff in until there seems to be enough. The average backpacker's choice is a bag extending *two-thirds of the frame length;* sleeping bag and pad are carried outside, strapped to the frame bottom. Some frame models, though, permit the two-thirds-length bag to be placed in any of several positions—at the frame top normally, or at the bottom to keep weight low for better balance in ticklish terrain.

The typical bag is a *top-opener,* with a metal *hold-open frame* to maintain the bag profile or a loose top closed by drawstrings. Over the top goes a *storm flap* tied to the lower bag by straps and buckles or cords and toggles; tent or tarp may be carried under the flap.

A top-opener may be *undivided,* the interior a single large cavity;

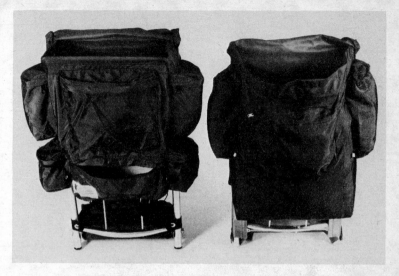

Representative packbags. Above left: two-thirds-length bag, divided. Main compartment top-opening with hold-open frame, lower compartment zippered. Above right: two-thirds-length bag, undivided, top-opening with drawstring closure. Below left: two-thirds-length bag, divided, back-opening with compression straps. Below right: full-length bag, divided, sleeping bag stowed in lower compartment

about half of all hikers favor this style for the general ease of stowing gear, especially bulky or long items. The other half likes the neat organization allowed by a *compartmented* bag and doesn't mind fiddling around to fit in gear of awkward dimensions. There may be two or three *upper compartments* separated by vertical panels, plus a *lower compartment* with outside access via zipper; the latter feature is transitional to the next style.

With a top-opener the hiker invariably discovers that any article he wants is at the bottom of the bag; he gropes and mutters and

144

finally dumps the whole mess on the ground. A *back-opener* eliminates this exasperation, but at a price. If there are three to five *hori-
zontally-layered compartments,* each item always is in its assigned
spot. However, the cubbyholes may be so small that tent poles have
to be lashed outside and the watermelon carried in the arms. If there
is a *single compartment* zippered on three sides, never is a frustrating
search required—lay the pack down, zip-zip, and everything is in
plain view. However, when the bag is overstuffed the zippers jam
and should they fail, let passersby guard their ears against the weeping and wailing; *compression straps* cinching across the back of the
bag press the load closer to the body and take strain from zippers,
lessening the worry.

Whether top-opener or back-opener, there may be provision, by a
frame extension or add-on crossbar and/or lash points on the bag,
for transporting a top load of equipment that can't be crammed inside, perhaps a tent or a duffle bag holding food or miscellany.

Outside *pockets,* ordinarily zippered, range in number from none
to nine, possibly including a map pocket in the storm flap. Extra
pockets may be purchased and sewed to the bag or, in designs with
proper attachment points, clipped on.

STUFF BAG

With the most-favored pack-bag style, extending two-thirds the
length of the frame, the sleeping bag and perhaps sleeping pad normally are lashed to the bottom of the frame. These being light by
comparison with dense food and stoves and cameras, the method
helps keep weight high on the body.

Particularly in wet climates and in brush or rough terrain, the
sleeping bag should be stowed in a stuff bag. The best for all purposes is abrasion-resistant *waterproof nylon,* with a drawstring closure
and a weather flap to cover the opening; weight, about 5 ounces. A
laminated *polyethylene* stuff bag, 1 to 5¼ ounces, is less practical because of its tendency to snag and tear but serves well inside the pack
bag, where one may also use light nylon stuff bags, about 1-1½
ounces, or *poly bags* in various sizes weighing a fraction of an ounce.
Cotton stuff bags are cheaper but weigh about 1 pound and are not

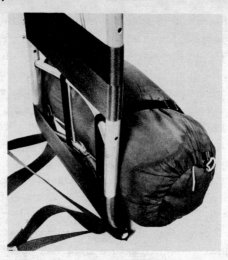

Attachment of sleeping bag stuff bag to frame with two straps

waterproof. A *compressor* stuff bag has outer lacing to facilitate squeezing to tiny size.

The stuff bag is attached to the packframe by two (not one) straps with buckles, 36-40 inches long (or longer if tarp, poncho, or whatever also is to be carried here), wrapped *around* the two lower horizontal frame bars and *outside* the two vertical center bars. Elastic shock cords are not recommended; they may catch on brush or rocks and pull away from the pack, possibly letting the stuff bag escape and certainly throwing the hiker off balance.

Duffle bags are not for backpacking as such, but are useful on long trips to the trailhead by public transportation—airplane, boat, train, bus—when heavy loads in the pack could subject it to severe strain, such as while being tossed around in baggage compartments or from boat to dock. It's discouraging to arrive at the start of a North Cascades trail and find the packframe has been destroyed by a baggage-butcher somewhere between Chicago and Stehekin.

CHOOSING A PACKFRAME AND BAG

The waters being now thoroughly muddied, time for an important announcement: despite the staggering array of options, it's hard to go far wrong in choosing a packframe and bag from the stock of a reputable outdoor outfitter. There is not, for each person, one and only one pack exactly right with all others hopelessly wrong.

The years of inventing and field-testing and refining and tinkering have established a standard, upheld by all the principal manufacturers whatever variant paths they have taken toward the Ultimate, that is very high indeed. Some trail veterans become fussy about straps and pads and zippers and toggles and even novices often are fascinated by intricacies of compartment design and stitching; manufacturers love to correspond with such connoisseurs—it makes them feel appreciated. However, the ordinary hiker can be perfectly happy with any of the excellent models on the market.

What is the most back-easing *frame style?* Who knows? Bodies are infinitely varied and so are opinions. A person with an "average" body (whatever that is) probably mates as well with one standard design as another. Those with deviant bodies (short torsos, narrow shoulders, thinly-covered bones) may wish to experiment with the intricate models; they do well to seek the counsel of experienced hikers of similar build or a mountain shop clerk who seems to know what he's talking about.

More critical than style is *frame size,* and here it must be stressed

A family on the trail for an overnight or longer hike. Father, son, and daughter carry various representative packframe-bags in sizes large to small. Mother hauls the baby in a Gerry Baby Carrier, her gear on the other backs

that a person's height is less relevant than the length of his or her torso. Ideally the novice should spend an hour or two in a shop, marching up and down the aisles wearing various packs—loaded, or nothing is learned. If a shop with rental service is handy, much more instructive is taking several packs out on the trail before purchase. Adjustable models should be tested with crossbars, backbands, and shoulder straps in a number of positions. Non-adjustable models usually come in two to four sizes; more than one should be tried.

Every *bag size* on the market is adequate for a weekend, or for a week if outfit and commissary are planned precisely. However, a lot

of bags are too skimpy for 10-day trips in rough and stormy wildernesses which demand considerable bad-weather and emergency gear. The little tiny bags that look so chic in the shop may be dandy for travels in benign meadowlands but are infernal nuisances in a trackless alder bottom, where the gear lashed and draped all over the outside tangles constantly with bushes.

A pack is useless in itself, providing neither shelter, calories, nor entertainment, so *weight* is a consideration. However, packs all weigh about the same, between 3 and 5 pounds, 4 the average. Those on the low side (the range drops to 2 pounds) require extra-careful handling; those on the high side (the range rises to 6 pounds) may be sturdy or accessory-cluttered beyond any normal requirement.

Doubtless a majority of novices select the first pack largely on the basis of *price*. At any shop of sound reputation the rule is you pretty much get what you pay for. Due to economies of scale a best-selling pack costs less than a slow mover of equal value; generally, though, price reflects (1) quality of materials and care of manufacture, factors which determine durability, and (2) the number of special conveniences, each of which adds expense. The novice must ask: "How much durability and convenience do I really need? And how much can I afford?" The hiker whose rambles are limited to trails in Appalachian forests or High Sierra meadows needs less pack than the masochist plunging into British Columbia jungles or trudging Yukon glaciers.

POVERTY ROW (UNDER $25)

With all due respect to your friendly neighborhood Handy Dandy Super-Thrifty Discount Drugs and Surplus, packs sold by retailers of this ilk must be viewed with suspicion. Simply to look at the $5 "Scout-type" pack sends shooting pains up and down the spine. One approaches a $9 "cruiser-style" pack in fear and trembling. However, for short trips such packs are not crippling. Certainly, the hiker so destitute he sets forth in tennis shoes and his uncle's rotten old World War II feather sleeping bag may see great merit in a $5 pack. Better that than stay home. Never forget, through all the pre-Kelty Dark Ages packs no better than these were carried by generations of hikers and relatively few are actually in traction.

The Trapper Nelson lives, and there are many who say if it was good enough to go to Minya Konka in 1932, then the highest summit attained by Americans, it's plenty good for tramping trails today. Priced at about $20, the Trapper is rugged and trustworthy and only with loads above 40 pounds puts a permanent crimp in the back.

A $20 "overnight" rucksack, discussed earlier, serves very well for initial weekend experiments and thereafter for any short trips.

Mass-merchandisers and a few mountain shops stock Asian imports which on quick scan appear identical to packs of much higher cost. Why pay more, wonders the novice, when here is a $25 Kelty? No reason at all if one plans merely several lightly-loaded (under 30 pounds) backpacks a summer and is willing to give very tender treatment and take along a repair kit of wire and cord. A beginner who hasn't made up his mind whether backpacking is his game ought to consider this option.

ECONOMY TOWN (UNDER $45)

Until recently the emptiness of the vast gap between the poverty packs and the Kelty class was relieved by a single offering, the REI Cruiser, which in various frame-bag combinations (two frame sizes, bags of expedition and two-thirds length, undivided and compartmented) sells for $30 to $40. The rugged REI Cruiser has been used to satisfaction from rain forests to the summit of Mt. Everest, has earned a reputation as dependable if not fancy, and is the best-selling pack in America.

Now other manufacturers have entered the economy market, among them Kelty with a $38 Basic Pack (distinguished from its famous Standard Pack), Sears Roebuck with the $35 Hillary II, Eastern Mountain Sports (EMS) with the $45 Heliomaster, and Jan Sport with the $45 Cascade 2.

These models have been described by consumer product-testing groups as "for moderate use only," implying they are fragile. Nonsense. Any pack can be broken by overloading and stupid handling, but failures of the models noted above are very rare. To be sure, some packs in the Kelty class are stronger, but only under exceptionally cruel circumstances is the "surplus" strength needed. The lower cost is explained not by shoddiness but by less costly (yet reliable) materials and construction methods, few special convenience features, and volume of sales.

MAIN STREET ($50 ON UP)

The hot spot in contemporary design is the $50 to $80 region. Prices go as high as $150; the packs above $80 generally are for the expeditioner or the connoisseur of exquisite taste.

Dozens of manufacturers are active and their entries run into the hundreds. Every year they improve old models and invent new ones. Kelty, of course, is synonymous with quality; indeed, "kelty" has entered the language as denoting *any* modern packframe-bag. This is not entirely fair, since superb Main Street packs also are made by Adventure 16, Alpine Designs, Alpenlite-Sierra Designs, Eddie Bauer, Camp Trails, Cannondale, Gerry, Himalayan, Jan Sport, Mountain Master, North Face, REI (with its Superpak), Stephenson's Warmlite, Sunbird, Trailwise, Universal Field, and others—and others.

It's folly to wrangle over which are best, that being a matter of personal opinion, even if dressed up as an "objective rating" by a consumers' organization. A week or two of examination by a half-dozen experts is no substitute for being hauled a million miles by thousands of assorted hikers, average, un-average, and weird. A fair rule is that if a model has been around a few years it has met the test of the trails with at least passing marks. If brand-new it may still be worthy, though it may have to wait a while for wide approval.

Perhaps a majority of hikers, if they continue backpacking long enough, eventually want a Main Street packframe-bag. Having made a choice from the bewildering array, they may become fanatic loyalists, exalting their mate above every competitor. Or, they may go through life flirting with each pretty face.

PACKFRAMES AND BAGS FOR CHILDREN AND SMALL ADULTS

The above packs serve persons from around 5 feet 3 inches upwards. People shorter—or somewhat taller with unusual torsos—must look elsewhere.

Jan Sport has two models easily adjustable to "grow" with the kids and well-liked also by small adults. The Mini is for loads up to 25 pounds or so. The frame is 25 inches high; the bag has two outside pockets. Total weight is 1¾ pounds and the price about $23. The Scout, for loads up to 35 pounds or so, has a 29½-inch frame and a bag with three outside pockets. Total weight is 2⅝ pounds and the price about $30.

The very large and comprehensive Camp Trails line includes two models for youngsters. The Bobcat, 1¾ pounds, has a cotton duck bag spacious enough for everything a 5-10-year-old can carry and sells for under $20. The Tracker is intermediate in size and price between the Bobcat and the Medium REI Cruiser.

The Kelty Sleeping Bag Carrier, not a packframe, consists of a pocket large enough for lunch and cup and a toy, shoulder straps attached, and bottom straps for lashing on a sleeping bag and/or clothing. The device, good roughly for the 4-7-year-olds, weighs ⅜ pound and costs about $10.

USING A PACKFRAME AND BAG

Backpacking techniques are treated in Chapter 2 but certain rules about use of the pack itself may be stated here:

Once on the trail, experiment with adjustable components (shoulder straps, backbands, hip belt) to find the most comfortable fit. Periodically, perhaps several times a day, tighten the backbands so they literally sing when snapped by a finger.

Any packframe, no matter how sturdy, can be broken; never drop a loaded pack, especially on rocks—always lower it gently. Keep the pack away from fire or excessive heat. In camp remove all food to disinterest animals, both mouse-type nibblers and bear-type slashers.

Carry a repair kit of spare clevis pins and locking wires (or whatever is suited to the particular packframe-bag brand) and nylon cord for emergency lashings in the rare case of the frame failing at a joint or the bag ripping.

In loading the bag, locate heavy items close to the back and up high—a process simplified by compartments. Keep metal objects away from the back; they may rub against the frame and quickly wear holes in the bag. In wet climates place all gear in waterproof nylon or poly bags so that if water finds an entry it doesn't soak the entire contents; be especially sure to put wet clothing in poly bags before stowing inside.

The sleeping bag is extremely important to keep dry and very hard to dry once wet; therefore, put it inside a large poly bag inside a waterproof nylon stuff bag. (The technique is to insert the poly bag in the stuff bag, *then* start stuffing.) Normally the loaded stuff bag is lashed to the bottom of the frame. Here, also, may be carried the sleeping pad—as well as a soaking-wet parka or poncho.

PACKS FOR CARRYING—AND BEING CARRIED BY—CHILDREN

Children on the trail are the subject of Chapter 18. However, following are a few words about the packs in which they are carried as infants and those they carry as toddlers, stumblers, and finally sturdy hikers.

CHILD-CARRIERS

For short walks with infants there are lightweight, frameless, cotton rucksacks (example, Gerry Pleatseat) weighing about 1 pound and costing about $6. The baby faces forward, held to the mother's (or father's, or older sibling's) back by the fabric and adjustable straps. The legs hang down through holes, the head rests against the hauler's neck when the baby sleeps.

For longer hikes, and children beyond infancy and thus heavier but still not toddling too well, a more elaborate vehicle is required. The Gerry designs are far and away most popular. The Gerry Baby Carrier consists of a tubular aluminum frame fitted with an adjustable seat below which is a storage area for baby-type gear; a cotton-duck seat; and padded shoulder straps. The pack serves for offspring from less than 4 months of age up to 35 pounds or so, weighs $1\frac{7}{8}$ pounds, and costs about $22. The Gerry Kiddy Seat is similar except the seat is not adjustable, there is no storage area, and the comfortable load limit is about 25 pounds. Weight is 1 pound and cost about $14. Many parents, when kids are becoming horrid lumps (more than 15-20 pounds) but still must be hauled, lash a Gerry carrier to a pack-frame.

In Gerry designs the child faces forward for safest riding and the happiest, since he or she always can see the hauler—who also is more comfortable with the child's weight close to the back.

Haulers who don't like busy little fingers in their hair and ears prefer a design in which the child faces rearward, despite the fact the babe tends to get lonesome and start screaming unless closely followed on the trail by the other parent or a sibling, and the further disadvantage that weight rides much lower on the body, tending to pull the carrier over backward. An example of this design is the Camp Trails Tote-a-Tot, with tubular aluminum frame, snap-out seat, safety belt, and padded shoulder straps. The pack weighs 2⅜ pounds and sells for about $20.

With the Himalayan Piggy Pack, similar in weight to the others and priced at about $18, the child can face either way.

CHILDREN'S PACKS

Any child being brought up as a backpacker, either because the parents think it's good for him or because they can't afford a babysitter, should be introduced to load-carrying almost as soon as he or she descends from daddy's or mommy's shoulders onto his or her own feet. Besides, at this age the kid generally demands a pack, imagining it to be some sort of daddy-mommy-type toy; before long the sorry truth is realized but by then the old folk have precedent working for them.

Often the first load is toted in a small rucksack, bought new or handed down through the family, the straps shortened to keep the bag from dragging.

Next may come a Kelty Sleeping Bag Carrier, or a retailored frame rucksack dating from the parents' half-forgotten free and simple past.

Finally arrives the time to buy the first packframe and bag—a Jan Sport Mini, a Camp Trails Bobcat, the smallest Trapper Nelson, or whatever. In a large or extended family or a wide circle of friends such a pack may serve many children over the years. Definitely, parents who love their kids must not yield to the temptation to saddle them with $5 drugstore torture racks, not if they want to keep the family together on the trail.

11:

MANY a backpacker with some way to go before total decrepitude remembers when the setting of the sun was a poignantly sad event—not for symbolizing the death of day, but for reminding that soon the hour would arrive to leave campfire warmth and begin the night-long ordeal by shivering. To be sure, there were rumors of better equipment available to those of immense wealth, but the ordinary hiker carried a rectangular wool or kapok sleeping bag that weighed a considerable fraction of a ton and never kept out the chill on a summer night in alpine meadows. At that he felt luckier than his poor comrades who couldn't afford a bag and wrapped up in blankets. Boy Scout troops of 30-odd years ago often ended by morning as a circle of tight-packed bodies coiled around a fire.

World War II, which in its aftermath released a deluge of surplus gear to civilians at a tiny fraction of original cost, introduced a whole generation of low-income Americans to the down sleeping bag, formerly the raiment of princes and magnates, and to the revelation the night need not be miserable.

Unreconstructed veterans scorn modern refinements and survey the stock of mountain outfitters with hostility. They feel today's youth is being robbed of the full wilderness experience, that man ought to shiver at night for the good of his soul.

But as has been said, "The past is a foreign country: they do things differently there." The backpacker now accepts as inalienable his right to sleep warm and with contemporary bags there is no reason he shouldn't, most of the time, if he makes a proper selection.

There, again, is the rub. The sleeping bag is a very important garment, in which a hiker spends roughly a third of his life on the trail, and must be chosen with care. It is also one of the three costliest items every backpacker must own, and unlike boots and pack, which at large mountain shops can be rented, must be purchased outright.

But a single shop may stock 25 or more distinct bags and the number available from American outfitters runs into the hundreds. The beginner, having wrestled with the major problems of buying boots, then a pack, now must face the third of the Big Three decisions.

However, it's not really as complicated as portions of this chapter make it out to be.

First, for any average person planning ordinary summer backpacking, many different bags of various designs and prices will serve quite well. After a few years a hiker may become fussy about fine details but if a beginner were to walk into a mountain shop blindfolded and grab a bag at random the odds would favor him getting one satisfactory for his purposes.

Second, many bags can be ruled out simply on the basis of

weight. The person of average size and metabolism should sleep warm, in typical trail conditions, in a bag weighing less than 6 pounds and perhaps as little as 3. Bags of more than 6 pounds are designed either for car-camping or high mountaineering (or winter) and should be ignored.

Third, it is not necessary to wipe out the family fortune for a night's sleep. There are luxury bags offering lavish refinements in every detail of material and construction but also economy bags that never would win blue ribbons at international expositions yet provide comfort enough at reasonable prices.

Fourth, beware of strangers bearing gifts. Mass-merchandising emporiums, having recently noted the dimensions of the backpacker market, have taken to staging great big sales offering bags at astonishing prices. The bargains may or may not be genuine; the beginner, unless guided by an experienced, discerning friend or unless the retailer has an established reputation for good values, has no way of knowing.

So much for general preface. Time now to dig into the guts of the bag and see what it's made of, and why.

As in previous chapters, the novice may wish to merely scan or entirely skip the following section on intimate details of sleeping bag structure and proceed directly to the section after that, on how to select a bag. No hard feelings.

ANATOMY OF THE SLEEPING BAG

A sleeping bag is an article of clothing that retains body-generated heat by trapping innumerable tiny pockets of dead air. Not the components of the bag themselves but rather the air (a poor conductor and thus a good insulator) provides a barrier between the hot body and the cold, cold world.

The warmth of a bag is determined by several factors: (1) the kind and amount of insulating material—down, polyester, or foam; (2) the structure—the shape of the bag and the manner in which insulating material is compartmented; (3) the bag closure—by zippers and drawstrings; and (4) to a much lesser extent, covers and liners that may be added.

INSULATING MATERIAL (FILLER)

Many a material has been used in the past as sleeping bag filler and, as in the case of wool and kapok, eventually abandoned. Very likely new materials will be introduced in future, perhaps better than any now known. Of those presently common, down and polyester are overwhelmingly dominant.

Goose Down

Down, the fluff growing next to the skin of waterfowl, traps air more efficiently than any other readily-available lightweight substance yet allows body moisture to breathe out; compacts into a small bundle for carrying yet is extremely resilient, quickly expanding when released; and withstands thousands of compression-and-expansion cycles before getting too bent and broken to rise to the occasion.

Eider down, gathered from Arctic nests of the eider duck, is reputed to be the finest of all downs. Few backpackers ever will have the chance to test its virtues; the total world supply is perhaps 100 pounds a year and the current price around $100 a pound.

The reigning champion is the goose. But there are geese and geese. The best down is from a large, mature domestic fowl raised in a cold climate, the plucking done in early winter when the down is thickest and sturdiest. However, with the demand going up at the rate of 50 percent a year, merchants are combing the planet for geese of any kind, from anywhere. A scrawny Formosan goose disrobed in summer has little to brag about. Further, geese are raised strictly for eating, the down a mere byproduct, and since a tender youngster tastes better than a tough old bird, relatively few live to full prime-down maturity.

Constantly more and more backpackers (and other down-consumers) means more and more recourse to warm-climate and young geese. And since suppliers are now refusing to sell their best down by itself, rather mixing it with otherwise unsalable down, the overall quality is declining; the fill power or loft (see below) of today's typical top-grade down is about a quarter less than that of a decade ago.

To confuse the issue, what *is* "down"? The Federal Trade Commission requires a "down" product to contain at least 80 percent down; articles manufactured in states where laws are not stricter (as some are) than the federal regulation may contain "goose down" that is up to 16 percent goose feathers, 2 percent chicken, turkey, and pigeon feathers, and 2 percent "miscellaneous" (floor sweepings).

The merchants who buy raw mixed feathers and down from traders then launder, separate, blend, and grade the down. They then sell a number of grades for a variety of commercial purposes. Each merchant swears his top grade is the supreme and gives it a fancy but meaningless trade name. In fact, merchants argue about what makes a good down. Despite convincing evidence that color is irrelevant, a few stubbornly insist white is better than gray. Some point with pride to a low feather content (all down has from 8–20 percent feathers and miscellaneous, since hand-separation of down from tiny feathers would be prohibitively expensive); others brag about feathers, stressing the fact that a certain proportion is essential for strength and resiliency.

The consumer's life would be much easier if every down bag carried a hang tag stating its insulating characteristics. The insulating value of down is determined to about 60 percent by *fill power,* or *loft,* the ability to fluff up and trap air; and to about 40 percent by *recovery power,* the ability to spring out to full expansion after being crushed. Loft is measured in a cylinder to determine how many cubic inches of space an ounce of down can fill; the present industry norm for a good down is 550 cubic inches. Recovery power is measured by another simple procedure. Why are the results so rarely given by sleeping bag hang tags? Because fill and recovery power vary with humidity, cleanliness, and other factors and no uniform measuring standards have been universally adopted. Many a manufacturer is reluctant to tag his bags with their "honest loft," which may look bad by comparison with a competitor's "dishonest loft." Until uniform standards are adopted and enforced, figures given for loft will be useful in comparing the bags of any one supplier but possibly misleading in comparing bags of different suppliers.

The subject is altogether too arcane for a layman to comprehend. The average hiker does well to forsake his attempt to pursue consumerism to the last percentile of perfection in favor of patronizing trusted outfitters who utilize the best materials they can obtain and whose standards far exceed those set by the most rigorous federal regulation or state law. Beware of Super-Thrifty Drugs and War Surplus. But feel fairly safe at a reputable mountain shop.

Duck Down

Everything said above about geese applies also to ducks. Only under a microscope, with difficulty, can duck down be distinguished from goose down. In Canada a distinction usually is not made and both are mixed in "waterfowl down"; eventually this may become the rule everywhere.

If a goose and a duck were raised side by side to the same age, the goose down would be superior to that of the duck, mainly because the goose, and thus its plumes, would be larger. However, a good duck is better than a bad goose. The quality difference in their downs as marketed often is minimal, or even in favor of the duck.

The top-grade duck down in most mountain shop bags has a loft in the range of 480–520 cubic inches (but is available to 550), overlapping the 500–550 cubic inches of top-grade goose down. Weights of filler and construction details being equal, a duck bag may be ever so slightly less warm than a goose bag; but because snobs are driving up the goose price faster, the duck bag costs less.

Polyester

Polyester, a synthetic fiber, is not a new sleeping bag filler. Bags have long been manufactured with Dacron 88, Fortrel, and Kodel.

Despite an insulation value very inferior to down, these bags are so much less expensive—one quarter the cost of goose down bags—that they have had, and still have, a definite place in the outdoor world, notably in car-camping.

The "old" polyester is not dwelt upon here because for backpacking it has been largely superseded by a second-generation polyester introduced in 1971.

The new polyester (Dupont's Dacron fiberfill II and Celanese's Fortrel PolarGuard) has a number of virtues: (1) Unlike down,

Representative mummy bags. Above: with half-length top zipper. Middle: child's bag with half-length side zipper. Below: with full-length, two-way side zipper

which once soaking wet doesn't dry completely for days, the fiber absorbs less than 1 percent of water by weight. Crawl into a wet bag at night and by morning it will be dry from body heat alone. (2) Unlike down, which clumps up, flattens out, and losses much loft in humid conditions and all loft when saturated, even if drenched the fiber loses only about 10 percent of its loft. Wring out a sopping bag, shake it vigorously, snuggle in and be warm. (3) Unlike down, which flattens to zero loft under the sleeper, the fiber resists compression and gives a certain amount of bottom insulation. (4) Unlike down, the fiber is nonallergenic, can be washed regularly and easily to get rid of dust, and thus is the forced choice of people who sneeze at feathers and dust.

Confronted by the challenge, are feather merchants declaring their industry a disaster area? Not at all. Even its boosters admit the new polyester has only 70–75 percent the insulation value of down. Down loyalists turn the mathematics around, saying goose down with a fill power of 550 cubic inches has 70 percent more insulation value than polyester. Consequently, depending on which statistics you buy, for equal warmth a polyester bag must be 1 or 2 pounds heavier than a down bag. In addition, being not so nicely compressible, polyester requires more effort to cram into a stuff bag.

As good down grows scarcer and costlier, polyester looks better and better. But to be a spoilsport, those who expect a sensational bargain are doomed to disappointment. Cost of filler is just one element in the cost of a bag. Polyester bags designed for warm weather can be simply constructed and very inexpensive; a cold-weather polyester bag of complex construction sells for less than down yet still is far from dirt cheap.

Economy is not the new polyester's chief boast. The resistance to water is. Hikers who mainly travel areas of high humidity (say, Eastern America in summer) or of cruelly persistent rain (say, Northwest America in every season) may be so overjoyed by the warm-when-wet attribute of polyester that they don't mind carrying an extra pound or two of bag.

The Down-Polyester War isn't enough of a fuss. There also has to be a Polyester Civil War. The new polyester is marketed in two dif-

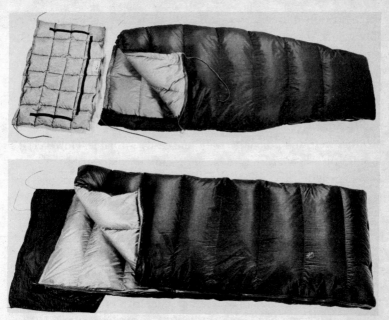

Above: *representative barrel bag with full-length side zipper; detached hood may be worn separately or attached to the bag with Velcro ("sticky") tape.* Below: *representative rectangular bag*

ferent versions. PolarGuard is cut in fibers 100 or more inches long which are resin-coated to keep them in stable position. Dacron fiberfill II is cut in 2-inch fibers which have no bonding agent applied but are held in position by being enclosed in a backing of Tyvek, a cobweb-like material that tangles with the fibers and prevents extreme shifting; the fibers are treated with a lubricating silicone that lets them slide easily, thus allowing the compressed bag to be rapidly refluffed to full loft. Hearing these claims, the PolarGuard people politely hide sneers. Fiberfill II is said by fans to maintain loft better than PolarGuard, whose fans disagree. PolarGuard promoters say the longer fibers are easier and thus cheaper to handle when making bags; fiberfill II promoters confess they had to develop new construction methods but say the problems have been solved. Claim is met by counterclaim.

Let it be remembered that the new polyester has been on the mar-

ket in quantity only since 1973. By 1980 intensive field-testing probably will settle the arguments between Fortrel PolarGuard and Dacron fiberfill II—and between polyester and down.

Foam

A polyurethane open-cell foam has the air-trapping capacity of
down, retains full loft when wet, doesn't go flat under the body,
breathes well, and is nonallergenic and easily washable. However, it's
heavier than down for equal warmth, quite incompressible and thus
extremely bulky to carry, soaks up and wicks water like a sponge, and
perhaps most disconcerting, doesn't cuddle a sleeper.

Nevertheless, foam is so much less expensive than down and so
relatively simple for manufacturers to work with that it has the
potential of providing very cheap bags—so cheap that many hikers
would be glad to adapt to the idiosyncrasies. But at present they
aren't particularly cheap. Why not? Doubtless because limited demand so far has made impossible the economies of mass production.

If the full-foam bag hasn't thrilled the masses, a few people have
become quite excited about bags with foam bottom and down top.
Again, more reports from the field must be awaited.

Chicken Feathers and Whatnot

No survey of sleeping bag fillers would be complete without a
wary glance at certain other materials.

Very decent "50–50" bags are sold here and there. The filler of
half down and half feathers is a good compromise for the hiker short
of cash.

Approach with caution bags advertised as "duck down" or just
plain "down" and at ridiculous prices, as low as $20. The filler may
truly be down—but stripped from scraggly goslings and ducklings
in a torrid jungle and having as much loft as fried lettuce. It may be
—despite the strictures of law—an outright fraud. During the Ko-
rean War the U.S. Army invented the Tan-O-Quil-Qm process to
increase the curl and thus the loft of chicken feathers. The Army
decided that the end product was junk but rumors abound of shifty
entrepreneurs pushing it.

Your neighborhood Handy-Dandy Super-Surplus Bargain Basement may tout "fiber fill" or "acetate" or "acryllic" bags for under $20, even under $10. Whatever these cheap synthetics may actually be, they are not warm or durable.

Fast-buck artists advertise a $4 bag, filled with golly knows what, as "good for up to 2 weeks" and promote it as "disposable—don't pack it back." There is even a "7-day disposable bag" priced at 99¢. May Heaven forgive them. We can't.

STRUCTURE OF THE BAG

The insulation value of a bag is determined partly by the kind and amount of filler and partly by various aspects of the structure. In order of importance as affecting warmth are (1) the shape of the bag; (2) the method employed to stabilize the filler; and (3) the construction of the inner and outer shells (the fabrics which hold the filler).

Shape

Other things being equal the smaller the bag the warmer, since there are fewer interior air spaces to be heated and more of the insulation is near the body rather than off in distant corners. The configuration of the upper opening, where the sleeper extends some portion of his face or head out of the bag, also is significant; the brain receives 20 percent of the body's blood supply and thus the head area can radiate a great deal of heat.

165

The warmest design is the *mummy* bag, contoured to the body and closed at the top by a drawstring that completely shuts off breezeways, leaving exposed, when desired, merely the sleeper's nose and mouth.

Though most mummy bags are substantially roomier than was once customary and some have a flare at the bottom for foot space, claustrophobics tend to prefer a *barrel* bag, which rather than tapering from head to foot bulges outward at the midsection to let elbows and knees maneuver. The design adds weight as well as comfort. Generally barrel bags are square-cut at the top with drawstring closure for sealing off the outer chill.

Roomiest and heaviest are *rectangular* bags, usually with no top closure, thus allowing heat to escape and breezes to enter; at low elevations and in warm climates this is, of course, an advantage. A *tapered* rectangular bag maintains the ease of ventilation and saves weight at the foot.

As a rough generalization, in bags of comparable filler and baffling (see below), barrel bags are about $10°$ colder than mummy bags and somewhat heavier; rectangular bags are about $20°$ colder and considerably heavier.

Compartments (Baffling)—Down-Filled Bag

If down were merely stuffed between an outer and inner shell it would soon lump up in certain spots, leaving others unprotected. Therefore some compartment system is required to hold the down in place. The aim of a designer is to get the most loft for the least weight of filler and compartmenting fabric; another consideration, especially in economy bags, is to do so at the least cost. Compromises are necessary on several counts and are evidenced by all backpacker bags.

The simplest and cheapest construction is *sewn-through* (*stitch-through*), where inner and outer shells are stitched directly together. The stitching lines offer no insulation and are "cold spots." This method is employed on down bags intended to be placed within outer bags for extreme cold.

Most down bags are built with panels (baffles) sewn to the inner and outer shells. Almost always the compartments run around the bag (*circumferential,* or the variant *"chevron cut"*) instead of in a line from top to bottom (*longitudinal*), in which pattern the filler tends to collect at the foot.

The panels commonly are of a nylon netting which is light, inexpensive, easy-breathing, and gives maximum compressibility. A few manufacturers prefer nylon cloth, a bit heavier and more costly but preventing movements of down between compartments.

A step up from sewn-through construction and eliminating cold spots is the *box,* in which the panels form right-angle compartments.

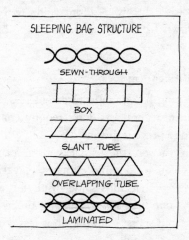

SLEEPING BAG STRUCTURE

SEWN-THROUGH

BOX

SLANT TUBE

OVERLAPPING TUBE

LAMINATED

Generally considered the most efficient design for down bags is the *slant tube* (*slant box, slant wall, parallelogram*), providing maximum loft for minimum panel weight and, in the judgment of a majority of experts, the greatest warmth per pound of total bag weight. When released the parallelogram walls straighten into rectangles, thus letting the down loft better than in ordinary boxes. Though construction expense is the same as with the box design, more baffle material is required, adding a bit to weight and cost.

The *overlapping tube* (*diaphragm tube, V-tube*) method holds the down very closely in place but somewhat restricts loft, thus giving slightly less insulation than the slant tube for equal amounts of filler. Also, construction expense is greater and the extra paneling increases weight and cost. (In the quest for perfect down control it is possible to "over-panel.")

A *laminated* bag has two sewn-through layers stitched together in an overlapping fashion to eliminate cold spots. Because of the weight of the additional fabric, few down backpacker bags are of this design.

Bags often have a *channel block,* a side-baffle opposite the zipper that prevents down from migrating around the circumference—and for that reason disliked by many hikers. They point out that down beneath the body is compressed virtually to zero thickness (thus the need for a sleeping pad, discussed below); before going to bed in cold weather they "chase" down from the underside of the bag to the upperside where it can do some good.

Batting Stabilization—Polyester-Filled Bag

Polyester comes to the sleeping bag manufacturer not in sacks of loose fluff but in rolls of batting. The batts don't require compartmenting but must be stabilized to prevent shifting.

Because of the ease of construction, the least expensive bags are *sewn-through* (see above), adequate for mild climates. A variation is the *sewn-through with a cover* that adds some insulation at the cold spots. Another is the *edge-stabilized sewn-through,* stitched only around the edges to minimize cold spots; stabilization is less effective and the batts may migrate within the shell.

Bags in a middle range of cost and warmth are *edge-stabilized without sewing-through,* the batts sewn to the shell around the edges but never through the batt.

Bags designed for cold weather usually are *laminated* (*double-quilted*), with two separate batts all around, sewn-through but with seams staggered so thin spots on one batt overlap thick spots on the other. In a still warmer variation, a *third edge-stabilized batt* is sandwiched between the two quilted layers of the bag top, which thus is one-third thicker than the bottom.

The second-generation polyester is so new that bag construction, notably batting stabilization, is in a period of experimentation and field-testing. Experience gained in years ahead will decide which of the present methods is best—and perhaps will lead to invention of better methods.

The Shell—Outer and Inner

Nearly all backpacker bags have shells of nylon, which is many times stronger than any other readily-available cloth, easy-breathing, wind-resistant, and effective at keeping filler from escaping; on the inside the slippery surface lets the sleeper revolve without the whole bag turning.

Cotton offers the advantages of lower cost and less vulnerability to campfire sparks, but being heavier for the same strength is mainly used for car-camping bags.

The nylon may be either taffeta or ripstop.

Taffeta, a flat-weave fabric, comes in many grades. The varieties customary in mountain-shop bags have a somewhat higher thread count than ripstop and thus are about the same strength. Taffeta has a softer, more comfortable texture, and for what it's worth is widely considered to have a more pleasing appearance.

Ripstop, which has extra-heavy threads every 3/16 to 1/4 inch that stop tears from running and form a reinforcing web which distributes stresses widely, also comes in many grades and weights. The cloth used in backpacker bags ranges in weight roughly from 1.5 ounces or less per square yard to 2 ounces; obviously the former is lighter and the latter more durable. Lightweight ripstop loses its *calender* (the flattening and pore-sealing given during manufacture) after repeated flexing and bending and thus rather early on starts leaking down (actually, the feathers usually escape first).

Though ripstop can be stronger than taffeta for equal weights, perhaps the main reason for its current dominance is the magic-word factor; ripstop is "in." Reputable suppliers use both fabrics in high-quality bags and the average backpacker is unlikely to discern any important difference.

Pages of precise logic and passionate rhetoric are devoted by mountain shop catalogs to debating the optimum way to cut the shells.

Many bags are *differentially cut (concentric cut),* which is to say the inner shell is smaller than the outer. The theoretical advantages are that the filler is permitted to loft more freely and that sleepers (especially those who thrash around a lot with knees and elbows) cannot so easily press the inner shell against the outer and create cold spots. Proponents claim such bags are warmer for equivalent amounts of filler.

Some manufacturers disagree and use a *space-filler cut,* with inner and outer shells the same circumference. Their theory is that the inner shell folds around the sleeper and fills air pockets. Proponents claim such bags are not only simpler and less expensive to make but have less inside air to heat and thus are warmer. They also say that in any event the concentric cut doesn't prevent cold spots as claimed.

Innocent bystanders suspect it doesn't make any difference how the shells are cut.

The body gives off not only heat but water vapor; while retaining the former the bag must freely breathe out the latter. Though beginners often ask for a waterproof sleeping bag, if such existed it would sweat the sleeper like a Turkish bath. Unwary hikers have been known to ruin bags by applying waterproofing compound.

OPENING AND CLOSING THE BAG: ZIPPER AND DRAWSTRINGS

Insulating material and structure have much to do with the warmth of the bag; the method by which it is closed (to freezing blasts) and opened (to cooling zephyrs) also affects warmth, and the overall comfort and convenience as well.

Incidentally, so much moisture is exhaled in the breath that even on the coldest nights a sleeper should try to keep his nose outside the bag to avoid dampening the interior. In extreme cold he may wish to protect the nose from freezing by breathing through a sweater.

As noted above, the head of the bag is a particularly critical area and thus may be treated first, followed by a discussion of zippers.

Head of the Bag

Rectangular bags ordinarily are wide-open at the top, though some have a drawstring.

Mummy and barrel bags usually have a drawstring closure to shut the airway. There may be a drawstring at the shoulders plus an extended *hood* which can be left flat in warm weather or drawn tight around the face with another drawstring. Or there may be a single drawstring around the top to form a hood.

For easy opening, to avoid a trapped feeling, a hiker does well to use a *toggle,* a spring-loaded clamp, on the drawstrings, or a *cord-block.*

Some manufacturers offer a down hood, or *collar,* which either can be sewn to the top of any bag or attached by Velcro ("sticky") tape.

Also available is a completely-detached hood that can be worn with any bag—or without one, as far as that goes.

Zippers

Very light bags dispense with a zipper altogether (the more zipper, the more weight) and the sleeper wriggles and slithers in from the top.

Some designs have a *center* or *top* zipper. Partisans claim these

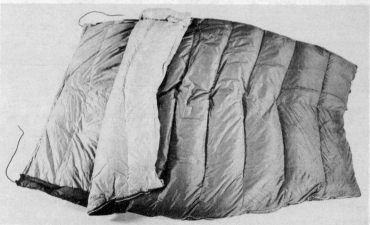

Above: *elephant's foot, normally used in combination with a down parka, but by itself good as a child's bag.* Below: *two side-zipped barrel bags zipped together to make a double*

advantages: the sleeper can lie on either side without being atop the zipper and can zip and unzip while on his back; the bag can be spread flat to use as a quilt; and when two top-zipped bags are joined (see below) the zipper is on the outside rather than in the middle.

Others have a *side* zipper, which may be on either side (*left-opening* or *right-opening*). Partisans claim as advantages that ventilation is most easily controlled and hoods can be used when two bags are joined.

Those hikers (perhaps a majority) who flop around a lot in the night find no important difference between top-zipped and side-zipped bags.

Mummy bags often have *half-length* zippers some 36 to 40 inches long, extending about halfway down from the top; as a general rule the less zipper the less of a cold spot and thus the warmer the bag.

Other mummies and barrels and most rectangulars have a *full-length* (70-inch or so) zipper. Some have a zipper running the *full-length and across the foot* for complete temperature control in warm weather, or *full-length zippers on both sides.*

Hikers who travel mainly in warm climates prefer a lot of zipper to avoid night-long stewing in their own juices. Cold-country hikers generally want much less zipper: when a full-length zipper fails (which occasionally happens even with the best) the sleeper is faced with either a shivering night or a massive hand-sewing job by flashlight; when a short zipper fails the comparatively small opening can be adequately closed with several safety pins or by clutching the fabric with the hands.

Two bags with full-length zippers can be joined—if the zippers are compatible—to make a double bag. Many couples like to have this option, either for the theoretical warmth of snuggling or simply for togetherness. (Wildland swingers, mindful of the adage that "a bird in the bag is worth two in the bush," check zipper compatibility when playing the trail version of the dating game.) Another advantage is that a small child can be accommodated, saving the weight of an extra bag. However, some couples (old marrieds) declare that in cold windy weather so much heat is lost through the top that a double bag is like no bag at all, and that sleeping with a squirming, kicking infant is no sleep at all.

Bags of different fillers can be combined for versatility (again, if the zippers are compatible). For example, if a couple has one bag with 2 pounds of down, another with 3 pounds, the two can be joined with the 2-pounder on top for warm nights, the 3-pounder for cold ones. Similarly, a polyester and a down bag can be combined, the former on the bottom since polyester compresses less and gives better ground insulation, and the down on top for its better air insulation.

The best zippers are nylon (a polyamide plastic) or Delrin (an acetal plastic), which unlike metal do not conduct heat, freeze, or rip the shell fabric when snagged. The highest-quality bags have "oversize" or "heavy-duty" zippers for greater dependability.

As with all special features a *two-way* (*two-slide*) zipper adds expense but is convenient in allowing the bag to be opened from either the top or bottom; in warm weather, the feet may thus be ventilated without chilling the shoulders.

Since the zipper is a line of zero insulation, in the best bags it is covered by a *down-filled tube* (*draft tube*) to prevent heat loss. (Incidentally, when buying two bags not the same model that are intended to be joined, make sure the insulating tubes overlap; otherwise the zipper will be uncovered, a full-length cold spot.)

Covers and Liners

A separate sleeping bag *cover* of cotton or nylon may be slipped over the bag to protect it from wear, to keep it clean when cooking and eating while stormbound in a tent, and for extra warmth. Covers are used mainly by climbers and winter hikers; few backpackers find the added protection worth the weight.

A sleeping bag *case* of ripstop nylon with a coated bottom, built-in foam pad, and drawstring hood is designed for extreme cold, such as sleeping on snow, and is of little interest to the average hiker.

Many hikers insert a light *liner* of nylon, cotton flannel, or cotton-polyester to keep the inner shell of the bag clean or because they prefer to sleep within snuggly cotton rather than slippery nylon. A liner adds a bit of extra warmth; during the night it also twists into interesting tangles.

Sleeping bags usually are carried in *stuff bags*; see Chapter 10.

SELECTING A SLEEPING BAG

The preceding section gives some notion of what dedicated, ingenious, idealistic, argumentative manufacturers are up to and the range of options and opinions they offer at every point. If, contrary to prior advice, the novice has ventured into that swamp, doubtless his indecision and anguish are now acute. Therefore, from motives of humanity, time for plain and simple talk.

There is no single sleeping bag ideal for everyone in the whole wide world. Choice of this intimate garment depends on very personal needs.

Most obvious is the matter of *body length/bag length*. Bags come in various lengths and obviously the bag should be long enough to contain the entire body, keeping in mind that a 6-foot bag is insufficient for a 6-foot sleeper; the body is longer when lying flat than when erect, and also extra inches are essential to let the toes flex and the neck stretch. However, for reasons of warmth, weight, and expense a person should buy the smallest bag into which he fits comfortably. A complicating factor is that some suppliers list the inside length of their bags, others the outside; at any shop, therefore, one must ask which system is used and what bag lengths are recommended for various body lengths. (When in doubt, better to choose a too-long bag than suffer cramped knees and neck.)

The backpacker may rather easily determine proper bag dimensions. Not so simple to unravel are the three central and intertwined considerations of weight, cost, and warmth.

(*Note:* Here and hereafter, the weights and prices given are for "regular"-size bags designed for the average-size adult body. Weights and prices are lower and higher for "short" and "long" sizes.)

As a generalization about *weight,* down bags range from about 3 pounds to 6, those on the lower end meant for mild temperatures, on the upper end for extreme cold. The most popular choice is roughly 4 pounds, suitable for most hikers in most areas. In polyester bags the range is from about 3½ to 6½ pounds, with 5 pounds perhaps the most popular. The beginner who sticks near the midrange won't go too far wrong.

If a bag is to be carried long distances, weight matters a lot and the hiker may wish to sacrifice warmth for the sake of a light load. On the other hand, if the bag is for short backpacks, an extra pound or two is insignificant.

Paralleling weight is *cost,* the sum of many factors—method and care of construction, type of filler, and special niceties of zipper and all. Down bags of interest to the average backpacker range from about $50 to $125, polyester bags from about $30 to $70.

If a hiker has all the money in the world he'll never look at a bag's price tag until satisfied with its warmth and weight and conveniences. On the other hand, a thin wallet may influence him to carry an extra pound or shiver a little to save $25 or $50. Still, he should buy the highest-quality bag he can afford; with proper care a good bag can outlast a series of make-do substitutes and be more economical in the long run—and more comfortable in the short run.

It's when a hiker investigates *warmth* that he finds himself plunging through thick mists, staggering from sinkhole to quicksand, deafened by creatures of the mercantile jungle screeching conflicting opinions. For orientation, the explorer must plot his route with careful attention to two considerations—how much warmth is required, and how much a bag provides.

First, *how warm a bag does the hiker need?* If most trips are planned for summer and/or low elevations, the choice should be a lightweight, inexpensive bag, perhaps rectangular. Adequate ventilation to avoid sweltering is important, meaning a full-length, possibly two-way zipper. If many trips will be in high mountains and/or winter a heavier and costlier bag is essential, of mummy or barrel shape and with minimum and/or heavy-duty zipper.

Two other factors influence choice. Hikers who sleep in tents don't need as much bag as those who sleep under tarps. In still air the interior of a closed tent is about 10° warmer than the surroundings; in a wind the differential is greater (see the wind chill chart in Chapter 6). Individual metabolisms vary enormously in their abilities to produce heat. Generally a beginning backpacker already knows if he/she is a cold person or a warm person; a cold sleeper may shiver on a tropic night in a bag designed for the South Pole, while a warm sleeper wrapped in an old horse blanket may snore up a storm on an icecap. (Incidentally, a cold sleeper can raise his thermostat setting by eating a supper high in fats, which during night-long digestion generate a great deal of heat.)

Second, *how warm is a bag?* Here is the arena of claims and counterclaims, bickering, opinion, nonsense, and little objective data. Testing programs have commenced to measure the thermal efficiency (and thus warmth) of down bags under laboratory conditions. Results to date suggest that not type or quality of down, not method of construction, not amount of loft, not care of workmanship, and certainly not retail price are clear indicators of thermal efficiency, which seems to be determined by a complex and poorly-understood relationship among shell, baffles, and filler.

Perhaps in coming years, as testing continues, industry-wide standards will evolve, cooling the arguments. Ultimately every bag may have a hang tag stating a federally-approved rating of thermal efficiency; a purchaser then will know exactly what he's buying. (Dream on, dream on.)

While hoping for a better future, how to cope with a lousy present? Some suppliers give a *warmth rating* (*minimum temperature rating*), saying a bag is warm down to 32° or 0° or whatever. Such figures must, of course, be treated with caution, since no scientist has studied sleeping with the thoroughness devoted to more athletic bedtime activities. None has measured the difference in cold toleration between fatties and skinnies. Moreover, such ratings assume a dry bag, brand-new, untouched by wind, and therefore are very approximate. Still, when provided, they at least permit comparison among bags offered by any one supplier.

Most manufacturers and retailers stress the bag *loft* as the best available indicator of warmth. Before going on, a distinction must be noted. As previously discussed, *down loft* is measured in a cylinder, yielding a figure for the number of cubic inches an ounce of down will fill when fluffed. *Bag loft* is measured in conditions of standard temperature and humidity by spreading out a bag, closed and fully fluffed, no weight inside or on top, and counting the inches from bottom to top. This is the *total loft.* However, because the bottom half of a bag is squashed more (with down) or less (with polyester) flat by the weight of the sleeper, many suppliers give only the *top loft,* which is to say, the loft of the upper half. (Some shops don't make clear whether they're speaking of total or top loft; bad cess to them.)

The problem is that the U.S. Bureau of Standards has not approved any set of rules for measuring bag loft and methods vary from one manufacturer and retailer to another, leaving much room for maneuvering, misrepresentation, and misunderstanding. Nevertheless, loft figures are excellent for comparing bags in any single shop, though not necessarily from one shop to the next.

Assuming a manufacturer has not goofed in his design and prevented full fluffing, the amount of loft is determined mainly by the *amount of filler*. Down bags in the "regular" size, meant for "average" conditions, contain from 2 to 3 pounds of down, which provide a top loft of roughly between 2½ and 5 inches. For summer trips in high mountains where night temperatures frequently drop to freezing, most hikers are content with 2½ pounds of down and a top loft of 3 (true) inches. For mild climates or warm sleepers, 1½ pounds and 2 inches may be perfectly satisfactory. Partly it depends on how often a person is willing to shiver a bit.

Second-generation polyester bags in the regular size have from 1½ to 4 pounds of filler, a top loft of 1½ to 3½ inches. Most hikers find that a bag decent enough for high mountains in summer has about 3 pounds of filler and a top loft of 2¾ inches. Again, less suffices for warmer climates.

Now, how does the hiker decide between down and polyester? Cost is a factor, though a well-made polyester bag is not tremendously cheaper than a down bag. The crucial criterion should be the wetness—including both humidity and raininess—of the intended area of travel. For long-distance, heavily-loaded hikes in realms of bitter cold and moderate-to-little moisture, down is the unbeaten champ. But where the water-laden atmosphere makes inescapable the sorry reality that a bag is going to be half-soaked half the time, polyester is the winner.

The following paragraphs describe several representative bags. The key word is "representative"—these are a very few points on a continuum of hundreds of bags. In a particular mountain shop the hiker may find nothing exactly matching details given here, certainly he will observe innumerable variations, and will encounter a wide range of prices, reflecting convenience features as well as basic quality. However, the examples suggest the range of choices available.

CHEAP STREET—UNDER $35

If a troop of Boy Scouts of the 1930s somehow, through courtesy of a time machine, could read this chapter, they'd be struck dumb with awe. When they recovered the explosion of laughter would echo and re-echo from the peaks. "What sissies are these hikers of the future!" they would cry. "Why, the bags they disdain as purely for the poverty-stricken would make *us* feel like *kings!*"

True enough. If all a hiker of today can afford is a $15 or $20 bag of "old" polyester, he's still better off than the ordinary backpacker of 35 years ago, and is no worse off with the Handy-Dandy-Super Surplus $10 Hot Bargain.

Nevertheless, a few dollars more allow a step up into modern times. For the beginner on a slim budget, and for any hiker whose camping is mainly in valleys in summer, occasionally in high country with near-freezing temperatures, a bag that will serve well enough is one of mummy shape, 2½ pounds of second-generation polyester in a sewn-through batt with cover, a top loft of 2 inches, total bag weight 4¼ pounds, price about $30.

COUNTING DOLLARS CAREFULLY—UNDER $70

In this price category the majority of backpackers can find true happiness or a reasonable approximation. Either down or polyester will do the job.

An example in down is a barrel bag with 2½ pounds of duck down, top loft of 2½ inches, total bag weight 4 pounds, price about $65.

One polyester example is a mummy bag with 2½ pounds of filler stabilized by sewn-through batting with cover, top loft of 2 inches, total bag weight 4 pounds, price about $50.

A second polyester example is a barrel bag with 3 pounds of filler in laminated (double-quilt) construction, top loft of 2¾ inches, total bag weight 5¾ pounds, price about $60.

These bags are comfortable for the average person at temperatures down to freezing or thereabouts, which means they serve not only for valleys but also for the summer highlands.

Warm enough for 0° or below is a mummy bag that combines fillers, with 1¼ pounds of goose down on top for excellent air insulation, 1¼ pounds of polyester on the bottom for good ground insulation (and warmth when wet, as bag bottoms have a way of getting), top loft of 3½ inches, total bag weight 4⅝ pounds, price about $70.

THE VAST MIDDLE CLASS—UNDER $90

In the upper economic realms the price of a bag can be misleading, affected as much by special features, useful or not, as by the fundamental characteristics of materials and construction that mainly determine warmth. Reference here is to a good basic bag, not fancy but honest.

In the past, before second-generation polyester offered a lower-cost and wet-climate alternative, this price category was where most of the action was; here were the countless bags, all filled with down, designed for temperatures down to $0°$, thus shiver-resistant in often-cold summer highlands, in often-icy valleys of spring and fall, and in any but the most vicious tempests of winter. Being so versatile, they have been the typical choice of habitual backpackers who carry loads long distances and travel in every sort of climate, but aren't rich enough to use dollar bills as kindling.

Among scores of slightly-differing models, one example is a mummy bag filled with 2½ pounds of goose down, top loft 3 inches, total bag weight 4 pounds, price about $85.

HANG THE EXPENSE—FROM $100 TO THE MOON

In the economic stratosphere, so rarified that barely a scattering of hikers can breathe it, are night garments many dream about but few have any earthly use for.

The price of a bag may be sky-high for one or more of four reasons: (1) More down, very costly, is used. (2) More special features, for warmth and convenience, have been added, ballooning a good basic $85 bag to $125. (3) Manufacture is done with tender loving care in home workshops by meticulous craftsmen totally oblivious to cost control. (4) The bag is a ripoff.

The examples cited here chiefly show the influence of reason #1 and to some extent reason #2. The bag gourmet should check the catalogs for examples of products fully displaying reason #2, and tiny little ads in backpacker/climber magazines for those deriving from reason #3, all the while bewaring of reason #4.

A fine bag for cold, cold nights (or cold, cold sleepers) is a mummy with 3 pounds of goose down, top loft of 3½ inches, total bag weight 5 pounds, price about $100.

For the icecap rovers is a mummy bag with numerous special features, 3½ pounds of goose down, top loft of 4½ inches, total bag weight 6 pounds, price about $140. The person who doesn't sleep warm in this bag is dead.

SPECIAL SLEEPING BAGS

Double bags, mummy or rectangular, may appeal to couples certain they always will want to sleep together; for equivalent weights such bags are warmer than two singles united; of course, they lack the separate-bed option.

The "elephant's foot" ("half-bag", "footsack"), extending on the average adult from feet to stomach, is designed as a climber's bivouac bag to be used in combination with a down parka. A hiker in a hurry may appreciate the combination; a typical "foot" weighs only 1⅞ pounds, costs $40. It can also do duty as a child's bag.

SLEEPING BAGS FOR CHILDREN

One reason many married couples buy sleeping bags that can be zipped into a double is to make room for little kids. The weight of an extra bag is saved and the kid (or kids) can snuggle between mommy and daddy—which is perhaps the only place they will sleep in the strange environment of the wilderness.

Family togetherness is, however, a disaster for everyone concerned if the kids kick and squirm all night. In any event, beyond a certain size the child cannot snuggle with parents and needs a separate sack.

Long-time hikers with a basementful of old gear often take a worn-out bag, chop off the bottom, patch as needed, and thereby make a child's bag with no cash outlay.

When a bag must be purchased the same rules given above apply. Children, though, being smaller and generally having better circulation, don't need bags with so much insulation or weight (or expense) as adults to gain equivalent warmth.

Important note: down bags should be used for children only after they are potty-trained; repeated cleaning destroys the loft (see below). Polyester is best for bed-wetters of any age.

CARING FOR THE SLEEPING BAG

There is no formula for predicting the life span of a sleeping bag. Every-night use for months on end, as during an expedition, may pretty well finish it off. If slept in only a few weekends a summer, it may last years. However, more important than the amount of use is the manner of use. Proper care can greatly extend a bag's life and carelessness can kill it while still new.

The nylon shell of the typical backpacker sleeping bag is strong but very thin and thus must be protected from wear and especially snagging. Therefore—and also to keep the bag dry—a layer should be placed between bag and earth, such as tent floor, sleeping pad, or ground sheet, and the bag should be carried within a stuff bag. The hiker's repair kit should include a roll of ripstop tape for patching holes through which filler might escape.

Nylon shells must be scrupulously guarded against fire; even a tiny spark instantly melts a hole in the fabric—and could kindle a smolder in the filler. Using an unprotected bag as a seat cushion for campfire seminars usually leads in the course of an evening to several holes per cushion, despite constant cries of "Spark! Spark!"

Even more perilous is steaming out the residue of a rainstorm. All fillers require some time to dry and down takes forever and during the long process spark holes are inevitable. And patience becomes exhausted, one moves closer to the flames, the fabric is scorched and disintegrates, and it's time to buy a new bag. All the more reason not to let the bag get wet in the first place.

Down bags should never be stored in the stuff bag between trips. The more time the down spends tightly compacted the more it bends and loses resiliency and thus loft and warmth. Instead, the bag should be loosely rolled, or better, hung on a wall or draped over a line in the basement or a hanger in the closet.

By the same token a down bag should be thoroughly fluffed before it is slept in. The rule is, as soon as camp is reached and the tent or tarp rigged, the bag is unrolled, shaken vigorously, and placed under the shelter to finish attaining full loft.

Any bag, but down especially, should be air-dried after each trip to avoid mildew and rot and to prevent the filler from matting. Indeed, on multi-day hikes the bag should be aired every day or two, weather permitting, to dry body moisture breathed into the filler at night.

HOW TO CLEAN?

Ideally a sleeping bag should be kept clean, not only for reasons of hygiene and social acceptability but to prevent the shell from rotting or being nibbled by small creatures (in the mountains or in the basement) which lust after salt and oil. Further, some people are allergic to the dust that collects on filler.

With polyester bags there is no problem; they can be safely washed in warm water with a mild soap either by hand or in a front-loading ("tumble") machine adjusted to the gentle or delicate setting. Polyurethane-foam bags can be rinsed out in the bathtub.

Down is something else. Experts agree that more down bags are ruined by improper cleaning than by all other causes combined, including long, hard use. Because of the perils, suspicious conservatives declare absolutely: "Never clean a down bag! If it gets too dirty for fastidious tastes, buy a new one."

However, sanitation is not the real issue. Body oils absorbed by down attract dirt which mats the down and in time destroys its resiliency. Dirty down loses loft, and thus warmth, and if dirty long enough loses its power ever to be lofty again.

Nevertheless, there is merit in the argument of the conservatives. The hiker should not become a purity fanatic. With average use, one cleaning a year is sufficient to maintain loft and protect the down. The more often the cleanings, the greater the danger of quickly killing the bag; and the question is open as to how many cleanings, however careful, a bag can tolerate before the down turns to string.

Each of the two usual cleaning methods has advantages—and hazards.

Dry-Clean the Down—But Afterward Breathe With Care

Safest for the bag and simplest for the bag-owner is dry-cleaning, the method employed by manufacturers and retailers. However, these people know precisely what they're doing. Does the average hiker? Not often. Because cleaning solvents are toxic and have killed sleepers in the night, the U.S. Bureau of Standards warns against dry-cleaning as altogether too risky.

Partisans say there is no danger if a mild petroleum-based compound (such as Stoddard Solvent) is used and the bag completely air-dried afterward—for at least a week—until the solvent odor is gone. Though they admit that the solvent lessens the water repellency of the nylon shell and attacks the down's natural oils, already largely removed by processors, they think that the harm done by one cleaning a year is acceptable.

But the chlorinated hydrocarbon (perchlorethylene) used by most dry-cleaners turns down into string and remains lethal to living creatures even when the odor is barely noticeable.

Cautious hikers, trusting their local dry-cleaner exactly as much as the friendly used-car dealer, say: better dirty than dead.

Wash the Down—But Gently, Sir!

Most experts recommend that the hiker clean his bag by hand-washing, unquestionably safe for the hiker and safe for the bag *if done right*. At any of a number of points, though, one false step and the bag is wrecked. Following are precise instructions:

Use Fluffy, a soap made in Holland especially for down, available at many mountain shops and by far the best cleanser available. If the product cannot be found, any *mild* soap (Ivory) may be substituted, but not detergent. The cost of a capsule of Fluffy, enough for one bag, is about $3, a high price but worth it.

Dissolve the capsule in 10–12 gallons of warm (never hot) water in a bathtub—or better, a large top-loading washing machine. (But *do not* use the wash cycle of the machine.)

Press the bag into the soapy water, starting at one end and keeping the other end dry (to allow air to escape more readily) until most of the bag is submerged. Squeeze out remaining air so the bag will stay submerged. Let the bag soak at least 12 hours, turning it *gently* a couple of times. (Once the bag is sopping wet it must *never* be roughly handled or abruptly lifted—the weight of the saturated down will instantly tear out the baffles and for all practical purposes the bag is a total loss.)

After the soaking period, scrub off surface dirt with a sponge or soft brush. Drain water from the tub and press as much as possible from the bag; in a washing machine, do the job by setting the control on the spin cycle. Refill the tub or machine with fresh warm water and gently knead the bag to work out the soap solution. Drain again, rinse again, and repeat until the water is clear and free of soap, residues of which will clump the down. Again remove all possible water—in a tub by hand-pressing, in a machine with the spin cycle. Lift out the bag—carefully, both hands underneath. Place it in a centrifuge or automatic washer, if one is handy, to extract excess water.

The safest and most economical method of drying, and one that gives excellent results, is air-drying. Gently drape the bag on a line (*don't hang it*) in a warm, dry place. After a day turn it inside out. As the down dries it begins to expand. Gently pat and shake the bag occasionally to aid the fluffing. Complete drying may take 3–5 days.

Drying time can be reduced by use of a large commercial drier that can be set at very low heat; however, so many cycles are required, possibly a dozen or more, that the cost is considerable. Many bags have been ruined by attempting to dry them in home driers, most of which are too small to hold a fluffed-up bag.

Some experts recommend what they claim are safe procedures for washing a bag in an automatic machine. In practice, few hikers ever are successful. Better hand-wash than be sorry. Or buy a polyester bag.

BETWEEN BAG AND GROUND:
SLEEPING PAD, AIR MATTRESS, GROUND SHEET

Disillusioning though it surely is for the beginner to hear, a down sleeping bag does not provide all-around insulation; the protection against cold is almost entirely on the air side, with little on the ground side. A polyester bag gives some bottom insulation, but both it and a down bag lack significant cushioning value.

THIS IS A "NO NO"

If the ground is warm, dry, and soft, no matter. But more often the ground is chilly and steals heat from the body, and/or wet, dampening the bag and speeding heat loss, and/or hard or bumpy, unkind to tender flesh and bones.

The bag, therefore, is only one of the three parts of the "sleeping system." Another, the tent or tarp, is the subject of Chapter 12. The third is what goes between bag and ground.

The old-style backpacker sought to live off the land. In high meadows he luxuriated in the grandest of earth's mattresses, a clump of heather. In forests, when ground was wet or snowy, he cut branches from living coniferous trees to build a bough bed.

Farewell, pioneer! There is not enough heather in the remaining wilderness of America, not enough greenery of trees, for these scarce resources to be utilized for *sleeping*. There is barely enough for *looking*.

As a friend of the Earth, entitled to all the responsibilities thereof, a backpacker must carry a complete sleeping system and not improvise a missing part by attacking the scenery with ax or knife or saw.

FOR INSULATION ONLY—THE SLEEPING PAD

The most popular sleeping pads, all of closed-cell foams and thus watertight, are: *ensolite*, ⅜ inch thick, 28 by 56 inches, weighing 1¾ pounds, costing about $8; *white polyethylene*, ¼ inch thick, 24

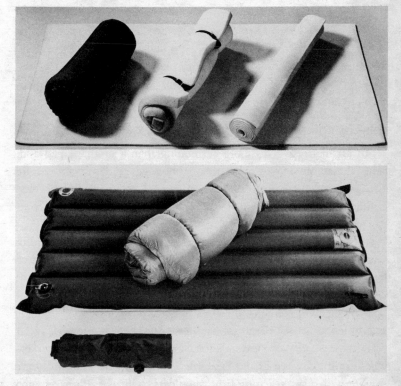

Above: *sleeping bag in stuff bag, 1¹/₂-inch urethane sleeping pad, and ¹/₄-inch ensolite pad—displayed on an ensolite pad spread out for use*
Below: *nylon air mattress, shoulders-to-hips length, inflated and deflated*

by 72 inches, weighing ¾ pound, costing about $5; *blu-foam poly-ethylene,* ⅜ inch thick, 24 by 48 inches, weighing 6 ounces, costing about $4. These sizes are adequate for the shoulder-to-hips area where most body weight rests on the ground; they weigh very little and the pads roll into small diameters. Pads come in lesser and greater widths and lengths with weights and prices to match.

Some hikers prefer a *urethane* (*polyether* is similar) pad 1½ inches thick, giving not only insulation but cushioning. The most popular 24- by 48-inch size weighs 1¼ pounds and costs about $4.

Urethane is an open-cell foam, much softer and more resilient than closed-cell foams, which eventually fatigue and stay compressed. However, because of the softness about three times the thickness of closed-cell foam is required for equivalent insulation. Also, open-cell foam is literally a sponge, wicks water from damp ground into the bag, and when wet is as cold as a water bed; in damp terrain it thus must be used in conjunction with a ground sheet. (But then, body moisture may condense on the ground sheet and be absorbed by the foam.) Another disadvantage is the major effort required to roll 1½-inch urethane into a diameter less than enormous.

FOR CUSHIONING MAINLY—THE AIR MATTRESS

An air mattress gives more cushioning than a urethane pad and, being deflatable, makes much less bulky baggage. However, despite also giving wetness protection, when used alone its insulation value is minor; convection currents in the air cells efficiently carry heat from bag to ground.

Another disadvantage of air mattresses is the evening-and-morning time needed to inflate and deflate. Another is the aggravating habit of letting the sleeper down in the night, either from a tiny puncture invisible to the naked eye, a valve failure, innate crankiness, or practical jokes by surly companions.

Full-length mattresses are splendid for weekends but too heavy (3 pounds or more) for extended backpacks. Long-distance walkers whose thinly-covered or old bones demand pampering generally are content with a size reaching from shoulders to hips. A 28- by 50-inch *nylon* mattress weighs 1⅞ pounds and sells for about $12.

Cheaper and a bit lighter are *vinyl* mattresses. A 22- by 46-inch size weighs 1½ pounds, costs about $6. Vinyl punctures even more easily than nylon, almost at the sound of a harsh word; however, one can carry a kit of cement and patches and while away many an hour in camp, day and night, searching for and repairing holes.

The *airlift* mattress consists of nine air tubes, 2 inches in diameter, enclosed in a ripstop case. Inflation at night is easy, about two puffs a tube, and deflation in the morning is quick. Even if one or two tubes develop leaks the sleeper is still in business. Patching is simple and replacement tubes cheap. The "shortie" size costs about $16.

If a mattress is used for comfort an ensolite pad may still be wanted for insulation between mattress and bag. An alternative recommended by snow-camping veterans is to sleep semi-nude and put trousers, shirt, and sweater between mattress and sleeping bag; they swear the method gives all necessary insulation.

A few hikers appreciate an air or polyester *pillow* weighing 5 or 6 ounces, costing about $3. Others improvise a pillow from the stuff bag filled with extra clothing or a boot wrapped in a sweater.

FOR BOTH INSULATION AND CUSHIONING

Cushioning *and* insulation can be obtained from an ordinary air mattress by slowly, patiently inserting down. As little as 2 ounces suffice for a cosy-warm sleep even on snow. The drawback, major, is that a pump thereafter must be used to inflate the mattress to keep the down dry. Even so it may find a way to get wet.

Far superior is a recent invention, the ingenious *Therm-A-Rest mattress,* consisting of a pad of open-cell foam within an airtight skin of the highest-quality waterproof nylon, extremely durable and leak-resistant.

Upon arriving in camp, open the valve and the mattress self-inflates as the foam sucks up air and within a few minutes attains a thickness of 1½ inches. (More time is required in extreme cold.) Close the valve to trap air in the foam and go to bed. The cushioning is superb and, since the interior air can't circulate well through the foam, so is the insulation.

In the morning, open the valve while getting final winks and body weight presses out much of the air. Finish the job by rolling up the mattress to a diameter of 4–6 inches, close the valve to prevent self-inflation on the trail, and away you go.

The Therm-A-Rest is 19 by 48 inches, weighs 1½ pounds, costs about $23.

FOR MOISTURE PROTECTION—THE GROUND SHEET

For any sleeping bag—no matter what the filler—to get damp or soaked in the course of a trip is always a minor or major catastrophe, to be avoided by every available manner and means.

Neither pad nor mattress can be trusted to keep the bag absolutely separated from wet ground; during the night a sleeper inevitably slops over the edges. The tarp-camper therefore must carry a ground sheet. (The tent-camper, with a floored tent, needs no sheet to keep his bag dry but may want one to prevent abrasion of the expensive floor.)

As example, a polyethylene sheet 7 by 8 feet, large enough for two or three sleepers, weighs 1⅜ pounds, sells for about $4. Among other sizes, a sheet 12 by 14 feet, sufficient for four or five adult bodies, weighs 4½ pounds, costs about $7.

12:

TENTS AND TARPS

Look back several decades, deep into the memories of veterans still pounding trails despite trick knees and backs, broken arches, stretched tendons, and miscellaneous physical and psychic scars earned in the era of nailed boots, wood-frame packboards, wool sleeping bags, and non-dehydrated food.

In the mind's eye see a band of these pioneers sack out in a mountain meadow under a clear sky. What is between them and the stars? Nothing but the thin envelope of Earth's atmosphere and millions of miles of space. See them fall asleep, and soon begin to shiver, and periodically, wakened by the cold and rolling over to find a closer approach to fetal warmth, glance up to make sure the stars remain bright. And when the stars turn watery and vanish? Shivers lessen with the great tarp of clouds strung over the meadow, reducing heat loss by radiation. But sleep grows expectant, broken by frequent glimpses upward, hoping for stars to sparkle through. Then, "pit!" Instantly alert, though still asleep, waiting for the "pat!" With "pit-a-pat, pit-a-pat" comes mid-consciousness. Then "SPLAT!" and sadly they crawl from bags, gather gear in arms, stumble across the meadow to the forest edge, and snuggle up to trees, hoping it's not a 3-day blow that will saturate the whole blessed world.

Why are these pioneers naked to the sky? Are they improvident idiots?

In the mind's eye see—on the same night in the same meadow—a second band of hikers smugly bedded down in tents. They sleep sounder than the others, partly because they are wealthy enough to own tents and rich people always sleep better, and partly because they

are much wearier from having hauled pounds of heavy fabric into the highlands. They are not wakened by the "pit," the "pat," or even the "pit-a-pat." But they stir with the "SPLAT" because the blob of rain is not stopped by the tent, only broken into fine spray. After an hour of "SPLAT-SPLAT-SPLAT" they are awake and damp and miserably aware that if it's a genuine 3-day blow they will despite their wealth get as wet as the poor boys cuddling the trees.

The choice for backpackers then was between: (1) carrying a heavy tent (assuming one could afford it) and thus reducing the miles-per-day traveled, punishing a back already suffering under the weight of other primitive gear, and gaining in exchange meager protection; or (2) carrying no tent or tarp at all, trusting to good weather, the interwoven branches of trees, overhanging rocks, the trail cabins and lean-tos then numerous and uncrowded, and accepting the inevitability of now and then being blasted right out of the wilderness in a retreat-from-Moscow stagger.

A few gimpy old pioneers continue to this day the no-tent-or-tarp tradition. They feel that just as shivering is good for the soul, man needs the humility that comes from total vulnerability. Sophisticated modern gear, they say, nourishes the "conquering nature" syndrome.

In shelter as in many other matters World War II was the boundary between the old days and the new. With V-J Day and the war-surplus bonanza the back country of North America blossomed in a glory of orange-and-blue 7- by 11-foot liferaft sails made of the new miracle fabric, nylon, lightweight and strong, coated to be completely water-proof, and given away by surplus stores for a dollar or two. Pioneers rigged them as tarps or converted them to tents, confessing they had previously trusted to luck mainly for reasons of poverty.

Since then, in what some hail as the perfection of the sport and art of backpacking and others view as one more sign the end of the world draws near, hikers of moderate means and weight-carrying capacity have become confident they can always build a snuggly wilderness home secure against all but the most fanatical assaults by nature.

The expectation is excessive in some climates, some elevations, some seasons. In general, though, it is true the modern backpacker, for small expense and weight, can gain protection against the elements beyond the dreams of his parents and grandparents.

Is this good or bad? Some of both. However, just as nobody really wants to go through another Depression (also now said to have been good for the soul) no hiker really wants to get soaking wet or frozen half to death or bug-bitten to insanity.

The option of purism remains as open as ever. The difference is, in the pre-World War II pioneer past it was compulsory to be uncomfortable. With modern gear the hiker has a choice.

CHOOSING A SHELTER

Where rain is infrequent (say, the High Sierra in summer), some hikers never carry shelter and accept the rare thundershower drenching as the price for an always-lighter pack. Where rain is at least as common as sun (say, the windward slopes of Pacific Northwest mountains), some hikers still do not carry shelter, depending on the lean-tos which dot many trails and/or certain famous trogs.

(An aside about lean-tos. Rarely nowadays can a party count on finding them vacant. Moreover, they typically have been so overused and abused, become so rancid and moldy, as to be occupied by fastidious campers only in desperation; here and there managers of public lands are gradually eliminating lean-tos and cabins as attractive nuisances that breed slums; they are, however, opposed by those who consider lean-tos to be "historic sites" as worthy of preservation as covered bridges and old homesteads.)

To carry shelter or not? And if so, what? Before making the decision a beginner should understand that rain protection is only one service provided by portable shelter and not always the most important.

RADIATION, SUN, WIND, PRYING EYES, AND BUGS

Sleeping under stars is one of the grandest experiences in backpacking. It may also be one of the coldest because the body-and-bag unit, together with all the rest of the world, radiates heat to the sky.

On overcast nights the clouds usually reflect heat back to earth but on clear nights it goes straight to outer space; especially in the thin air of high meadows the ground cools and so do uncovered sleepers. The starry nights are chilly. They may also be wet when next-to-ground air is cooled below the dew point and beads of dew or crystals of frost form on the sleeping bag. A shelter, whether tent, tarp, or thick-branched tree, greatly reduces the radiation heat loss and gives a warmer (and drier) sleep.

In hot, open country it is quite possible to get too much sun; a tent or tarp may well be wanted for a shady retreat.

Wind is a vigorous, even vicious coolant, as well as a carrier of sideways-blowing rain and fog. Hikers who customarily sleep in tents can carry lighter sleeping bags (and are less likely to get them wet) than those who trust to tarps. Partly because of protection from radiation heat loss, which a tarp also provides, but largely because of the conservation of body heat, the interior of a tent is usually about 10° warmer than the outside, much more in a wind.

In popular camps many hikers grow sensitive to being stared at by close neighbors; a tarp offers a partial screen but only a tent gives complete privacy, particularly appreciated by—for example—unliberated females who don't enjoy undressing in public.

Finally, in some places at some seasons by far the major menace to comfort and sanity is not moisture or cold or voyeurs but bugs, both those with wings and also the creepy-crawlies. A tarp puts no obstruction in the paths of insects or small beasts; a floored tent with netting keeps intrusions to a tolerable level.

TENT OR TARP?

Once a beginner has decided to carry shelter the first question is whether to buy a tarp or a tent. In addition to the above-noted distinctions there are other considerations in choosing between tarp and tent, and between various categories of tents.

As a rule of thumb, shelter weight should be no more than 4 pounds per person. Most backpacker tents stocked by mountain shops are designed to stay under this upper limit. With some tents the weight allotment can be much lower and with tarps as little as a few ounces. Generally, of course, the less weight the less protection and/ or living space. If the shelter is to be carried only short distances an extra few pounds is of minor concern; on long, multi-day hikes every ounce matters.

The hiker's range of options depends on *how much he can afford to spend.* A simple tarp and accessories, shelter enough of sorts for several people, can be purchased for less than $5, and elaborate tarps for up to $30. In the intermediate category of "tarp-tents," which offer somewhat more convenience and protection, prices run from roughly $20 to $40. But "true" tents begin at about $75, a substantial investment for the beginner faced with the essential Big Three acquisitions of boots, pack, and sleeping bag; tents offering the most

refinements, the least weight, and most space cost $100, $150, $200.

Possibly a majority of backpackers eventually want a "true" tent. However, it is unwise for any but the wealthiest beginner to buy until he has spent enough time on the trail to determine by experience how much protection, and against what, he needs and wants.

For example, those who camp often above timberline in wet and cold mountains may want a storm-tight "mountain tent." On the other hand, those who hike mainly in forests or warm, dry climates may find their major requirement is for a "bug tent," or "mist tent," or "sun tent," or "dust tent."

Another factor is the number of people the tent usually will hold —one person, two or three friends, a married couple with one or two small children or several children of assorted sizes.

Because of the expense and complexity of tents the beginner does best to start with a tarp of the simplest, cheapest kind. Later he may move up to a sturdier tarp and eventually, after careful study, to a tent—or tents.

Let it be noted, though, that for economic, esthetic, or philosophical reasons many backpackers never in their lives proceed beyond tarps.

TARPS

To repeat, a tarp protects against vertically-falling rain, heat loss and dew accumulation through radiation, and hot sun but bars only mild winds (and the horizontal rain or mist they may carry) and few prying eyes and bugs. (Some veterans partially dissent, declaring an expert tarp-rigger can be as cosy in high winds as a tenter—especially one who doesn't know how to pitch his tent properly.)

On the positive side, a tarp provides its limited shelter at minimal cost and weight. In addition, tarp-campers live more intimately with nature than tent-campers in their wombs—not only with wind and bugs but also views of shooting stars and the Moon and the dawn and incoming clouds, scents of pine needles and flowers and grasses, sounds of tiny creatures in the darkness. Feeling vulnerable they experience more, and in retrospect their wilderness nights are as memorable as the days.

A tarp is simplicity itself; still, there are variations on the theme both in construction and rigging.

VARIETIES OF TARP

Hardware stores and the like sell very thin (.002-inch, or "2 mil") and cheap transparent polyethylene ("poly") tarps intended for such purposes as painters' drop cloths. A 9- by 12-foot size, large enough for two or three adult sleepers and their gear, weighs about 1 pound and costs around a dollar. (Mountain shops stock "emergency shelter" tarps a bit stronger and more expensive but essentially the same.) The material is waterproof until punctured or ripped or abraded—which happens very easily. Hikers often carry two or three of these tarps, perhaps one for shelter, another, doubled, for a ground sheet, another for covering gear left outside the tarp or at the rain-unprotected edges. Unfortunately, the cheapness and the fragility cause some hikers to leave these tarps all over the landscape; the invention of plastic is a mixed blessing, what with the air and water pollution its manufacture causes in industrial areas and the trash in wildlands.

Mountain shops generally begin their tarp line with various sizes of polyethylene sheets .004-inch ("4 mil") thick, a translucent white to reflect sunlight (which transparent tarps do not, a serious flaw in blistered country where a sun shade is badly wanted), with no grommets. Visqueen is a common trade name. The 9- by 12-foot size weighs 2 pounds, costs about $4. The 12- by 12-foot size, accom-

modating four adults or a married couple and several children, weighs 3 pounds, costs about $5. Such tarps are heavier than drop cloths but far more resistant to tearing and puncturing.

Available from a few shops is polyethylene reinforced with heavy nylon threads; tarps of this material weigh and cost more but are extremely tear-resistant, though they can be punctured.

Poly tarps with grommets installed weigh and cost a bit more because of the grommets.

Much tougher and thus less likely to rip to shreds in a wind or to be punctured by sharp sticks, and very abrasion-resistant, are tarps of polymer-coated and thus waterproof 3.1-ounce nylon in blue or yellow or other colors. These tarps last for several or more years with proper care, compared to a summer or two (or one wild storm) for poly tarps; the coated nylon also weighs less. Equipped with eight grommets the 9- by 11-foot size (for three sleepers and gear) weighs 2 pounds and sells for about $20.

Some mountain shops offer more elaborate nylon tarps with dozens of grommets and tie loops for versatility in rigging. These may cost as much as $40, a lot to pay for a tarp.

GROMMETS AND SUBSTITUTES

The simplest way to attach rigging lines to a poly tarp lacking built-in grommets is to bunch up the corners and tightly wrap them with a

number of turns of cord. This method allows only four attachment points—the corners—which may not be enough to hold the tarp even reasonably close to the ground in a wind or to prevent it from sagging under the weight of rain.

A better technique is to push a rock, pine cone, or wad of paper against the tarp to form a protuberance around which a rigging line is then wrapped. A line can in this manner be attached at any point along the edge or in the middle.

The Visklamp, consisting of a metal ring and a rubber ball, complicated to describe but easy to use, does the same job, working like a garter. The Versa Tie employs a disc rather than a ball.

Tie loops can be improvised at corners and along the sides with cloth adhesive tape or nylon-reinforced Scotch tape, both of which adhere firmly to polyethylene and withstand much jerking by wind, as do the stick-on Tarp-Tys grommets when attached correctly.

Grommets may be installed and some shops offer complete kits for the purpose, but poly tarps tear so readily it isn't worth the trouble and nylon tarps generally have enough grommets as sold.

Tarp-campers do well to carry a roll of 2-inch cloth tape with adhesive backing to reinforce tarps where they show signs of pulling apart and to repair rips and holes.

RIGGING A TARP

A tarp can be spread belatedly as a blanket when the party has gone to bed without erecting a shelter and doesn't feel like getting up

Polyethylene tarp (4-mil, translucent) rigged as shed roof, adequate protection against gentle rains, radiation heat loss, and glaring sun

to cope in any more elaborate way with sudden showers. However, in the course of a full night exhaled body moisture condenses on the inside of the "blanket" and thoroughly dampens sleeping bags.

Accompanying photos show the two most common tarp rigs—the *shed roof* and the *A-frame.*

Convenient trees or tall boulders, if any, can support the tarp, or dead branches lashed in pairs as bipods. Rocks, logs, or sticks can be used to anchor the ground edges.

However, to avoid living off the land, ecology-sensitive tarp-campers carry poles and pegs (see below). Two poles and eight pegs, properly chosen, weigh no more than 1½ pounds total and allow a party to leave nature unmolested. As a bonus for the virtuous, a tarp

Nylon tarp with built-in grommets, quickly and easily rigged as A-tent by use of two aluminum poles and eight lightweight pegs

can thus be pitched wherever desired and in minutes—a great advantage when arriving late in camp, perhaps in darkness, and lacking the energy to prowl and scrounge for a perfect match-up of tarp-supporting trees and ground smooth enough for sleeping, to lug rocks and logs from their natural positions, and to improvise bipods and stakes.

With skill that comes from practice a tarp can be rigged as a hemisphere, the edges pegged down all around and the middle propped up at several points with poles, ice axes, and packframes. The resulting poor man's mountain tent is very weatherproof.

PRELIMINARY REMARKS ABOUT TENTS

Ever since English scramblers in the Alps ventured beyond chalets and barns, in the age before the building of high huts, mountaineering literature has been full of arguments about tents—of what materials they should be made and how.

Many long-standing debates have been settled in the past generation. For instance, the invention of nylon in the era of World War II spelled the beginning of the end for other fabrics in use for backpacker tents. Cotton, though still favored by a few traditionalists, is as expensive as nylon, heavier for equal strengths, and demands great care to prevent mildew and rot. Dacron is occasionally used where its lack of stretch is desirable, as in the outer walls (rainflys) of double-wall tents, but costs much more than nylon. Virtually every backpacker tent currently offered by American mountain shops is of *nylon taffeta* or the lightest, strongest material available, *ripstop nylon* (for definitions of these see Chapter 11). To illustrate the strength of the latter, two specially-built ripstop tents were pitched at 27,500 feet on Mt. Everest and 3 weeks later, after two severe storms with winds in excess of 100 miles per hour, were still undamaged.

Though rain protection is only one purpose of a tent, it is the most difficult to attain and has engaged the ingenuity of tentmakers over the years. If the tent is completely waterproof no rain gets in but also no moisture breathes out through the fabric; since a human body exhales approximately a pint of water a night, in a sealed tent the result by morning is a thoroughly damp interior. On the other hand, if the fabric is breathable to let body moisture out, it lets hard rains in.

Out of this dilemma have emerged two quite different species of tent.

The *single-wall* tent, or *"tarp-tent"* as it may be called for present purposes, is generally made of completely-waterproof coated nylon. Body moisture is carried out by horizontal ventilation between ends that are either completely open, or have flaps that can be opened wide. Often there is no floor.

The *double-wall* (*"true"*) tent consists of an inner or main tent with walls of lightweight, breathable, taffeta or ripstop nylon, a floor (and perhaps a partial sidewall) of tough, waterproof, polymer-coated nylon, and a separate (or sometimes attached) rainfly of waterproof nylon. When the only protection desired is against fog and misty rain, snow, wind, radiation heat loss, voyeurs, flying bugs and creeping beasties, the rainfly need not be rigged. For protection against hard rain the fly is rigged at some distance from the inner tent to allow airflow space—a greater distance in warm weather, when it may also be used for sun protection, and a lesser in cold weather, when it also adds warmth.

Backpacker tents are of various *sizes*, from one-man to two-man (that can hold three) to four-man (that can hold six). By far most popular is the two-man—comfortable for two adults and their gear, in some designs large enough in a squeeze for three adults or two adults and two small children. The four-man tents are excellent for a group of constant companions or two parents and several offspring.

For ordinary backpacking the *color* of a tent is mainly of psychological concern. In wet climates a soft orange or red gives a warm feeling and feeds the illusion it is sunny outside. In hot climates a cool blue seems to blunt the assault of the sun. Green blends into the background of forests and meadows, appreciated by campers who don't like to be gaudy.

Idiosyncrasies of design exhibited by contemporary tents are discussed below in the course of describing representative examples. As with other gear the tents stocked by various mountain shops differ considerably in details, as well as in quality of materials and the care in manufacture, and the range in prices reflects these factors. However, the diversity is considerably less bewildering than that of boots and packs and sleeping bags and the current offerings fall into several logical groupings.

WELL, I THINK IT'S A GOOD EXAMPLE OF OVER-TENTING!

To once more echo an old theme, hikers should take care to buy no more tent than is required by the climate of the areas they will be traveling. Some models stocked by mountain shops are aimed for high-altitude, winter, or expedition use and though in many instances superb for summer backpacking, may have features that add weight and cost and are of little or no value to trail-walkers. For low-elevation backpacking a tent need not be anywhere near so strongly built and elaborate as for high mountains; it can also be constructed of lighter and less-expensive materials.

TARP-TENTS

The term "tarp-tent" as used here denotes a broad category which at one boundary is nothing more than a shaped tarp and at the other verges on a "true" tent. The common characteristic is a *single wall*, in most cases waterproof. Prices range from as little as tarps to up around $50. Most are intended for one or two persons. Several representative examples may be described to suggest the diversity.

TUBE TENT (INSTANT TENT)

The simplest tarp-tent is a tube of .003-inch polyethylene 9 feet long, 3 feet wide at the base when rigged, weighing 1¼ pounds, costing about $5. Three grommets at each end allow easy rigging; in heavy weather cords threaded through the grommets can be used to draw the ends tight—though not for long without severe interior condensation. The tube—a ground sheet as well as a shelter—is large enough for one adult plus pack.

A typical two-man tube, 5 feet wide at the base when pitched, weighs 2½ pounds and costs about $7.

Tubes cost and weigh little, are quick-rigging ("instant"), and offer good rain protection; they are cramped inside and bar few bugs —nor any wind except with the ends drawn tight, at the expense of sweating. They can be lifesavers in sudden storms and thus are often recommended for emergency kits.

BUG TENT

In areas or seasons of calm weather but bad, bad bugs, a significant upward step is a floorless A-frame tent of waterproof nylon, the open

One-man polyethylene tube tent. In emergencies the corners need not be pegged, the weight of hiker and gear preventing wind from blowing the shelter away. String a line between two supports and the "instant tent" is erected.

ends guarded by mosquito netting. Protection is excellent against vertical rain and flying insects and the open ends give an airway which minimizes sweating. The wind, of course, blows free.

A two-man size weighs, excluding necessary poles and pegs, about 1½ pounds and costs about $25. Rigging is done as with a tarp from built-in grommets and tie loops.

ONE-END-CLOSED TENT

Exemplifying another compromise is a floorless A-frame of waterproof nylon, one end with a zipper-closed panel, the other open. The panel can be shut during gusty winds and excruciating bugginess and the open end partially blocked against wind by a pack, against winged bugs by an added piece of netting. Prolonged closure, of course, leads to sweating. Such a tent, some 7 feet long and 5½ feet wide and 3½ feet high, accommodating two people cosily, weighs 1½ pounds without poles and pegs, costs about $25.

Similar, but tapered to save weight, is a larger floorless tent of waterproof nylon, 7 feet long, 9 feet wide and 4 feet high at the front, 3 feet wide and 2 feet high at the rear. Three people can fit in chum-

Representative floorless, single-wall, waterproof-nylon "tarp tent". Rear end is closed, zippered front panel has crawl space at bottom. Mosquito netting can be draped over the front to make a bugproof tent. Many variations are available on the basic theme.

mily. The front has a zippered panel extending most of the way to the ground but leaving a crawl space underneath. The rear end is closed. Weight without poles and pegs is 1¾ pounds, cost about $30.

BORDERLINE CASES

A few single-wall tents dodge the dilemma of breathable-but-not-rainproof versus rainproof-but-sweaty by going this way or that, making no pretense of being all-purpose. In design they tend to closely resemble the inner portions of the double-wall A-frames discussed below.

For one example, some suppliers offer a "mist tent" of water-repellent (not proof) nylon which really is a double-wall tent minus the fly. Where bugs and/or wind are a central threat and the climate is of a sort that rare rains are mainly mists or brief showers, it serves very well—as does the inner portion of a double-wall tent.

Another example is a two-man tent with waterproof nylon roof and waterproof vinyl-nylon floor. The door must be kept open for

Example of one variety of "borderline" tent. Waterproof outer wall is rigged high for ventilation in dry weather and gentle rains, low during wind-driven rains. However, when rigged low a single-wall tent may sweat on the inside. Inner wall is a netting that lets breezes in but not bugs. Excellent "mist tent," superlative "bug tent"

cross-ventilation most of the time lest the aforementioned pint of water per person per night fill a swimming pool; in warm, wet, windless periods the pool will fill anyway. In certain areas and seasons this compromise may do a decent job at a third the cost of a "true" tent. Its faults, however, are responsible for evolution of the next items on the agenda.

A-FRAME, DOUBLE-WALL TENTS

By far the most versatile tent style and the most popular among backpackers in all the varied terrains of America is the double-wall A-frame. The triangle shape gives maximum interior area for minimum weight and the low profile withstands high winds. The inner tent can be used alone in good weather, the waterproof floor guarding against ground moisture and creeping bugs, the mosquito netting at all openings against flying bugs, the zipper-closed door barring the wind, and the breathable walls letting body moisture escape while keeping out fogs and misty rains and sun and blowing dust. In wet weather the rainfly can be rigged—well away from the inner tent to allow air circulation between the two. In stormy climates the double-wall tent is the only "true" tent.

The models stocked by mountain shops exhibit a number of variations on the basic design and depending on special features, materials, and workmanship range in price from about $80 to more than $170. A great many manufacturers have good-to-superb entries in the field; among those with the widest current distribution are Alpine Designs, Eddie Bauer, Berkeley Co-op, Bishop, Black, Camp Trails, Cannondale, Frostline, Gerry, Holubar, Moor and Mountain, Mountain Products, North Face, REI, SE-AB, Sierra Designs, and Trailwise.

There are two styles of A-frame: the *horizontal ridgeline* or "high-ender" (that is, the same height at both ends) and the *sloping ridgeline* or "low-ender" (that is, tapered from head to foot).

HORIZONTAL-RIDGELINE A-FRAME

The "high-ender" has much the roomiest interior of the two styles for comparable floor dimensions. Description of a representative example will help identify typical characteristics:

Length of the inner tent is 7 feet, width 5 feet, and height 3¾ feet. Two people and their gear fit comfortably, or three chummily, or two parents and a couple of small children.

Representative horizontal-ridgeline A-frame tent. Inset: *with rainfly rigged*

The inner tent is of breathable ripstop nylon with a waterproof, coated-nylon floor. Rigging is easily and quickly accomplished by two pairs of poles secured at each end forming an A-frame and six ground pegs. The front door is covered by a panel that opens with two nylon zippers from the peak, backed by a zippered panel of mosquito net. A small tunnel window at the rear provides cross-ventilation.

The rainfly of waterproof nylon is supported by the tops of the poles and anchored to the ground by four pegs.

Complete with rainfly, poles, pegs, tent-line tighteners, and carrying bag, the tent weighs 7 pounds and sells for about $100. The rainfly, which can be left home when only a mist-and-bug tent is desired, weighs 1¾ pounds.

Variations and Elaborations

Weight is saved on some designs by having a single vertical pole at each end or A-frame poles at the door and a vertical pole at the rear.

Side pullouts, tie loops attached to the centerpoint of the walls and anchored to the ground, eliminate center sagging and maximize interior space.

A neater and more expensive way to achieve the same end is to construct the tent with a *catenary cut,* in which the fabric is cut on a curve in such a way it pulls taut when rigged, eliminating flapping and sagging, and again enlarging the interior. The catenary cut (though still usually supplemented by pullouts) is characteristic of the best tents, substantially increasing their stability in storms.

On some designs the rainfly extends out from the door far enough to form a *vestibule* for extra wind and rain protection, storing gear, and cooking. On others a vestibule is an integral part of the inner tent. In either case the result may be a "2½-person tent."

A few models have an *integral fly,* permanently connected to the inner tent, with advantages of quick rigging and disadvantages of non-detachability.

Some tents have a drawstring-closed *tunnel entrance* instead of a zippered doorway—or perhaps a tunnel at one end, zipper door at the other. Since even nylon zippers can freeze or blow apart, the tunnel provides a fail-safe entry for high, cold mountaineering; for summer backpacking, though, it merely adds weight and expense.

A *frost liner*, a detachable inner wall of light cotton, collects ice crystals that otherwise would form directly on the tent wall and be shaken loose by wind to create an interior snowstorm; also, when the crystals melt, the cotton soaks up the moisture. The liner is valuable for temperatures below 20°F but not for most backpacking.

The pros and cons of cooking in the tent are discussed below. Since in high-altitude and winter mountaineering it may be necessary, some tents have a zippered *cook hole* in the floor so that spilled soup will run onto the ground or snow rather than into sleeping bags. The zipper can be a leak point and thus is not desirable for a summer backpacker tent.

Among other features found on the more elaborate mountain tents are pockets on the inner walls for storing small bits of gear and loops at the peaks for stringing a clothesline.

SLOPING-RIDGELINE A-FRAME

The "low-ender" saves weight by tapering the tent height from front to rear—thus reducing, of course, interior space.

Representative A-frame tent of more elaborate design, providing a spacious bad-weather vestibule for taking off muddy boots, storing packs, cooking. Inset: *with rainfly rigged*

Representative sloping-ridgeline A-frame tent. Inset: *with rainfly rigged*

In a representative example the inner tent has a length of 7⅓ feet, a rectangular floor 4½ feet wide, and a height tapering from 4 feet to 2¼ feet; the tent holds two people and their gear but usually not a third adult conveniently, though perhaps one small child.

Other details of material and structure are the same as in the representative "high-ender" except the waterproof floor extends several inches up the sidewalls. The complete tent weighs 6 pounds and sells for about $100. The rainfly weighs 1⅜ pounds.

The variations and elaborations described for "high-enders" are also found on "low-enders." In addition, some designs save more weight by tapering the floor width from front to back.

"FAMILY" (STAND-UP) TENTS

The A-frame or "two-man" tent is the best choice for the single hiker who may wish to invite a friend on occasion or for a couple, whether childless or with one or two small ones.

When the family (or the circle of constant friends and companions) numbers three or more adults and large children there are advantages to the category of tents which may be called "three-to-six-man," "stand-up," or "family." Though the tent is heavy, when it is occupied to full capacity the weight-per-person is the same or even less than with an A-frame. A family which might require two two-man tents possibly can save both weight and money with a single larger tent—which is, of course, less adaptable to parties of various sizes than two smaller tents.

ARE YOU SURE THIS IS WHAT THEY CALL "THE FAMILY TENT"?

An important virtue of the large tent is that its height allows comfortable maneuvering—one can, for example, dress standing up rather than by slithering horizontally. Further, if the party is confined to camp by long stretches of poor weather the spacious interior ameliorates tent fever. Particularly during days of rain when squirming kids must be kept reasonably content and their parents preserved from stark staring madness the "family" tent is a blessing. Some designs in this category are vulnerable to high winds, a matter of small consequence in ordinary backpacking.

Surprisingly, designs originally intended for expeditions may be excellent for backpacking. For example, the REI Camper is quick and easy to rig, supported by a single center pole and anchored by ground pegs. It is 7 feet high at the peak, has a waterproof nylon floor measuring 6½ by 8 feet with the waterproofing extended 18 inches up the sidewalls. The inner tent is breathable nylon and the rainfly waterproof nylon. A tunnel entrance and a tunnel vent in the opposite wall give cross-ventilation. Four adults and their gear have plenty of room, or a family of six in assorted sizes. Total weight including rainfly, pole, pegs, cord, cord-tighteners, and carrying bag is 10⅞ pounds and the cost about $150. The rainfly weighs 2½ pounds.

One example of a "family" tent, a "Logan" design, meant for expeditions but also good for ordinary backpacking. Inset: with rainfly rigged

Of the same basic design are the "Mt. Logan tents" offered by a number of shops. Examples are the Alpine Designs High Country Camper, Holubar Four-Man, and Sierra Design Three-Man. The sizes, special features, and prices vary, going as high as $250.

A quite different style with much the same advantages plus several of its own and specifically designed for summer backpacking is the Gerry Camponaire, supported by exterior poles, 5 feet high with 6- by 8-foot floor, comfortable for three adults (family of five) and gear. The weight complete with rainfly and accessories is 9¾ pounds and the cost about $150. A larger version, the Gerry Fortnight, is 6 feet high with a floor 8 by 9 feet, holds four adults (family of six) comfortably, weighs 12 pounds complete, sells for about $200.

Another example of a "family" tent. The same design comes in a still larger size. Many other designs are on the market. Rainfly not shown

The Alpine Designs Yosemite (the Sierra Designs Cathedral is similar) is still another unique design; the rainfly is actually the primary tent, with the breathable-nylon inner tent attached by nylon netting. Support is by a single, segmented A-shaped pole at the center and two vertical poles front and rear. The Yosemite comes in two-, three-, and four-man sizes. The latter, ample for a family of six, is (inner tent) 6 feet high at the peak, has a floor 7 feet long, 6¾ feet wide at the front, 7½ feet wide at the peak, and 5¼ feet wide at the rear; total weight is 9¼ pounds and the price about $140.

The Famleehut, with a 6- by 8-foot floor, 5 feet high at the peak, weighs 8 pounds complete, costs about $160, and holds three adults and gear or a family of five.

The North Face Morning Glory, resembling two A-frames joined at the center, holds four adults, weighs 10½ pounds; costs $250.

The above are a few of the "family" backpacker tents most commonly stocked by mountain shops; there are others of similar or related design.

SELF-SUPPORTING TENTS

The tents discussed to this point share two characteristics: (1) dependence from poles anchored to the ground by stakes; (2) basically flat surfaces.

Recently interest has been increasing in self-supporting tents which (1) are free-standing, independent of staking, and (2) have rounded walls.

One style approximates a *half-cylinder* (or is "barn-shaped"), with flexible aluminum or fiberglass poles which arch across the ends, fitting through loops or sleeves. Examples (varying considerably in details) spacious enough for two to three persons, weighing complete with rainfly about 7 pounds, costing from $130 to $200, are: Bishop's Ultimate, Eureka Draw-Tite Alpine, MSR Two-Man and Three-Man, and Stevenson's Warmlite.

Example of a self-supporting tent, half-cylinder design. Most tents of this style lack a rainfly and thus are restricted to cold-weather use, where a frost liner catches interior condensation

Another style is the *dome*, the arch formed by glass-rod poles slipping through sleeves. One example is the Adventure 16, a 2½-man half-dome selling for $130. Jan Sport has several: the two-person Trail Wedge, weighing complete with fly 6¼ pounds, costing $125; the three-person Trail Dome, 8½ pounds, $165; and the Mountain Dome (large size) for four to five persons, 13½ pounds, $270.

A central virtue of self-supporters is an aerodynamic shape that lets violent winds flow around rather than smacking into flat walls and setting them flapping. Thus they appeal chiefly to mountaineers who often camp in the realms of roaring winds, at high elevation or in winter. A second advantage is that since they are erected without stakes (which, however, certainly should be used during gales lest the entire tent, when the occupants crawl out, go sailing away into

Example of a self-supporting tent, dome design. The large sizes are excellent "family" tents. Inset: with rainfly rigged

the sky) self-supporters can easily be picked up and moved from place to place or tilted on end to shake out dirt.

The flexibility of the frame is not always worth bragging about; in certain sorts of blustery, shifting winds a self-supporter does a lot more "dancing" than a flat-waller supported by semi-rigid poles. Also, in some models the rainfly canot be rigged at sufficient distance from the inner tent to minimize interior humidity in warm weather. Finally, the self-supporter usually lacks a fly-covered vestibule where mucky-snowy-soggy boots and parkas can be doffed before entering the main room.

All things considered, the ordinary run of backpackers probably will continue to prefer more traditional designs. Nevertheless, for some hikers and many climbers the self-supporters are superb.

TENT AND TARP ACCESSORIES

Since "true" tents are sold complete with everything required to set them up, the following paragraphs are of less interest to tenters than users of tarp-tents and tarps, for which rigging accessories must be purchased separately.

POLES

Most poles are aluminum; a few are fiberglass. Some telescope into nests, other break into sections held together by shock cord (see below) which aids in assembly, prevents loss, and automatically holds the pole together.

Any design that extends to 5-7 feet serves the purpose. The tarp-camper, with his innate concern for lightness, easy portability, and low cost, should choose poles (usually he wants two) which weigh no more than ½ pound each, break down or collapse to a length of no more than 3 feet, and cost not much more than $4 each. A number of poles sold by mountain shops meet these criteria.

Note: the insides of nesting poles must be kept clean to prevent jamming. Especially at the ocean, where salt air rapidly corrodes aluminum, they should be wiped thoroughly and frequently.

PEGS (STAKES)

The typical tarp-camper kit includes eight pegs weighing in total about ½ pound or less. Following are representative examples of the pegs found in mountain shops; all are very inexpensive.

Curved aluminum pegs nest together to save space in the pack and hold well in all terrains except rocky ground. The 6½-inch length, ¾ ounce, is sufficient for most conditions. The 8½-incher is good in soft ground (beach sand). The 11¾-incher is strictly for snow. The same stake made of galvanized steel is a bit cheaper and weighs al-

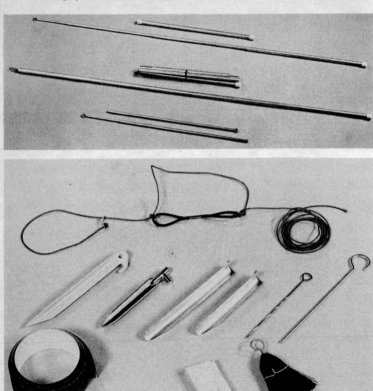

Tent and tarp accessories. Above: telescoping pole, closed and extended; sectional pole, apart and together; short telescoping pole for low end of tapered tents, closed and extended. Below: tent-cord tightener and shock cord, shown on a rigging line; a sampling of pegs; ripstop repair tape, sponge, whiskbroom

most twice as much.

Chrome-moly steel wire drives into rocky ground (moraines) that resists other stakes. In the 10-inch length, weight is 1½ ounces.

Cast-aluminum stakes are very strong, never deform; they are a bit heavier than others—1½ ounces for the 6½-inch length—and cost a bit more.

Stakes of high-impact plastic penetrate easily and hold well and are especially good in beach sand. They make a larger hole than others, objectionable in delicate meadows. Weight is 1½ ounces for the 9-inch length.

TENT-CORD TIGHTENER

A cord tightener is a device made of nylon or aluminum that does the job of the traditional taut-line hitch, which probably only a handful of contemporary backpackers know how to tie or care to learn. With one of these gadgets on each tent or tarp line, ground pegs can be placed approximately and the proper tension in lines obtained by adjusting the tighteners rather than repeatedly relocating pegs. Weight and cost are insignificant.

CORD IN GENERAL, AND SHOCK CORD SPECIFICALLY

For tarps and tarp-tents sold without rigging lines, nylon cord may be purchased in a variety of sizes and strengths, ranging from 3/32-inch, 285-pound test, to ¼-inch, 1100-pound test.

When a tarp is to be strung along a ridgeline the 3/16-inch cord, 900-pound test, is the minimum and ¼-inch better; an amazingly heavy load is placed on the line when the tarp is soaked by rain and flapped by wind.

The ⅛-inch cord, 520-pound test, serves for anchoring corners and edges. Most tarp-campers carry a 50-foot coil (weighing several ounces) and cut pieces as needed for anchor lines, pack repairs, spare bootlaces, and miscellaneous.

A *shock cord* of rubber stringers sheathed in nylon or cotton stretches in wind gusts, then returns to original length and tautness. Shock cord should *not* be used to guy an inner tent because it allows flapping that strains the fabric; better in such case to let the less-expensive pole be bent. However, shock cord should always be used with a rainfly, which balloons in the wind and, being of a coated fabric, may come apart unless strain is transferred to the cord.

REPAIR TAPE

As mentioned above a hiker always should carry tape to repair sparkholes or rips or punctures in tarp or tent.

A 2-inch-wide cloth tape with adhesive backing serves for polyethylene, coated fabrics, and other non-porous materials; 2-inch ripstop repair tape is recommended for tents of ripstop nylon.

CARING FOR TENTS

Though a tarp or rainfly can be replaced at moderate cost, the inner portion of a "true" tent is expensive and therefore must be treated gently. The principle threat to any tent (or tarp) is fire. If sparks from blazing logs are observed blowing toward a nearby tent or tarp, either the fire should be damped down or the fire or shelter moved.

Generally speaking a tent is not meant to be cooked in. Moisture from steaming pots adds enormously to interior wetness, commonly to an extent that cannot be alleviated by cross-ventilation or breathing-out through the fabric. More dangerously, with many stoves there is the chance of a flare-up that might instantly melt a huge hole in the roof. Cooking is best done outside the tent, or at least in the vestibule, if any. Expeditioners may have to take the risk frequently, but back-

packers rarely. (Nevertheless, there are wildland veterans who always cook in tents when wind frustrates the stove or bugs devil the chef, not to mention when the weather is plain lousy miserable. But they do so carefully—*very carefully*.) As of 1975 many tents sold by mountain shops are treated to be *fire-retardant;* they thus will not go off in one great life-endangering torch, but they are not immune to hole-melting and spark-stabbing.

To protect the tent floor from being gummed up by pitch and other nastiness and abraded by rocks and twigs it is wise always to place a lightweight poly sheet underneath.

A tent should never be washed but may be sponged off occasionally; better, really, to let it gradually acquire a dignified grime and character.

However, gritty dirt tracked or blown inside should be scrupulously swept out to avoid sandpapering the fabric. Fastidious hikers carry a small whiskbroom for the purpose—and perhaps a sponge to mop up puddles.

Moisture inevitably accumulates in a tent during a trip, if not from blown-in rain or tracked-in water then from exhalations of human bodies. Nylon *can* mildew, develop a musty odor, and rot. Thus, before a tent is folded for extended storage it should be erected in the yard in sunny weather, or in the basement or spare bedroom, and thoroughly air-dried. (And meanwhile swept clean.)

Though spray-on and paint-on compounds are advertised as doing the job, once nylon loses its water-repellency attempts at re-waterproofing are fruitless. However, it is useful to occasionally paint the seams, where leaks are most likely, with seam sealant or cement.

13:   KITCHEN GEAR

MANY a novice backpacker mentally picturing a wildland kitchen doubtless is influenced by a certain genre of American art, the calendar painting. In his mind's eye he sees, all in florid color, a band of hardy woodsmen gathered around a wall tent and elaborate fireplace, wearing Bowie knives and pistols, surrounded by double-bitted ax, chopping block, crosscut saw, rifles, fishing poles, enormous frying pan, huge iron kettle, coffee pot, Dutch oven, sides of bacon and sacks of flour and salt and beans, table and chairs hewn from logs, laundry lines strung between trees, antelope suspended from a pole tripod, scores of trout in a smokehouse, and a faithful Indian guide skinning out a bear—and the dozen horses or fleet of canoes which carried the half-ton of equipment and supplies.

Led astray by such portraits of a vanished past a person may seek to duplicate, to the limit of his carrying capacity, the classic frontier kitchen. However, the old classic must be considered as extinct as the passenger pigeon and vast herds of bison. The new classic, that of the modern ethical hiker, is kept as simple as possible to avoid serious damage to fragile ecosystems.

After the spiritual anguish and financial pangs of selecting and paying for boots, pack, and sleeping bag, the beginner can relax when assembling his kitchen. The few, light, inexpensive elements are: (1) a fire; (2) cooking pots; (3) eating tools; and (4) miscellaneous accessories. A number of handy gadgets are available for gracious living but the novice does well to start with nothing but the basics and add frills very gradually, if at all.

FIRE—WITHOUT STOVE

WOOD FIRE

As explained in Chapter 4 the backpacker increasingly must grow accustomed to camps and kitchens lacking that old symbol of the wilderness home, the wood fire. It's sad to see grand traditions recede into ancient history but the world changes and not always for the better.

Cooking with a wood fire, using a lightweight metal grate. On driftwood-littered beaches, wood fires long will be possible in good conscience, unlike many other provinces of American trail country.

Still, a wood fire is not yet everywhere morally a sin or legally a crime punishable by fine and/or imprisonment. To cook with wood several bits of equipment should be carried.

Matches, of course, a main supply in a poly bag, an emergency supply in a waterproof packet or box of foil, plastic, or metal. The ordinary city match is acceptable but inferior for obvious reasons to matches that are waterproof, windproof, or both. Gadgeteers may be intrigued by a "metal match" or "flint stick" which when struck or scraped emits a shower of high-temperature sparks. A much better gadget is a butane lighter.

Hikers depending on wood fire in wet country should carry a *fire-starter*, such as a "fire ribbon" (a jelly that squeezes from a tube), candles, or solid hydrocarbon "fuel tablets" (Hexamine, Heatabs).

The easiest way to cook on a wood fire is with a metal *grate* or grill. For backpacking the weight should not be much more than ½ pound and preferably less, the width small enough to slip easily into a pack (enclosed in a poly bag to avoid sooting the interior), and legs omitted as worthless. Few outdoor shops stock designs that can be recommended. One is a "U" of stainless steel tubing 15 inches long, 5 inches wide; weight, 6 ounces; cost, $3. Another is a rectangle of stainless steel tubes with a center tube, some 16 inches long and 5 inches wide; weight, 3 ounces; cost, about $5. Cake racks, found in the kitchenware section of any department or variety store, make excellent grates, weighing and costing very little.

SOLID CHEMICAL FUELS

The fuel tablets mentioned above as firestarters, and also "canned heat" (Sterno—jellied alcohol), can be used for rudimentary cooking. The simplest method is to ignite them between two rocks arranged to support a pot or cup. Folding canned-heat stoves and Heatab stoves give wind protection and easy pot support; a more elaborate cooker set includes a windscreen and a 1-pint pot.

These fuels generate relatively little heat and rarely can be made to boil water. However, they often serve well enough for a person dining alone, wanting only to warm a can of stew, fry an egg, or get water hot enough to dissolve cocoa. Since fuel tablets cost next to nothing a penniless beginner with no pretensions as a gourmet can get by with them until he's financially up to purchasing a stove.

STOVES

In choosing from among the dozens of stoves on the market, the backpacker must first resolve to ignore the heavy models designed for car-camping, canoe-camping, and other trips where weight doesn't matter, and focus on those of around 1–2 pounds. He must then decide which fuel he prefers: gasoline, kerosene, butane, propane, or alcohol.

GAS STOVES

The appropriate fuel is *not* automobile gasoline but "white gas." Purchasing in bulk from a service station is risky: the white gas may be old and partly decomposed, in which case it will gum up the stove; it may in sordid fact be paint thinner, which burns poorly if at all. Though more expensive, far safer is brand-name appliance gas sold in cans—Pressure Appliance Fuel, Blazo, Coleman Fuel. The product is filtered clean and is stabilized to stay good 3 years in a sealed can or 6 months after being opened.

White gas is the most volatile of backpacker fuels and thus easiest to ignite—and requires greatest care to avoid catastrophe. Just as a Molotov cocktail can disable a Tiger tank so can an improperly-used gas stove wipe out a tent.

For generations outdoorsmen have used "primus" as a synonym for "gas stove." However, due to a rearrangement of corporate structures, there no longer is such a thing as a Primus gas stove; there still is a Primus butane stove but the former Primus gas models now are

Cooking on a stove, no fuss, no muss. When the party leaves, no sign of its stay will remain except temporarily flattened grass.

sold exclusively under the Optimus name. (The same company also makes the Svea.) No matter—they're as dependable as ever, performance-proven by hundreds of thousands of hikers. Moreover, replacement parts are available at large mountain shops, some of which (including Recreational Equipment Inc.) offer a top-to-bottom repair service, over the counter or by mail.

The most popular model is the Svea 123, with a built-in windscreen and a cover that inverts to serve as a small pot; weight is 1⅛ pounds, cost about $15. Next in popularity is the lower and more stable Optimus 8R, which stows neatly in a steel box (the Optimus 99 is identical except the box is aluminum); weight is 1¾ pounds, cost about $19. The Optimus 80 (formerly the legendary Primus 71L) is virtually the same as the Svea except it comes in a steel car-

Popular gas stoves. Clockwise from left: *Optimus 111B, Optimus 8R, Optimus 80, Svea 123 with stovelid/pot and pot lifter*

rying box that acts as pot support and very effective windscreen, making this the easiest of all models to start and keep going in high-country winds; weight is 1¼ pounds, cost about $15. Larger and heavier, giving more heat and equipped with a pump for faster starting and greater dependability in cold weather, is the Optimus 111B, weighing 3½ pounds, costing about $30 and ideal for hikers who normally cook in groups of six to eight; the blowtorch-like flame lets it do the job of two smaller stoves.

Though few other gas stoves are widely distributed at present, some are excellent, notably the Phoebus models and the MSR 9. Requiring mention is the "Taiwan Svea," a crude copy of the original, selling for as little as $6, fairly reliable, but with no replacement parts, no repair service.

Fuel Carriers and Accessories

The fuel for gas stoves (and kerosene as well) must be transported in a leakproof metal container—not glass, which breaks, and not poly bottles, which are leakproof for other liquids but not fuel.

The favorite is an aluminum *fuel bottle* with screw cap and rubber gasket, very sturdy and fitting easily into an outer pack pocket—far and away the best place to carry fuel since some fumes inevitably escape from any container and if within the pack permeate food and clothing. A most desirable accessory to avoid spillage is a *vented pouring spout*. The plain-finish pint bottle weighs 4 ounces and sells for about $2; the quart size weighs 5 ounces and costs a bit more. Anod-

Stove accessories: aluminum fuel bottle, plastic funnel, vented pouring spout for the bottle, cleaning wire, and eyedropper

ized bottles are corrosion-resistant but should not be used to carry alcohol, booze, or acidic fruit juices; these tend to dissolve the lacquer, for example turning a white wine to a red.

A tin-coated *fuel flask* with vented pouring spout has a flat shape for easy storage but must be handled with care to avoid crushing. Just as with a "tin can," when the plating is eroded through or cracked the underlying iron rusts. The pint size weighs 4½ ounces, costs about $3; the 1½-pint and quart sizes weigh and cost more.

When using carriers without pour spouts a small *funnel* of nylon, polyethylene, or aluminum, preferably with a filter (of value in any event to keep garbage from the fuel tank) is essential to avoid spillage.

An *eyedropper* is handy for starting a gas stove, as described below.

Using a Gas Stove (Some Remarks Applicable to Other Stoves)

Except for the pump-equipped Optimus 111B, Phoebus 625, and MSR 9, all the gas stoves described above operate on self-pressurization from heat, similar to gasoline blowtorches.

Before firing up, the tank should be filled—but not to more than 75 percent of capacity; with a too-full tank the gas lacks proper room to build vapor pressure for optimum operation; also, when the stove gets hot the expanding fuel shoots from the burner in a frightening flame and leaks from the cap and ignites, making for a generally hectic kitchen. (In the case of kerosene, a too-full tank prevents bleeding air to the outside to lower the flame.)

Next the *cleaning wire* supplied with some models should be plunged two or three times into the gas vent in the burner head to ensure free passage for the vaporized fuel. The wire pushes tiny bits of soot or whatever out of the way, so that they may cause no problem. If the chunks of trash are large, interior pressure may push them back to the vent once the stove commences operation. When a stove grows impossibly cranky it usually is because of such chunks; the cleaning wire avails naught and the only recourse is complete disassembly and clean-up. (The Optimus 8R and 111B, Phoebus 625, and Svea 123 have a built-in nipple-cleaner that pushes trash *out* rather than in, a superior procedure.)

The first step in actual operation is to preheat the vaporizing tube located between the tank and the burner head. One method is to extract gas from the tank or fuel bottle with an eyedropper, fill the small depression at the base of the vaporizing tube, and (with the control valve in closed position for safety) ignite. (Alcohol is much cleaner, since it leaves no soot.) When the outside gas (or alcohol)

has nearly burned off, open the control valve; with the gas in the vaporizing tube now heated to the vaporization point the stove—hopefully—roars into life. If not (as perhaps in cold wind) try again. The goal is to get the stove as hot as possible before opening the control valve *without* starting a conflagration that scares the wits out of everyone in camp and perhaps over-ventilates tents.

In windy weather the stove must be shielded by barrier walls, such as rocks or logs or aluminum foil; otherwise the cooling makes initial pressure-generation difficult and gusts may blow out the flame repeatedly. Snow or very cold weather requires insulating the tank, perhaps by wrapping it in an old sock, to maintain pressure. However, a warning: *do not over-insulate,* as by burying the stove in dirt, or using an Optimus 80 with the front flap of the case closed, or using a Svea 123 *with windscreen inside a Sigg cooker;* the stove can overheat and blow the safety valve.

For several reasons the flame should be regulated by the control valve to somewhat less than maximum output:

First, flame pouring out around the sides of the cooking pot wastes heat and fuel.

Second, overheating can blow the safety valve. Usually the valve prevents the tank from exploding like a bomb, but the scene is only a little less dramatic when a valve lets go, releasing vapor which instantly ignites in a 3-foot stream of fire. When this happens the proper action is to kick the stove off in the weeds or run like hell.

Third, the major cause of stove malfunction is a scorched wick. The cotton wick draws fuel from the tank up into the vaporizing tube, where, on contact with hot metal, vaporization occurs. If a stove operating wide-open and very hot abruptly runs out of fuel the now-dry wick is scorched and loses its wicking capacity. The re-lit stove sputters and stutters.

Gas stoves—and stoves in general—are simple contrivances but tricky and only practice makes perfect. The beginner should try his stove under ideal conditions, such as in the yard at home, before depending on it in a dark and stormy wilderness night.

Any stove should be kept clean and the fuel free of impurities. When unused for extended periods the fuel should be drained from the tank.

A gas stove—and the gas—must at all times be treated with caution. Never fill the tank near an open flame. Never refill a hot stove —let it cool first. (That's why the tank should be filled before starting a meal, to avoid having to stop in the middle, letting half-cooked food cool. Further, in cold winds only a near-full tank can maintain operating pressure.) Never operate any stove in a tightly-sealed area, whether tent or snow cave; fumes may cause sickness, oxygen-starvation and carbon-monoxide poisoning can be fatal. When a stove is used in a tent be super-careful, keeping in mind that house and home and all worldly goods might vanish in one great flare of flame; since the starting-up holds the most potential for drama, conduct the operation outside the tent—if wind allows.

KEROSENE STOVES

Kerosene has approximately the same BTU rating as white gas. Being less volatile, it's a bit harder to nourish into healthy flame, but by the same token is less likely to explode, making for greater peace of mind. (Incidentally, kerosene stoves also will operate on stove or diesel oil, should kerosene be unavailable.)

The most popular model is the Optimus 00, with roarer burner, weighing 1⅝ pounds, costing about $20. Similar but larger is the Optimus 48, with silent burner, weight 2½ pounds, cost about $20. (The Optimus 45 is the same as the 48 except for having a roarer burner.)

Popular kerosene stoves. Left: *Optimus 48.* Right: *Optimus 00. Burner plates available for both.* Front: *fire ribbon for priming*

A kerosene stove is started by putting a bit of "fire ribbon" or sterno in the cup at the base of the vaporizer and igniting. Once the vaporizer is hot, pressure is hand-pumped into the tank and the kerosene begins to burn.

Kerosene stoves generally do not have control valves. More flame is obtained by pumping; less, by opening the air screw on the tank. A safety valve is unnecessary since kerosene does not build up dangerous pressure.

Though white gas can be used in kerosene stoves equipped with roarer burners the practice is extremely dangerous. With no control valve and no safety valve, pressure builds up and up, the fire gets hotter and hotter. If the leaping flame frightens a camper and he opens the air screw wide to vent pressure, gas vapors may spew out and explode in a catastrophic ball of fire.

BUTANE STOVES

Among beginning hikers butane stoves outsell all others. The fuel is a liquefied petroleum gas contained under low pressure in a thin metal cartridge; when vented to atmospheric pressure by the control valve it instantly vaporizes—apply a lighted match and the stove is going. Butane stoves are quick and easy to start, dependable, virtually free of tricks, "tent safe," and the fuel is conveniently carried and used with no fuss, no mess. Unlike gas stoves, which when turned to a low flame tend to be blown out by every zephyr, they readily can be adjusted down to simmer or sauté or to fry a decent egg or pancake.

There are, however, disadvantages that lead many who try them to switch to gas or kerosene. First, the fuel is much heavier for equivalent heating values than gas or kerosene because of the cartridge. (It is also a dozen times more expensive, but even so the cost is still only pennies per meal.) Second, it freezes solid at 15°F, doesn't vaporize freely below 32°F, and the stove thus operates poorly in the cold of winter, high altitude, and strong winds. (Efficiency can be improved by insulating the cartridge with an old sock or whatever; one may have to sleep with it to be able to cook breakfast. Aluminum foil around the burner reflects heat against the cartridge to improve vaporization.) Third, butane emits less heat than gas or kerosene and cooking time therefore is substantially longer; also, as pressure in the cartridge drops the heat output lessens—the last supper may be lukewarm. Fourth, in the absence of a set of scales one never knows how much fuel remains in a used cartridge. Fifth, fumes leak from the cartridge and have a wretched smell—but this problem is easily solved by taping the orifice. Sixth, an "empty" cartridge contains enough vapor to be a bomb—*do not* change cartridges by a campfire. Finally, the "disposable" cartridge is now becoming a prominent component of back-country garbage—PACK IT OUT!

The pioneer model on the American market and still the most widely distributed is the Gaz S-200 (formerly called the Bleuet), bulky, tall, and so unstable that great care must be taken to position it on an absolutely flat surface. Complete with full cartridge the stove weighs 1½ pounds, costs about $10; the optional windscreen is a dollar more. Extra cartridges, each good for 3 hours, weigh 10 ounces full (5 ounces empty), cost about $1.

The Gaz is a *vapor-feed* stove; the butane goes directly from cartridge to burner, meaning that for efficient performance the entire cartridge must be kept warm. Other vapor-feed models are the Benzomatic ST880, Mountain Products Auto Stove, and Primus 2255 Ranger. All are very tall; squattier and more stable is the Rich-Moor Alp, with a rubber hose connecting cartridge to burner.

Popular butane stoves, with cartridges in place. Left: Gaz S–200 (vapor feed). Right: EFI Mini-stove, marketed under many brand names (liquid feed)

In a *liquid-feed* stove the butane flows from cartridge to a vaporizing chamber; since the chamber is the only part that must be kept warm for steady operation, there is little loss of efficiency in windy or cold weather; however, during start-up these stoves have a disconcerting tendency to flare. One example of the liquid-feed design is the Optimus 731 Mousetrap. Another is the E.F.I. stove, marketed under that name and such house labels as Gerry Mark II, Universal, Medalist, and Browning. Both Optimus and E.F.I. are low to the ground, compact and stable.

The Gaz stove and some others use the French-made Gaz C-200

cartridge. The American-made cartridge used by most liquid-feed models has the advantage that it can be removed from the stove with no loss of fuel and replaced later.

PROPANE STOVES

Propane, also a liquefied petroleum gas, is much superior to butane in cold weather since it vaporizes down to -50°F. However, it is kept under a pressure of about 124 psi (at 70°F) and thus must be contained in a fairly heavy steel cylinder—on a multi-day hike the empties grow weighty indeed. Though worthy of consideration by expeditioners, current models are unsuitable for ordinary backpacking.

ALCOHOL STOVES

Alcohol has about half the BTU rating of white gas and kerosene but is nontoxic and nonexplosive and appeals to nervous hikers who don't mind spending a lot of time cooking. At roughly $9 a gallon, the fuel is not cheap.

A major problem with alcohol stoves is finding one. A few mountain shops carry a very simple, foolproof, light (4 ounces), inexpensive (about $3) model.

WHICH STOVE TO BUY?

Most factors involved in choosing a stove have been discussed above. Obviously both stove and fuel should weigh as little as possible. Ease and convenience of use are considerations, and cost (both of stove and fuel), and safety. Personal preference in these matters mainly determines whether a hiker goes for gas, kerosene, butane, propane, or alcohol—each of which has virtues and faults—or any particular model. For what it's worth, beginners prefer butane by a wide margin, veterans who try butane as often as not go back to gas or kerosene, especially if they travel much in cold and wintry country.

Of minor consequence on short hikes but very important on long, multi-day trips are *fuel consumption* and *heat output*. The accompanying table compares these and other attributes of the most popular stoves.

In theory a supper for three persons, at low-to-medium elevations, in reasonably calm weather, can be cooked—if quite simple and carefully scheduled—in about the time required to bring 3 quarts of water to boil, *each quart separately.* That is, first a pot of soup, then a main course, then the water for cocoa-coffee-tea-Postum. Thus, to use the Svea as example, burning time for supper might be as little as 20 minutes, perhaps half that for breakfast. One ⅓-pint filling of a Svea with a burning time of 1 hour therefore might cook (on the average) two suppers and two breakfasts, and 1 pint of gas approximately suffice for a three-man 6-day trip.

Similarly, a Gaz cartridge with a burning time of 3 hours but a lower heat output might cook three suppers and three breakfasts so that two cartridges would serve the same trip.

That's the theory; the practice is something else. First, many soups and main courses must be not merely brought to a boil but boiled for 10-20 minutes, especially at higher elevations. Second, some gas is inevitably spilled, some heat inevitably wasted. A good rule of thumb is to double the theoretical figure and for that three-man 6-day trip with a Svea to carry a quart of gas, and 2 quarts if the meals are at all elaborate.

Beginners on short trips can eliminate worries about uncooked food by always carrying plenty of gas or kerosene or many butane cartridges; in the process they will gain some notion of how much fuel is about right for their purposes.

Statistics in the table may be used (with all due caution that they are approximate) in calculating the amount of fuel required for extended trips.

POTS AND PANS AND ALL

A beginner who must save a few dollars can improvise a cooking kit from Number Ten cans, coffee cans, and kitchenware picked up at thrift shops for nickels and dimes. Indeed, some sentimental veterans insist food doesn't taste right unless cooked in a Ten Can. However, pots stocked by mountain shops have many advantages, such as bails or handles, tight-fitting lids, ease of cleaning, and the compactness of nesting sets; they are also light and not really expensive, though admittedly more so than a coffee can.

STOVES RECOMMENDED FOR BACKPACKING

These are currently the most popular among the many models available.

Note: No two stoves of the same model operate with exactly the same efficiency; the operation figures are those of tested samples and may be somewhat different in other samples. No wind and a moderate temperature are assumed.

Fuel	Stove Model	Capacity of Tank or Cartridge (pints)	Approximate High-Flame Burning Time of One Tank Filling or One Cartridge (hours)	Approximate Time to Boil 1 Quart Water (minutes at sealevel)	Weight without fuel **weight of full cartridge (pounds)	Approximate Cost without fuel *cost of one cartridge
	Svea 123	1/3	1	6–8	1 1/8 *	$15 *
White Gas	Optimus 80	1/2	1 1/4	6–8	1 1/4 *	$15 *
	Optimus 8R and 99	1/3	3/4	7–9	1 3/4 *	$19 *
	Optimus 111B	1	2 1/2	3–5	3 1/2 *	$30 *

Kerosene	Optimus 00	1	2½	4–6	1⅝*	$20*
	Optimus 48	1¾	4	5–7	2½*	$20*
	Gaz S-200 and Gaz cartridge	¾	3	10–12	⅞* / ⅝**	$10* / $1**
Butane	E.F.I. and cartridge	¾	3	10–12	½* / ⅝**	$10* / $1**
Alcohol	Simple burner	⅓	½	8–10	¼*	$3*

The backpacker should avoid the heavier pots intended for car-camping. Beyond that his choice depends on how many people will be in the cooking group; a lone person needs nothing more than a small kettle and a cup while a group of four or more may require several pots in various sizes. Outdoor shops offer a number of styles in a number of brands; the following examples suggest the alternatives.

The *Sigg Tourist Cooker* includes a Svea 123 stove, aluminum pots of 2½- and 3½-pint capacity, a lid which can serve as a fry pan (and makes a good double-boiler, used with any pot underneath, for fondues), a stove base and wind screen. Total weight, 2¼ pounds; cost,

Above: *Sigg Tourist Cooker, on left disassembled; on right assembled for carrying, stove and all.* Below: *Nesting billies, disassembled on left, assembled for carrying on right*

about $23. By itself the set suffices for three people—or more by adding another pot or two.

A set of *nesting billies,* three aluminum pots with capacities of 1, 2, and 3 quarts, individual lids that double as plates or fry pans, the inner pot large enough to hold a Svea 123 stove, weighs 1¾ pounds, costs about $9, and serves four–five people. The large pot can be left home for two-man groups; a lone person may want to carry only the small pot.

Incidentally, lids are very desirable to keep out stray ashes and flying bugs and to speed the cooking. They can be improvised for Ten Cans and coffee cans from aluminum foil but never fit tight and blow off in the wind.

Nesting kettles heavier and more expensive than billies, in sizes from 1-5 quarts, are less good for extended backpacks where weight is important.

Cook sets are most popular with Boy Scout troops and large families of novice hikers who appreciate the all-together feature; the sets include some eating utensils in addition to nesting pots. One example is a set of lightweight aluminum with two kettles (2 quart, 6 quart), a coffee (hot water) pot, a lid that serves as fry pan, four plates and four cups; weight 3 pounds; cost, about $7; capacity, four people. Similar sets can handle six people and up. More elaborate ones of heavier aluminum are better suited to car-camping.

Cook kits are for individuals or couples. The one-man Boy Scout kit of lightweight aluminum includes a ¾-quart kettle and lid, deep

Above: *Typical four-man cook set. Everything nests into the large kettle for carrying.* Below: *Typical two-man cook kit, disassembled*

plate, cup, and fry pan with handle that holds the kit together; weight, ⅝ pound; cost, $2. Comparable kits costing up to $5 serve one or two persons.

Though most pots have bails and many lid-fry pans have handles, a most desirable accessory to avoid burned fingers and the spillage of dinner that may result is a *pot gripper*. The best is a spring-loaded steel model that gives a strong hold on loaded pots; weight, 3¼ ounces; cost about 85c. Some hikers prefer a pair of *pliers* which can also be used to work on the stove, open jammed fuel bottles, and extract teeth.

A *stirring spoon* with a long handle is useful; wooden ones don't melt or get hand-burning hot if left in the soup.

Hikers who do a lot of frying, as of fish, hotcakes, and omelettes, often become disenchanted with lids of nesting pots or pieces of

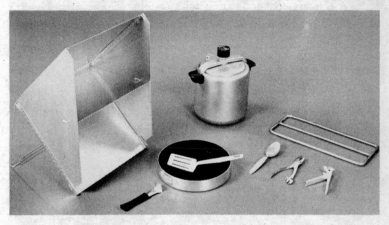

Kitchen accessories. Clockwise from left: reflector oven (folds flat for carrying), pressure cooker, grate, pot-gripper, pliers, stirring spoon, Teflon-coated aluminum fry pan with nylon spatula

aluminum foil and carry an honest-to-gosh *fry pan.* Some declare it's impossible to fry properly except with steel; a pan 8¾ inches in diameter, weighing 12 ounces, costs about $4; a light steel spatula completes the unit. Others like an easy-to-clean Teflon-coated aluminum pan, 9½ inches in diameter, weighing 15 ounces complete with the nylon spatula that must be used with Teflon (wood is also suitable); cost $3.50.

Though admittedly a very fussy luxury, a *reflector oven* is a magnificient contributor to trail cuisine when wood fires are possible (or the party has three-four efficient stoves) and the group includes a devoted baker seeking to amaze and delight friends with biscuits, coffee cakes flavored with blueberries picked along the way, and other goodies. A folding aluminum oven weighs 2½ pounds, costs about $12.

High-altitude hikers may wish to consider a *pressure cooker*. At sealevel water boils at 212°F; at 5000 feet the boiling point is 203°F and cooking time is increased by half or more; at 10,000 the boiling point is 193°F and cooking time is nearly quadrupled. Those who frequently camp at 10,000 feet, as in the Wind River Range and parts of the High Sierra and Colorado Rockies, may find advantage in the pressure cooker's ability to cut cooking time approximately in half. A 4-quart cooker suitable for two-four people, of heavy-duty aluminum, with two perforated separators and a solid one for segregating foods, 6½ inches high, 6½ inches in diameter, weighs 3 pounds and costs about $20.

EATING TOOLS

Any number of methods are satisfactory for conveying food from pot to mouth. It is surprising how finicky some hikers are about the technique—but then, the more time one spends on the trails the more one becomes a creature of fetishes.

Eating tools. Above: plastic plate, bowl, and cup. Below: cutlery, pocket knife, and stainless-steel cup

There are those who cannot eat happy unless all solid elements of the entire meal are spread before them at once on a *plate*. The lids of billies and other kettles can be employed, or the plates included in cooking sets and kits, or pieces of aluminum foil, or plates of plastic or aluminum. Other hikers cannot abide cereal except in a *bowl*—the shops have them, mainly of plastic.

Most experienced hikers do all their eating from a *cup*—whether the food is soup, coffee, steak, pancake, or salad. While plate-eaters move now to this item, now to that, back and forth, cup-eaters go at

the meal one course at a time, finishing this before starting that. Plastic cups, light and cheap, are most popular; stacking (nesting) mugs of large capacity weigh ¾ ounce, cost 30¢. A measuring cup with quarter-cup graduations doubles as a chef's tool, saving much guesswork about quantities of ingredients and avoiding too-watery pudings and stews.

A traditional favorite is a stainless steel cup with wire handle (called "Sierra Club cup" in California and among Northwesterners of long memory the "Ome Daiber cup"). It can serve as a small pot, such as to heat water for a spot of tea. Weight is 3 ounces; cost, about $1.50. The capacity is just over 9 ounces—a good thing for the cook to remember (1 cup equals 8 ounces.).

Plastic cups have the enormous virtue of the "cool lip" but may absorb and retain tastes of certain foods; steel cups, cool at the rim but not elsewhere, are easy to keep clean and pure; aluminum cups are a disaster—when contents are hot the edge burns the lip and when the edge is cool enough for the lip the contents are cold.

The *pocket knife* every hiker must carry (see Chapter 15) serves all ordinary cooking and eating needs; if it lacks an effective *can opener* a separate one must be included in party gear.

A *spoon,* stainless steel or plastic, transports food to the mouth.

Some hikers carry a *fork* as well, feeling frustrated unless they can spear their meatballs. Asians and a few American show-offs like chopsticks.

FOOD CONTAINERS

Mountain shops stock many kinds of plastic (mainly polyethylene) bags, bottles, and jars for hauling foods, including water.

Strong, light, transparent *poly bags,* in sizes from 5-by-8 to 15-by-18 inches, costing from 1-10¢ each, have many uses noted in Chapter

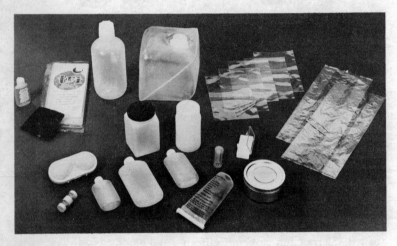

Dishwashing gear and food-carriers

4 and elsewhere in this book. Similar bags in which bread and produce are sold are free. The bags may be closed by rubber bands or, better, paper-wrapped wires.

Poly boxes, square or round, with snap-on lids, are good carriers for lettuce, grapes, tomatoes, peanut butter, and other foods which are crushable or sloppy. In various sizes the boxes cost from 20–30¢. *Poly vials* handle pills and spices and the like. (A friendly neighborhood pharmacist may supply, for free, pill jars in assorted sizes and shapes.)

Poly squeeze tubes are excellent for jam, honey, peanut butter, margarine, and other oozy foods—except in cold weather when the contents may adamantly resist squeezing. The tube has a clip at the bottom to permit refilling.

Plastic egg boxes have obviously limited utility.

A plastic, two-compartment *salt-and-pepper shaker* is convenient. If a larger supply of salt is carried separately, as customary on long hikes, the other half of the shaker can be filled with garlic salt, cinnamon, or some other favorite spice.

A major use of flexible, translucent-white *narrow-mouth poly bottles* with screw-on caps is as canteens; only a few traditionalists nowadays carry the old "canteen-shaped" canteens of aluminum or rigid plastic. The bottles come in shapes from oval to round, capacities from 2 ounces to 32 ounces (1 quart—the most popular canteen size), prices from 20–90¢, weights from 1½–3½ ounces. In the kitchen they serve as containers for liquid detergent or cooking oils or the ingredients of an aperitif, as shakers for mixing the morning orange juice, and so on.

Wide-mouth poly bottles, round or square, are intermediate between narrow-mouth bottles and poly boxes and do some things as well as either and some things better. Their advantage over boxes is a screw-on lid far less likely to let honey butter and margarine and other semi-liquids escape. Their advantage over narrow-mouth bottles is ease of access: fresh eggs can be broken inside, carried a couple (cool) days without spoiling, then fried with the yolks unbroken; peanut butter and mayonnaise can be reached with a spoon; snow can be stuffed in quickly and easily. Sizes range from 1 pint to 2 quarts, weighs from 2–4 ounces, prices from 50¢ to $1.25.

In desert travel usually and elsewhere occasionally, a party must haul more water than canteens can accommodate. One alternative is a large *collapsible plastic water bottle* that folds up and packs easily when empty. Capacities range from 4 quarts to 5 gallons, weights from 2–7 ounces, prices from 40¢ to $2.50.

DISHWASHING

The tools of dishwashing are simple enough.

First is some device to loosen food particles (and charcoal) from utensils, particularly cooking pots. Oldtimers did the job with sand

and gravel; much neater is a scouring pad available in any grocery store or a length of nylon netting purchased at a fabric shop.

Second is a means of cutting grease. Hot water alone serves very well but a small amount of soap or biodegradable detergent, liquid or solid, speeds the process and minimizes consumption of hot water, which may be in short supply when cooking on a stove for which the fuel has been carried a long, long way.

An inexpensive product which doubles as pot-scraper and grease-cutter (and hand-and-face washer) is the Tri Soapy Towel, a tough, rough-textured paper toweling impregnated with detergent.

Note: If aluminum utensils are not thoroughly cleaned and dried, acids are formed which dissolve the metal with amazing speed.

14:   FOOD

ONCE upon a time in the Great Depression a CCC crew was building a road near Hood Canal. Several of the guys, all from Eastern
cities, began wondering about the interior of the Olympic Mountains
and decided to spend a holiday exploring. None ever had seen a
mountain or trail before so they asked an experienced hiker how such
a trip should be done. After hearing the complexities of packboards
and food lists and boiling oatmeal and rice on campfires a mile above
sealevel their leader said, "The hell with it, we won't take any food.
We're only going to be gone 3 days."

Off they went into the Olympic wilderness, some 50 miles up and
down valleys and over passes and along ridges, and were too enrap-
tured to care about having nothing to eat. These Depression youths
had felt hunger often enough to know it wouldn't hurt them in 3
days.

In fact, a person in average health can miss a lot more meals than
that without damage; from a perspective of history and a glance
around the world today one almost might say that on the ordinary
backpack of up to a week or so food is a frill.

To make a fast retreat before the wrath of all the mountain rescuers on the continent gathers into a single bolt of lightning: without a

fairly constant supply of calories the body slows down and weakens and becomes prone to stumble, the mind tends to make errors in judgment, and the system loses resistance to cold. Hikers should keep stoking for reasons of safety if not pleasure.

Still, it is true enough that most backpackers worry excessively about food. Beginners especially, not having experienced the Depression, or the daily existence of millions of people on this Earth who feel lucky to have a supper of a bowl of rice and the tail of a fish, are likely to think they will faint and fail and die within hours of their departure from the road unless they maintain a regular succession of "well-balanced meals."

The first common mistake of novices is to haul too much food— twice as much as they can eat and four times more than they need.

The second mistake is to fret about the proper mix of protein, vitamins, and minerals—not realizing that on any hike up to a week or two in length the only important physiological need is calories. (Unless one tends to suffer from constipation and requires a certain amount of roughage, in which case a cup of prunes a day keeps the suppositories away.) To be sure, with an exceptionally bizarre diet minor vitamin deficiencies could occur, perhaps causing night-blindness, but in so short a time there is absolutely no risk of scurvy, beriberi, or rickets. And anyway, whatever foods are carried (unless one tries to subsist solely on sugar cubes) will have enough of the essential elements to prevent significant imbalance. As for fears of a deficiency in protein, even during strenuous exercise the body uses relatively little for muscle replacement; Americans happen to like and be able to afford protein and consume vastly more than the world average, but most of it is converted to energy (and fat), not muscles.

Before leaving the point let it be noted that Americans of the affluent class that does the bulk of the backpacking generally can well afford to drop surplus pounds in the wildlands by deliberate undereating—which reduces not only body but pack weight.

The above discussion omits something: it's a pleasure to eat. And never more so than on the trail. Indeed, some long-time backpackers confess they are not sure whether they eat to hike or hike to eat. Though perhaps never in their city lives having visited a gourmet restaurant, and at home hardly able to recall at breakfast what they had for supper, they will rapturously describe the famous glop they created at Pretty Meadows on a magic evening 25 years ago.

Whether necessary or not, then, eating is a pleasure few hikers forego. But what to eat? There is the question with a thousand answers, all correct. The choice is almost entirely determined by personal tastes, including passionate likes and dislikes that develop with age and experience. Assemble a seminar of trail-toughened veterans and ask them to reveal the secrets of their backpacking success and they'll talk boots and pants and packs—but eventually will end up in a loud debate about the virtues of Logan bread versus pilot bread versus pumpernickel and how many smoked oysters per man are essential for a 9-day trip. Then they'll settle down to swapping recipes, which leads to arguments about brown versus white sugar, the ideal way to rehydrate a meatball, and whether the one-pot supper is the greatest invention of mankind or a sign that civilization is rushing toward total collapse.

Indeed, try to plan a week's menu that will perfectly satisfy each of four old trail hands and chances are the party never will leave town. Two may insist on Thuringer sausage, one can't abide anything but salami, and the other vows to boycott all lunches lacking Goteborg. The Appendix notes a number of books containing calory charts, food lists, menus, and recipes; the diversity of their advice abundantly demonstrates the wide range of opinion and taste.

The following exposition does not probe deeply into trail cuisine and is not intended for the experienced backpacker, who already knows what he likes and is certain to object more or less violently to whatever is said on the subject. Rather, the treatment is aimed at the absolute novice and is designed solely to assist him in selecting the first trail meals. Having fed himself a few times in surroundings beyond electric stove and refrigerator he soon will make stupendous discoveries, become as opinionated as the veterans, and start pressing recipes on strangers encountered in wilderness camps.

THE SHORT AND THE LONG OF IT

Opening a can is within the capacity of a majority of beginning hikers, given a can opener. Nearly all are able to strip a banana and assemble a jelly sandwich. No higher order of culinary skills than these are required to make out well enough on short trips. As miles and days mount, though, wildland cookery becomes slightly less simple—but nowadays never really complicated.

DAY HIKE

For an afternoon stroll a chunk of chocolate or an apple or packet of nuts may add to the pleasure of a rest stop; food, however, is purely optional.

On a full-day hike the only meal is lunch, usually consumed in several instalments from second breakfast through high tea—and supper and breakfast too if an accident or loss of route forces an unplanned night out. Any menu will do—sandwiches, crackers and cheese, smoked salmon, grapes, cookies, carrot sticks, cherry pie—whatever the people enjoy. Any amount will do so long as there is enough for a possible emergency—too much is unlikely to damage the back. (Unless the example is followed of a group of climbers who once hoaxed an Eastern photographer at a lunch stop high on the Nisqually Glacier of Mt. Rainier, and through him the readers of

Life magazine, by casually pulling watermelons from rucksacks and slicing them up as if this were standard alpine fare.)

Even in well-watered (and pure-watered) country the party should have a canteen supply, if not to drink (perhaps mixed in the cup with lemonade powder) then for first-aid purposes. For thirst alone canned fruit juices or carbonated beverages are delightful; they also give a quick shot of sugar to cure an acute case of that pooped feeling.

Do not drop along the trail or toss in the brush candy wrappers, orange peels, or cans. (What you can pack in full you can pack out empty.) And don't bury them—every loose rock beside popular trails already has garbage underneath. *Pack it out*! *Pack it ALL out*!

OVERNIGHT

The same rule that applies to day-hike lunches extends to weekend lunches—and breakfasts and suppers. The rule is there is no rule. Too little food doesn't cause intolerable misery and indeed adds zest to hamburgers and milkshakes at the drive-in Sunday night. Too much food rarely leads to a permanent stoop.

However, a basic choice must be made prior to the trip: between walking far and fast or eating in the style of the last days of Pompeii.

At one extreme are meals essentially a succession of quick lunches; ham sandwiches make a satisfying supper and unheated hash fresh from the can resembles dog food but is amazingly tasty, especially with a splash of ketchup. To quote a saying famous among climbers, "Though the food is cold the inner man is hot." Civilized stomachs are conditioned to feel vaguely incomplete lacking at least one hot meal a day; amid grand scenery the sensation passes.

At the other extreme is wilderness feasting, where backpacking miles have as their goal the sharpening of the appetite. Sybarites may devote the afternoon and evening to a supper of: aperitif of choice and hors d'oeuvres of sesame crackers spread with truffled paté; tossed salad or slices of lemon-washed avocado; Cornish game hen foil-roasted in coals and served with corn on the cob; biscuits baked in a reflector oven and topped by frozen strawberries and whipped cream; wines and brandies and cheeses at the discretion of the maitre'd.

The average weekender meals fall someplace in the middle. For example, supper may be cherry tomatoes, optional soup, canned beef stew, bread and butter, stir-and-serve pudding, and instant coffee, tea, or milk. Breakfast may be orange juice, oatmeal "cooked" in the cup by addition of hot water, and instant coffee-cocoa. Thousands of other menus have been published in the literature. Ad infinitum, ad nauseum.

LONG BACKPACK

Beyond a 3-day weekend eatery demands thought. Depending on the backs and appetites involved, somewhere around 4 or 5 days and certainly by 6 or 7 days the distance from the road forces a qualitative change in cuisine.

Above all it becomes essential to *go light*. An extra half-pound per person per meal matters little on a weekend with a maximum of 4 meals, matters much when the meals number 12 or 27—6 or 13 extra pounds on each suffering back makes for a slow and painful pace.

Through use of dried foods and those naturally low in water content, shucking cardboard packaging, and moderately careful menu planning, it is possible to feed the average hiker to repletion on 2 pounds of food per day. By more precise planning the job can be done with 1½ pounds. And if the party members are willing to leave a bit of lard along the way and endure pangs while stomachs shrink, with

1 pound. At this point, though, about the fifth evening the hiker will look into the setting sun and see not the majestic drama of day's end but only a great fried egg dripping hot butter.

This general rule concerning pounds of food per person has so many exceptions it is hardly a rule at all. Exercise stimulates the appetites of some, who grow ravenous several days out and go mad at the aroma of peanut butter and begin to lust after chipmunks and prowl tidal pools for edible seaweed. Others eat less the harder they work— perhaps because their systems, freed from habitual city overstuffing, are slimming down for re-entry into the natural life of the wilderness.

And of course, an 80-pound human requires less fuel than a 250-pounder. Although, contrarily, a person with hyperactive metabolism, the sort who eats and eats and is always skinny (or in the case of females, "lithe") needs more food than the person whose inner plant is so efficient a single kipper adds an inch to his girth.

And again, on extended backpacks as on day walks, the choice must be made between lightness and luxury. On long trips lightness dictates most decisions, but there are no words to convey the ecstasy of salted cucumber slices 6 days from the road; the extra ounces of such an occasional special treat may be worth the added strain.

Cooking time is another consideration. When the intent is to cover a lot of ground, walking every day from early morning to late afternoon, and/or when all cooking is to be done on a stove, most meals should be medium-fast and some instant-quickies, requiring only hot water for supper and cold water for breakfast. On less frantic trips, though, a few meals should be fancy—for rest days or days of rain at camps where wood fires can be built. For example, the ingredients of a pancake-bacon-eggs breakfast contain no surplus water and thus are very efficient in the ratio of weight to calories. A pancake breakfast ordinarily lasts to lunchtime, but when mists are driving through the flowers, or rain drizzling among the trees, or the camp is a marvel, and there is no need to march on, who cares?

For obvious reasons the subject of foods for long backpacks is the most controversial among veterans—and the most baffling to novices. Thus, to guide through the confusion, a new section must begin. In fact three sections, one after the other.

LONG-HAUL FOODS: SUPERMARKET

Thirty-odd years ago, before food-processors ran amok, the diet of the long-distance backpacker was restricted and his cookery a formidable art. Few dried foods were available (it was possible to get quite sick of prunes and chipped beef) and those naturally dry were not treated for quick cooking. Pasta (noodles, macaroni) was relatively easy to make digestible but rice took an hour or more at high altitude and usually ended as a gruel punctuated by tiny pebbles; beans were an overnight project. Even oatmeal and farina required an eternity of smoke-swallowing and stirring and generally burned on the bottom.

Nowadays, however, supermarkets are cornucopias of low-in-water, fast-cooking products. By prowling the aisles and checking cooking times carefully, avoiding tempting packages that call for a $400°$ oven, the backpacker can assemble any number of lightweight, nutritious, delicious, alacazam meals. To stimulate the imagination, following are some of the innumerable supermarket foods suitable for long-haul backpacking.

For breakfast: quick-cooking and instant-in-the-cup oatmeal and farina; compact no-cook cereals such as Grape Nuts; pancake flour; bacon; dried fruits; powdered juice mixes; "instant breakfast"; sugar; dried milk; instant cocoa and coffee.

For lunch: dense and durable breads and crackers; margarine;

A sampling of long-haul foods available in supermarkets. Above: breakfast ingredients. Middle: lunch things. Below: supper stuff

cheese; peanut butter; jam and honey; candy; nuts; dried fruits; sausage; powdered juice mixes.

For supper: dried soups; instant potatoes and dry gravy mixes; quick-cooking noodles with cheese (Kraft Dinner); rice that requires no boiling, only steaming, and may have various spices and garnishes included in the package; canned meats and fishes; hard sausage; chipped beef; cheese; Lipton's complete main dishes with freeze-dried meats, such as beef stroganoff and ham chedderton; instant puddings; cookies; instant coffee; tea bags.

The big problem is deciding how much of any particular food is enough for a certain number of people; the "serves four" on a package may mean four finicky mice. Trial-and-error experience gained on short hikes where mistakes in calculation are not serious is the best way to learn how to buy. If a shortcut is wanted, exact amounts of ingredients required for a myriad of menus are given by cookbooks listed in the Appendix.

DRIED FOODS

Time out now, before proceeding from supermarket to mountain shop, for a bit about the background of dried foods, which generally

THIS WILL FEED BOTH OF YOU FOR FIVE DAYS

weigh only 20-30 per cent or less of what they did before processing and are the key factor in the virtuosity of the modern trail chef.

Man's earliest means of preserving food was sun-drying, dating to prehistoric times and the original method of making raisins, prunes, dried peas and beans, beef jerky, and the like. Freezing perhaps came not much later as man moved into lands of cold winters. Probably the first use of artificial heat was in smoking meat and fish. The technology of preserving without tinning advanced little beyond this level of sophistication until the 20th century, when experiments with other techniques, stimulated by military requirements during and after World War II, led to the current state of the art.

HOT-AIR DRYING ("DEHYDRATED" FOODS)

Hot-air drying once was done in oven-like chambers by the batch, requiring much handling and consequent expense. An improvement was *tunnel-drying,* where foods are placed on trays and passed slowly through a long tunnel in which hot air blows end to end; emerging after 6 hours or less with moisture content below 10-12 percent, the food is transferred to finish-drying bins; moisture is there reduced to less than 5 percent, the point necessary for storage stability. Demanding more complicated equipment but offering greater efficiency and economy and providing better quality control and thus gradually replacing tunnel-drying are various *continuous processes.* An example is spreading the food on a wire-mesh belt which moves through a chamber perhaps 120 feet long; the air blowing through the food from various inlets may be very hot early on, then cooler. In 3-4 hours for large vegetable dices and 30-45 minutes for leafy vegetables, moisture usually is less than 5 percent, often eliminating the need for finish-drying in a bin.

Dehydration of highly-concentrated fruit or vegetable purees, such as mashed potatoes, yams, applesauce, tomatoes, and so on is by *drum-drying,* the "mash" spread on the stainless-steel outer surface of a large, internally-heated, rotating drum, automatically scraped off into a hopper and spread on another drum, and so on until done.

Some fruits (apples, apricots, peaches, prunes) may be processed by *vacuum-drying,* basically with hot-air methods but in a partial vacuum to avoid excessive oxidation and resulting discoloration. The older and still-common and less-expensive alternative is to replace the air in the chamber with sulfur dioxide gas; the obnoxious taste and odor inevitably linger.

Puff-drying (mainly of carrots) is a variety of hot-air drying in in which by some technique the vegetable is expanded for quicker re-hydration and cooking.

Spray-drying, conducted in a tall tower into the top of which tiny droplets are sprayed, dehydrating as they fall through heated air, is customary for powdered milk, coffee, and vegetable and fruit juices.

Upon rehydration foods treated by hot-air methods generally do not closely resemble the original in appearance or flavor, largely because when a plant or animal is air-dried to less than 10-15 percent of its natural moisture the cell structure tightens up irreversibly. A stewed raisin is nothing like a grape and rehydrated spinach flakes are only distant cousins to leaves fresh from the field. But then, a raisin is excellent eating in its own right and some hikers actually prefer trail spinach to garden spinach. Air-dried foods can be delicious and have the enormous advantage of much lower cost than the freeze-dried next discussed.

VACUUM SUBLIMATION (FREEZE-DRIED FOODS)

Vacuum sublimation, called the greatest breakthrough in food preservation since the tin can, combines the flavor-retention of freezing with the lightness of dehydration.

The food, cooked or raw depending on the product, is flash-frozen so that ice crystals cannot grow large enough to distort the cell structure, then placed in a high-vacuum chamber at very low temperature, perhaps down to -50°F, then exposed to radiant heat. The combination of heat and low pressure forces some 97 percent or more of the moisture to sublime—that is, pass directly from solid to vapor without ever becoming liquid, again preventing damage to the cells.

The process may have been invented by Incas in the high Andes when they placed meat on freezing rocks in thin air under intense sun. Not until recent years, however, mainly through the impetus of military needs (hikers riding piggyback on the soldiers), has the technique become economically practical, and it still is in a very early stage of refinement. Few companies are in commercial production; more are experimenting.

Partly due to the innate inefficiency of batch handling, freeze-drying currently is the most expensive of any method of food preservation; in time researchers surely will perfect an assembly line and the cost will drop considerably.

Not even high prices discourage the more affluent backpackers, who like freeze-dried products because they rehydrate quickly to virtually pristine shape and flavor and if correctly packaged keep indefinitely. Though economics pretty much restrict the technique at present to valuable, high-solid foods such as red meats, poultry, and seafood, it also works beautifully on most fruits and vegetables, coffee, and a great many other foods—though not all; cheese, for example, crumbles to dust.

PACKAGING

Many dried foods are shipped from manufacturer to retailer in large, tight-closed tins and packaged in poly bags shortly before sale. (Some mountain shops sell full tins of vegetables and fruits for big-time eaters.) A few dried products last for months in the poly but because the plastic is not absolutely impervious to passage of air many start to deteriorate in a matter of weeks. The hiker probably should toss out poly-bagged fruits and vegetables left over at the end of the season rather than saving them for next year; they will not become hazardous to health but may provide strange new taste sensations. Eggs packaged in poly definitely must be used the same season purchased. So should such foods as flour and beans; they will not spoil but over a long period may develop weevils, which do not detract from food value and indeed increase the protein content but are widely considered unesthetic.

Though aluminum cans are occasionally used, the most common container for freeze-dried meats and meat products and some vegetables is the *shrink pack,* where the food is placed in laminated aluminum foil, the air drawn out by vacuum, and the sealed foil covered by an outer layer of tough plastic. The package is very durable if protected from puncturing and preserves contents indefinitely. Even a tiny, perhaps invisible hole, however, permits freeze-dried meats to rehydrate, in which event they quickly spoil; if the food stinks or looks strange when the pack is opened, it must *not* be eaten.

LONG-HAUL FOODS: MOUNTAIN SHOP

Where the supermarket leaves off the mountain shop begins, offering dried foods and specialties with limited appeal, if any, for city use but making possible a variety, convenience, and quality of wilderness eatery inconceivable to oldtimers.

Generally, because of special processing (particularly freeze-drying) and packaging, a menu entirely drawn from mountain shop supplies is considerably more expensive than one depending partly on the supermarket. The hiker must let his pocketbook be his guide.

SEPARATE INGREDIENTS

A wide range of fruits, vegetables, meats, and miscellaneous foods are packaged separately, to be eaten alone or in combination with others, such as:

Air-dried and freeze-dried fruits and vegetables from apples to peaches, beets to yams.

Freeze-dried meats from meat balls and hamburgers to beef steaks and pork chops.

Beef jerky, dehydrated bacon bar and meat bar, powdered eggs, meat-flavored vegetable-protein chunks.

Fruit pemmican, English mint cake, maple sugar candy, fruit-nut bar, powdered beverages, pilot bread.

And more.

COMPLETE DISHES

A number of firms (Wilson, Seidel, Rich Moor, Chuck Wagon, and Oregon Freeze-Dried Foods, with Mountain House and Tea Kettle labels) package complete main courses and side dishes which are delicious and nutritious or at least edible and so simple to prepare as to be virtually foolproof; some require only the addition of hot or cold water to be ready to eat. To cite a very few from a great many:

For breakfast there are omelettes, pancakes, cereals.

For supper there are rice-beef-vegetable mulligans, beef stew, chili, Boston-style beans, ham and potatoes, noodles and beef, chicken romanoff, turkey tetrazzini, beef almondine, tuna a la neptune. And for dessert, puddings and gelatins—and no-bake pineapple cheese cake with graham cracker crust!

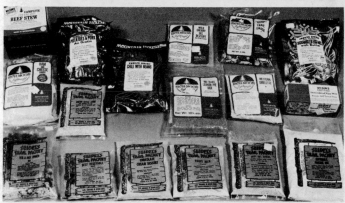

A sampling of representative long-haul foods offered by mountain shops.
Above: separate ingredients, some normally eaten alone, others commonly
mixed up in glops. Middle: complete dishes, all required components in
the package. Below: complete meals, the easy way out for the confused
novice

And drinks, snacks, and goodies galore.

Many of these splendid dishes cost two or three or five times more than the glops a hiker whomps up from supermarket foods—which doesn't matter to the wealthy or occasional camper but certainly does to the impoverished, inveterate, long-distance walker, who mostly eats at the Kraft Dinner level and considers freeze-dried hash a holiday treat.

It must be noted that most of these foods are unappealing in the city, barely tolerable on weekends, and don't become genuinely appetizing until about the fourth day on the trail.

COMPLETE MEALS

Several of the firms mentioned above provide the ultimate in convenience by packaging complete meals carefully tailored to the high-calory, low-weight, easy-cooking requirements of the hiker and accompanied by exact directions which can be followed by anyone able to boil water and scramble an egg.

Among the fans of complete meals are scoutmasters and other trail bosses who have neither the energy (or perhaps experience) to puzzle out a menu and shopping list for a dozen or a score gaping young mouths; using the shortcut they can buy food for a week in minutes and feed the mob very well.

The convenience has a price; the same or similar meals can be assembled at a fraction of the cost from separate ingredients purchased in supermarket-plus-mountain shop. Also, after the beginner has developed personal eccentricities he doubtless will prefer to structure his own menus. However, through packaged meals he gains the equivalent of on-the-job training in backpack cookery directed by experts.

WILD FOODS

Living off the country cannot be condoned or encouraged now that people-pressure is crushing the small scraps of wilderness remaining in North America. Still, in proper places at proper times hikers may gently crop the wildland without harm.

Fishing in lakes and streams is an obvious example, and gathering clams and other shellfish from ocean beaches. A person may harvest all the edible berries he can find without upsetting the natural order (though perhaps a bear) and thus explode a tart moisture within a dry mouth, or by saving a cupful for camp, boil up a superb topping for pancakes.

Mushrooms delicately sautéed in margarine add a gourmet touch to any outdoor supper. With a little study a half-dozen super-safe varieties can be learned.

Similarly, a number of greens may be harvested for a wildland salad—miners' lettuce is one. For fresh vegetables there are such delicacies as boiled skunk cabbage leaves—picked at the proper stage. The backpacker does well to know some of the common edible plants in the area of his customary travels, not only to vary menus on long trips and for survival when lost but to gain the increasingly rare experience of eating genuinely natural, completely unchemicalized, perfectly "organic" foods.

15:   ESSENTIALS

ENOUGH! The wallet is empty, the pack full, the back bent.

And yet *not* enough because to travel the trails happy and secure the hiker needs still more gear.

Keep cool—these last few bits cumulatively weigh not many pounds and cost not too many dollars.

But do not omit them—all are more or less essential either for safety or comfort or efficiency, as will be evident from their descriptions.

THE TEN ESSENTIALS

Back in the 1930s, when The Mountaineers began presenting an annual Climbing Course, the faculty soon discovered that while students were eager to haul axes and ropes and pitons they saved weight by eliminating less glamorous stuff. Novice Homer and Novice Chuck, inseparable companions, would arrange for one to carry a flashlight, the other a map and compass. Then the party scattered on the descent from a peak and the buddies were separated from each other and everyone else. Darkness came and Homer could see to walk but didn't know which way to go; Chuck knew which way to go but couldn't see to walk.

From innumerable such incidents, many miserable and not a few tragic, The Mountaineers drew up a list of Ten Essentials to be carried by every climber on his person or in his pack at all times. The list was really just a teaching device, since no experienced wilderness climber then or now ever would be caught without the Ten.

The rule is absolute for climbers; for hikers there is a sliding scale of necessity. The afternoon walker on a broad, well-marked, heavily-populated trail often can do without a single Essential. The overnight backpacker who sticks to turnpikes may need only several. Those who probe deep into wilderness, away from quick support of rangers or other hikers, and especially those who strike off cross-country, must have the full Ten.

A further qualification. A family that invariably stays together in a tight bunch may need some of the Ten only *as a group.* The more independent the party members the more important it is for *each person* to carry all Ten.

ONE: EXTRA CLOTHING

Chapter 9 sufficiently makes the point, which is to have in the pack more clothing than seems necessary when setting out on a sunny

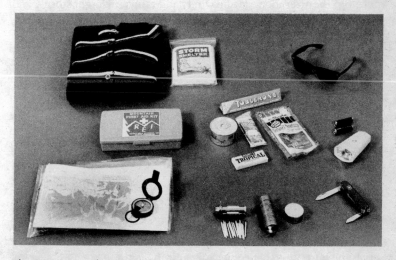

The Ten Essentials. Top row: extra clothing (here, a sweater and a storm shelter), sunglasses. Middle row: first-aid kit, extra food, flashlight (and extra cells). Bottom row: map, compass, matches, firestarters, knife

morning; the afternoon may be windy and rainy, the night stormy and freezing, and though the hiker doesn't intend to be on the trail that night a sprained ankle may leave no choice.

In wet, cold country each person must have *wool* clothing and some sort of protection from moisture of sky and ground (such as a light sheet of polyethylene) in case circumstances force a bivouac without camping gear.

TWO: EXTRA FOOD

The day-hiker's lunch may have to be stretched into a supper, a breakfast, another lunch—while the lost route is being found or the rescue party summoned. Thus the lunch must be substantial; the test is that on any trip *without* misfortune there should be food left over at the end.

A can of fruit-nut pemmican stowed permanently in the pack serves the purpose; few people will eat it in anything but an honest-to-gosh emergency. One Northwest climber carries a packet of dry dog food.

THREE: SUNGLASSES

In predominantly forest travel sunglasses are not essential; they surely are in desert country and open alpine regions, such as massive screes or felsenmeers (boulder fields) of light-colored rock. The extreme case is snow, where sunglasses are mandatory on bright days to prevent discomfort, pain, and even *temporary blindness and permanent damage.*

Mountain shops stock a variety of sunglasses and goggles in a range of styles and prices; for ordinary hiking any will do and choice is a matter of individual preference. For extended snow travel, however, glass lenses are best; some plastic lenses are virtually useless and few block enough of the eye-harming rays. Persons who wear prescription glasses should be careful to select sunglasses that fit comfortably over the regular lenses, or alternatively have an optician make a set of prescription sunglasses.

FOUR: KNIFE

Except for small children each hiker should carry a knife. Uses include eating (opening that can of pemmican), first aid, whittling kindling to start a wood fire (for cooking or for emergency warmth when trapped in storm or night by accident or loss of route).

No backpacker needs a "hunting knife" unless to bolster his manhood—a requirement felt most urgently by very young boys (of all ages). Big blades are for hunters, fishermen, and guerrillas.

While on the subject of weaponry let it be noted that the backpacker has no business hauling an ax or hatchet; they are heavy, totally unnecessary, and inevitably lead to clear-cut logging of campsites. And just as an ax triggers a compulsion to chop-chop-chop for the sake of chopping, a lightweight folding saw may cause even the sensitive hiker to engage in an orgy. It was a symptom that a frontier town was coming of age when the sheriff required transients to check their guns at his office, and it is high time now for wildland walkers to check their steel at the trailhead. If Sonnyboy is going out of his mind for a chance to try his new hatchet, keep him away from the trees, send him off to whack at billboards.

Returning to knives, the most popular is the Boy Scout type with single blade, can-opener, combination bottle-opener and screwdriver, and awl, costing from $2 to $7 depending on the quality of materials and manufacture. The cheapest is best for children, who lose knives instantly.

Many prefer the Swiss Army knife, strongly constructed of stainless steel and thus not rusting shut as happens with some less-expensive knives. Generally sufficient is the model selling for about $8 and having a blade, can-opener, bottle-opener, reamer, screwdriver, and file; the can-opener, incidentally, works much better than the Boy Scout design.

The "Japanese Army knife," including fork, spoon, complete kitchen kit, and a dozen other tools, entertains kids but is too heavy and cumbersome for grown-ups.

The hiker should own but not necessarily carry a whetstone for occasionally sharpening the blade.

FIVE: FIRESTARTER

Even where the wood fire is obsolescent or already forbidden it continues to have a role in emergencies. To be able to start a fire when one is urgently needed, as in a rainstorm when the hiker is lost and the wood wet, each person should carry a fire ribbon or a few candle stubs or fuel tablets (see Chapter 13).

SIX: MATCHES

To start the firestarter matches are required. In addition to those carried for routine purposes each person should have an emergency supply, either waterproof or in a waterproof container; windproof matches can be lifesavers in foul weather. So can a butane lighter.

SEVEN: FIRST AID KIT

Ideally every hiker venturing more than a few miles and hours from civilization should have first aid training and a complete kit; certainly anyone who spends much time in the back country should avail himself of instruction offered by the American Red Cross or mountaineering clubs and assemble a kit with sufficient materials to cover a wide range of eventualities. (See the Appendix for books and pamphlets detailing items essential for climbers and long-distance backpackers.)

At the very least the novice must be equipped to handle common ailments of the trail, some of which can be disabling even though not "serious" in a medical sense. If each hiker carries a small kit, supplies can be pooled for crises; if the group (say, a family) carries only a single kit it should be correspondingly more elaborate.

The following items constitute a *very minimum, one-man* first aid kit:

    Bandaids—Several, for minor cuts

    Gauze pads—Several, 3 inches and 4 inches square, for deep wounds with much bleeding

    Adhesive tape—a 1-inch or 2-inch roll for holding bandages in place, covering blisters, taping sprained ankles, etc.

    Salt tablets—to prevent or treat symptoms of heat exhaustion (including cramps) when sweating heavily

    Aspirin—for relieving pain and reducing fever

    Needle—for opening blisters, removing splinters

    First aid manual—one of the booklets or books listed in the Appendix, discussing diagnosis and treatment

Such a kit can cope with only the simplest problems; after a hiker has gained a bit of sad experience he will want to add many of the following:

    Moleskin or molefoam—for covering blisters

    Razor blade, single-edge—for minor surgery, cutting tape and moleskin to size, shaving hairy spots before taping

Gauze bandage—a 2-inch roll for large cuts

Butterfly bandaids—for closing cuts

Triangular bandage—for large wounds

Large compress bandage—to hold dressings in place

Halazone tablets—for treating drinking water of doubtful purity in regions where this is a problem

Antacid—for settling stomachs upset by over-exertion, unaccustomed altitude, and the cook's mistakes

Wire splint—for sprains and minor fractures

Elastic bandage—3 inches wide, for sprains, applying pressure to bleeding wounds, etc.

First aid cream—for sunburn, itches, scrapes, and diaper rash.

Antiseptic—Bactine, Zepherine Chloride, or other for cleaning minor wounds

Antihistamine—for allergic reactions to bee stings

Oil of cloves—for toothache

Darvon—for severe pain (prescription required)

Anti-diarrhetic pills—for terrible cases of the trots (prescription required)

Laxatives and/or glycerine suppositories—for prune-resistant constipation in persons congenitally suffering this affliction

Snake-bite kit—see Chapter 5

Mountain shops stock small kits containing some of the above items, weighing from 3-12 ounces, costing from about $2 to $7. The beginner should purchase one of these for a start and build from there.

EIGHT: FLASHLIGHT

Hikers often carry candles for camp use and many climbers like headlamps which free the hands; the standard "essential," however, is a two-cell flashlight.

The tool is secondarily for camp convenience and primarily to permit continued travel when caught by darkness. With the exception of small children who never will be far from parents, each person must carry his own light. (One in the party is not enough even if the group stays scrupulously together; flashlights presently on the market are notoriously undependable.) The obscurity of a forest night is total and the only safe way to navigate an unlit trail is on hands and knees, which makes for a very slow pace; off the beaten path, forget it.

Almost every year, somewhere in America, a benighted, light-less hiker keeps walking in an attempt to reach his destination, perhaps minutes away, and steps off the path, over a cliff, into eternity. And

Two popular "light kits." Left: C-cell metal-case flashlight with spare bulb and two extra zinc-carbon cells. Right: a matched pair of AA-cell Mallory flashlights (in case one fails) with spare bulb and four extra alkaline cells. Each kit supplies enough hiking light for an entire night

every year other hikers wisely give up the attempt and sit out long, shivering hours during which relatives worry and rescue parties mobilize; these hikers nevermore leave the flashlight home to save weight.

Liked very much by some (but hated by others) for ordinary hiking is the Mallory AA Compact Light, weighing complete with two AA alkaline cells only 3 ounces and costing about $2. At moderate temperatures the cells give continuous useful light (enough to walk a trail by, that is) for about 3-4 hours; a spare bulb should always be carried and at least one extra set of cells—more for hikers who habitually read in the sleeping bag. To prevent power wastage in the pack the switch should be securely taped in the off position. Though many people think the little Mallory quite rugged, others find it goes haywire at a frown; since it is unfixable except by practiced technicians, and not at all in a midnight storm, hikers may wish to take two, plus two extra sets of cells, sufficient illumination for an entire night if need be; the total weight of this very versatile package is 10 ounces and the cost about $6.

More widely popular are the bigger C and D flashlights, preferred for the larger beam and possibly greater durability—though as a commentary on contemporary manufacturing practices, no inexpensive flashlight made today is as tough and trustworthy as the products of 30-odd years ago. A typical C-size with two zinc-carbon cells plus a spare pair (roughly comparable in length of useful light to the doubled-up AA Mallory package) weighs 9 ounces, costs about $4.

Which are the best cells, the old zinc-carbon or the newer alkaline? Except for the AA size, where zinc-carbons give only about 1 hour of light at 70°F and ½ near freezing, the subject is good for debate. Certainly the alkalines are superior for prolonged use (night hiking, reading in the bag) and for cold weather. At 70°F the C alkalines provide useful light for perhaps as long as 15 continuous hours, compared to no more than 3 for zinc-carbon; at freezing the differential is greater, some 8 hours to about 1½. Other statistics could be bandied about to prove alkaline cells are the only ones worth carrying—as, indeed, many hikers believe.

Others, though, cite faults. The alkalines cost about three times more and weigh 50 percent more; even so, they still would have a clear advantage in terms of useful-light-per-ounce were that the whole story. But alkaline cells abruptly blank out when exhausted, unlike the zinc-carbons which go from bright to dim in a straight-line dwindling, warning when darkness is imminent. And once in a while alkalines have a mysterious tendency to drop dead very prematurely. And when slightly damaged they may leak gelatinous filler, losing all power and fouling the flashlight or pack.

A key matter is the definition of "useful" light. Cells that by manufacturer's standards have fallen below the minimum "useful" voltage in fact suffice for a hiker to follow a forest path. The lower the voltage accepted as "useful," the less the longevity advantage of the alkaline. More research is required.

The heavy-duty D zinc-carbon cell (Eveready Super 99) weighs the same as the standard zinc-carbon and has a 50 percent greater life-expectancy.

A thing to remember at low temperatures: cells apparently dead can be warmed to 70°F or so in pockets or by a fire (carefully—when too hot they explode) for additional life.

NINE: MAP

The kinds of maps and their use and where to obtain them are discussed in Chapter 16. Here, enough to say a party, and preferably each individual, must have a map of the area being traveled—and know how to read it!

TEN: COMPASS

The natural companion to the map is the compass, use of which also is treated in Chapter 16. The hiker should avoid the expensive precision instruments intended for complex navigation; he can do very

Representative hiking compasses. Above: *Silvara Polaris, SUUNTO Boy Scout, PASTO prismatic.* Below: *altimeter, Wilkie bearing compass*

well with a simple compass costing around $5 so long as it has a clear base with grid lines that can be aligned with a map reference line for orientation.

The *altimeter,* to climbers and cross-country roamers a routefinding aid almost as valuable as a compass, is never necessary for ordinary trail hiking but makes a nice conversation piece (and serves also as a barometer). Instruments calibrated to 12,000 or 16,000 feet in 100-foot graduations are available for about $25 and up.

OTHER (FREQUENTLY) ESSENTIALS

There is another category of items whose lack rarely imperils life or limb but can lead to major discomfort or inconvenience.

WHISTLE

Rescue authorities wish every lost hiker had a whistle, since the shrill blast carries farther than a yell and takes less effort. Parents often issue whistles to offspring—after sternly emphasizing they are *not* for scaring birds and aggravating camp neighbors but solely for emergencies.

SUNBURN PREVENTIVE

See nature boy strip to shorts and T-shirt in morning and walk meadows or desert or beach, joyously soaking up rays from the life-creating sun. By afternoon he notes his skin feels warm even when a cool wind blows, but is unaware of catastrophe until, in camp that evening, companions cry out aghast at the sight of him. Through the night he lies sleepless on his bed of pain. In morning he cannot move legs or head without wincing and to hoist pack on back is to scream and whimper. He will not again seek oneness with the solar furnace, this miserable nature boy. Next time he wants a tan he'll buy it at the drugstore.

In woodlands and poor weather a hiker is unlikely to receive more radiation than his skin readily can tolerate. But in all-day brightness, especially at high elevations and/or in snow, a burn can become a true medical emergency, requiring first aid with soothing creams and pain-killers and sedatives plus aspirin to reduce fever, possibly an unplanned layover, or in the extremity, evacuation to a hospital. Persons with dark complexions or deep tans slowly acquired can stand more sun than those with fair skins freshly exposed after months of encasement in city clothing, but not so much as they think; even black people can become gravely sunburned.

During the first bright trips of summer a hiker should cover up with shirt and trousers after no more than 2 hours or so; gradually the time of exposure can be lengthened, perhaps to a full day. The uncertain beginner should apply sunburn preventive to exposed

areas at the very start of an extended walk in the sun and every hour or so during the day and definitely *not wait* for "hot skin" or "red skin"; by then it's already 2-3 hours too late to avoid agony.

Unless a hiker spends a lot of time in snow or is supersensitive to sunlight (a condition he is likely to discover early in life) he doesn't need the clown white or glacier cream favored by climbers and skiers; any lotion or cream stocked by mountain shops or drugstores suffices. The main thing is to have *some* sunburn preventive—and to use it. Experience (a certain amount painful) tells the individual how much protection he requires.

A person whose lips are prone to burning and chapping should carry a lip salve or chapstick. (Lipstick works fine for women but not for men without risk of misunderstandings.) Similarly, people with flaring nostrils may appreciate one of the preparations available to prevent interior burns that cause runny noses.

INSECT REPELLENT

It is possible for hikers to be totally incurious about the water ouzel, golden eagle, varied thrush, and hummingbird. However, none is so stolid of soul and tough of skin as to lack a lively interest in mosquitoes, flies, gnats, no-see-ums, ticks, chiggers, and others of the afflictions visited upon man as a consequence of his fall from grace. These instruments of the Lord's anger, which drove Adam and Eve from the Garden of Eden, are considered at gruesome length in Chapter 5.

Tundra in mosquito time, forests and meadows in fly time, may force one either to cower in a tent barred at every opening or cover up completely with clothing, guarding face and neck with a *head net*.

Though no repellent answers the hiker's prayer for a zone of quiet, application can reduce the incidence of bites; the attendant cloud of wings just has to be lived with.

Still on the market and still with faithful adherents are liquid and rub-on stick repellents, dating from World War II, whose principal active ingredient is ethyl hexanediol; there are also arcane potions concocted by North Woods medicine men and transcending science. However, in the late 1950s the bug experts of the U.S. government concluded after extended research that *N, N, diethyl meta toluamide* is the most effective known chemical (safe for application to the human body) at discouraging insects.

By far the best buy is the Vietnam-born "jungle juice," a 75 percent solution of diethyl toluamide in alcohol, 2 ounces costing about 60¢. The alcohol quickly evaporates yet the odorless, invisible chemical stays and works for hours unless washed away by sweat or rain. The compound is so strong in this concentration one must be careful about use around the eyes, into which it may be carried by sweat and sting like fury. It may also irritate the tender skin of infants.

The popular Cutter cream, costing about $1.50 for 1 ounce of a 30 percent solution, is a dozen times more expensive for equivalent amounts of diethyl toluamide, a differential which raises a lot of questions. Despite the fantastic price many hikers prefer the cream because it feels good and is thought by some (not all) to last longer on hot uphill grinds where sweat is flowing free.

Aerosols and foams have more gas and package than repellent and weigh and cost too much for backpacking.

REPAIR KIT

A hiker awakes to find that during the night a goose apparently died a violent death inside the tent; then he notes the rip in his sleeping bag, exactly where he dried it by the campfire. On the trail he carelessly dumps pack from weary back, the frame hits just right (wrong) on a rock, a joint separates, and there seems no solution but to send out for a wheelbarrow. Nearing the road he lengthens stride and overstrained pants rip and modesty forbids him to enter mixed company.

These are only a few of the ills the best of gear is heir to, reasons why experienced backpackers carry some sort of repair kit. Following are typical components and examples of uses:

Cloth tape—for repairing tarps

Ripstop tape—for mending ripstop nylon parkas, sleeping bags, and tents

Thread—a spool of heavy, cotton-covered polyester for mending clothing and sewing on buttons

Needles—several in various sizes

Awl and very coarse thread—for sewing packbags, tent floors, and other tough fabrics

Safety pins—several large ones and lots of little ones for such emergencies as a zipper that goes off the trolley

Clevis pins and wires—for packframe problems (see Chapter 10)

Nylon cord—⅛-inch or so, for lashing together broken packs and sick boots

Light steel wire—for field reconstruction of gravely-wounded packframes

Pliers—for manipulating recalcitrant materials, in addition to kitchen use and expedition dentistry

TOILET KIT

A folk hero brags in an old ballad:

> I clean my teeth with river sand,
> Comb my hair with a tree,
> Wash my face whenever it rains,
> And let my wind blow free.

His gamy descendants know neither soap nor comb nor toothbrush nor handkerchief from start of trail to end, when they again submit to cleanliness, godliness, and all that.

Admittedly, years of wildland wandering are necessary to live content unsoaped and uncombed, and TV training is so ingrained most people never can blow their nose in the old way, finger against nostril, without feeling nasty. And in an age when sweating in public

is virtually a penitentiary offense, who dares spit anymore? Women especially, because of the all-pervading sexism (sugar and spice, feminine daintiness), rarely adjust to an environment of natural, healthy dirt.

Eventually the advertising-propelled steamroller of the Neatness Industry must be halted and a compromise found that allows people to pass downwind of each other without being stunned yet permits rivers to flow suds-free to unpoisoned oceans.

Granted, a clean body, even if it does not lead to a clean mind, has certain health values; the following simple toilet kit perhaps is ecologically tolerable if used in moderation:

Toothbrush and paste in carrying case

Soap or biodegradable detergent—a plain old bar, a tiny bottle of concentrated liquid solution, or Tri Soapy Towels—any of which doubles for dishwashing

Small cloth towel, reusable paper towel, or a packet of Handi-wipes

Polished-steel mirror

Comb

Handkerchief—if not for nose-blowing, for cleaning glasses, wiping sweat, binding wounds

Finally, the Eleventh Essential—toilet paper. It's amazing how many hikers, even the experienced, fail to plan ahead. The rule is, each person should carry his own roll to avoid the embarrassment of begging from others and carry enough to cope with the consequences of a cook's blunder.

NOT ESSENTIAL BUT SOMETIMES NICE

By now the beginner may well be yearning to say the hell with equipment and follow the fabled youth who gear-less, food-less, nearly naked, and supremely free, crossed the Olympic Mountains on a very cheap trip. Patience. A final few words about this and that—frills, really, but potentially adding much enjoyment.

Cameras and fishing gear are examples—for some hikers the photos or the trout make the trip.

In later chapters (namely, 17 and 19) a bit will be said about how ice ax, rope, snowshoes, and cross-country skis can expand hiking horizons.

Binoculars aid in puzzling out cross-country routes, identifying distant peaks, and gaining close-up looks at birds and animals. A good choice for backpackers is a set with a magnification of 6 or 8, weighing about ½ pound, costing about $20.

Curious about wind velocity? Air temperature? A wind meter weighs only two ounces, a pocket thermometer less.

Philosophers may leave watches at the car to symbolize renunciation of city routine and trust to sun and moon and stars to measure the passage of time, close enough for ordinary trail purposes. However, approximations can be far from the mark when heavenly guides are obscured by thick clouds; especially if boats or busses are to be met or many miles covered between dawn and dusk, a party generally takes along one or two watches. Climbers and other fanatics often carry an alarm wrist watch or lightweight alarm clock in order to be stirred from the sack at the properly-insane predawn hour.

Toys are fun. Flying a kite from a tall peak gives a feel for the sky and except for mystifying eagles causes minor disruption of the natural scene. But the use of some toys demands transport to a penal colony —such as, the pistol packed for "plinking" cans, bottles, trail signs, marmots, chipmunks, birds.

What to do when confined to tent or tarp for hours or days by storm? Sleep, of course, until that's worn out. Talk, until hostilities trend toward dangerous confrontations. Then, a deck of cards for a hot game of hearts ("Smoke it out! Smoke it out!") which harmlessly releases tensions, or a pocket chess set which does the same at a lower noise level.

A few days from the city compulsively literate folk become inordinately fascinated by lists of ingredients on food packages, a symptom of printed-word hunger. The syndrome can be controlled by carrying a paperback book, preferably with maximum words for minimum paper and slow enough going not to be run through hastily. An Ian Fleming romp fills a mere afternoon; for little more weight a single volume of Gibbon's *Decline and Fall* occupies the entirety of a 3-day blow; Durant's *History of Philosophy* has been known to outlast dozens of storms.

In bad weather and good, knowledge of wildlands is enlarged and appreciation deepened by guides to identifying birds, animals and their tracks, flowers, trees, mosses, mushrooms, rocks and minerals, planets and stars.

The scene may stimulate cravings for artistic expression with watercolor pad and paints.

Finally, a notebook and pencil stub have many uses. For leaving notes when the party is traveling in two or more sections. For keeping a trip log or diary. For composing letters to the makers of this book pointing out egregious errors and stupid blunders, objecting to provincial and freaky-veteran prejudices, and offering ideas for improving the next edition. (Speak and you shall be heard.)

Part Three
ELABORATING THE ART

16:   ROUTEFINDING

MANY hikers, even some with years of trail experience, stay on course through the back country entirely by watching the heels of the companion immediately ahead and never need any routefinding skill except that of boot identification, to avoid switching to the wrong boots at a crowded junction and following a stranger up the wrong valley.

However, there are serious disadvantages to the method. For one, the heels may disappear around a bend and be seen no more. For another, they may themselves be lost. And finally, the heel-watcher never feels independent and self-reliant.

Mastery of wilderness navigation requires considerable time and study and is far too complex for comprehensive treatment in these pages (see the Appendix). Still, even the raw novice should learn the fundamentals in order to have a better-than-average chance to reach his desired objectives and return without the assistance of a search party.

TOOLS OF THE TRADE

The basic equipment of routefinding is built into the human body; the skilled navigator, by use of eyes and ears and other senses, and

through habits of always watching where he's going and where he's been, constantly filing mental notes about landmarks, maintains a sort of internal gyroscope.

However, the "instrument" occasionally gets out of whack, particularly in fog or darkness and unfamiliar terrain, and other tools must be brought into play.

COMPASS

The compass needle always points north—right? Wrong. The needle has two ends and one points south; to avoid very gross errors the distinction between the ends must be kept in mind.

The needle always points north—right? Wrong. It does not point to *true* north—that is, the North Pole—but to *magnetic* north—that is, the North Magnetic Pole, located about a thousand miles to the south in the Canadian Arctic. The difference between true north and magnetic north is the *declination,* and unless this is known for the area being traveled the compass merely confuses the situation.

For example, the current declination in the state of Washington is approximately 22° east (that is, the needle points 22° east of true north), and in the state of Maine approximately 20° west. Some maps give the local declination but some don't, in which case the information must be obtained elsewhere before the trip. Trail navigation is not so precise the hiker must fret about declination down to the last exact several degrees. However, failing to distinguish between east and west, and thus adjusting for declination in the wrong direction, is a good way to see a lot of unexpected country.

Before use, the compass must be oriented. To do so, set it on a flat surface or hold it carefully in the hand, making sure no metallic objects are close, since their slight magnetism may distort the reading. When the needle stabilizes rotate the compass to the proper declination—that is, for Washington, until the north-pointing end of the needle points 22° east (right) of the north symbol on the dial, and for Maine, 20° west (left) of the symbol. The compass is now oriented and the north symbol on the dial indicates true north.

True north also can be found by spotting the North Star on a clear night. True south can be found with a watch: point the hour hand (standard time—not daylight saving) at the sun; true south lies halfway between the hour hand and 12.

Through experience a hiker learns to identify certain characteristics of vegetation and landscape in his home hills with certain directions—a greater frequency of cirques, avalanche paths, and snowfields on north and east slopes, or dry-habitat trees and shrubs on

Compasses oriented for various parts of America, showing declination

south and west slopes. But the lore is much less dependable than always carrying a compass and always knowing the local declination.

ALTIMETER

In areas accurately contour-mapped, knowing the elevation often permits climbers and off-trail ramblers to puzzle out their position even in thick fog. The altimeter has less utility for the average hiker but may serve such purposes as gauging progress when ascending a trail in dense forest.

An altimeter does not directly indicate distance above sealevel but rather, being in fact a barometer, measures atmospheric pressure, which varies not only with altitude but weather changes. Readings therefore are approximate; while sitting in camp a party may be informed by the altimeter it is gaining elevation at a mad rate—unsettling news, meaning air pressure is falling rapidly and a storm probably is moving in swiftly.

BINOCULARS

In cross-country travel a close-up look at distant terrain is extremely valuable in choosing a route or campsite, identifying landmarks needed for orientation, finding a skimpy trail invisible to the naked eye. Trail hikers more often use binoculars for nature study.

MAPS

Anyone who paid moderate attention to geography lessons has at least a rudimentary ability to interpret maps, sufficient for the elementary demands of trail travel; though only field practice makes perfect, mainly a novice needs to know which maps to use and where to get them.

A *planimetric* map shows lines (roads, trails, rivers, and perhaps ridge crests) and points (camps and peaks) in their horizontal relationship but without "depth." A familiar example is the gas-station highway map normally required to escape the maze of civilization.

A number of federal and state land-managing agencies, and in some parts of the nation private firms, publish planimetrics of back country. Most widely used are those from the U.S. Forest Service,

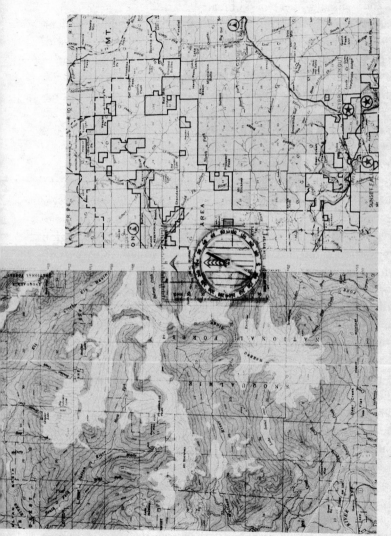

U.S. Geological Survey topographic (contour) map and U.S. Forest Service planimetric map, covering approximately the same area. Both are properly oriented by the compass.

given away or sold at ranger stations and (by mail) headquarters of National Forests. Government planimetrics generally are revised fairly frequently and provide the most up-to-date information about roads and trails and other works of man.

A *topographic* (*contour*) map contains all the data of a planimetric and in addition portrays the vertical shape of the terrain with *contour lines*—lines upon which every point is the same elevation above sealevel. With experience a hiker develops a stereoscopic vision that allows him to look at a topographic map and clearly distinguish ridges from valleys; however, even a novice can readily learn from the contours such crucial matters as whether a planned camp is at 6000 feet rather than 2000, or whether the trail ahead gains a lot of altitude or very little.

Topographic maps of the United States are produced and sold by the U.S. Geological Survey. For areas west of the Mississippi River order from U.S. Geological Survey, Federal Center, Denver, Colorado 80225; for areas east of the Mississippi, from U.S. Geological Survey, Washington, D.C. 20242. Index maps of the sheets available for individual states are free on request.

Topographic maps of Canada may be purchased from the Map Distribution Office, Department of Mines and Technical Surveys, Ottawa, Ontario. Mountain shops stock more or less extensive selections of topographic and other maps in their area.

Pictorial relief maps giving a bird's-eye view of the land and sketch maps published in guidebooks and alpine journals often offer supplementary data not found on the basic maps.

Rare is the map that merits absolute, unquestioning trust. Several factors determine the reliability. First is the reputation of the producer, the U.S. Geological Survey standing at the summit and other agencies at varying positions downward. Second is the date of the survey on which the map is based, usually noted on the sheet. Particularly in areas being heavily logged, such as multiple-use zones of U.S. National Forests and most of Canada, roads are built and trails obliterated annually and maps more than several years old may be ancient history in their delineation of the works of man. Third is the scale, since the larger the area represented by a map the smaller the amount of fine detail and normally the less painstaking the care in preparation.

Though maps are inexpensive if not free and can be easily replaced in the city, not so during a wildland storm, precisely when hikers may be wondering where the hell they are and how to get out; maps thus should be protected by being carried in a polyethylene bag—in windy, rainy weather the map can be folded for reading without removal from the bag.

VERBAL INFORMATION

Maps condense an enormous amount of data into small space but cannot tell all a hiker may wish to know about a trail—the special attractions that make it worth walking, the best season, the preferred campsites, the confusing junctions, and so on. For this there are hiking guides, more every year, until soon surely few portions of the continent will lack their full complements of "cookbooks."

Climbing guides, also madly proliferating, should not be overlooked from a sense of humility; in describing approaches to basecamps for summit ascents they often provide excellent recipes for trail trips and off-trail roamings. However, the hiker must not be tempted beyond his abilities; when a climbing guide says a route is "easy" it means easy for a trained climber, not every casual pedestrian.

Each guidebook must be checked for publication date, field-tested for accuracy, and accorded only the degree of trust it earns; among the guides regularly stocked by mountain shops are some very bad ones and even those prepared by authors of the highest integrity invariably include mistakes in observation, typographical errors, and data rendered obsolete by the passage of time and the advance of bulldozers and loggers.

Other valuable sources of verbal information are mountaineering and conservation journals, annuals, and magazines, which frequently print narratives of tempting hikes, descriptions of inviting country.

But only by talking (in person or by letter) to local folk—usually the rangers—can frequently-indispensable late news be learned—such as that spring floods took out a certain key bridge or that due to an exceptional winter the snow is still deep in meadows ordinarily now in flower.

ORIENTATION

Rescue-wearied, sleepless rangers, besieged at the height of the season by calls from worried relatives asking after overdue parties, sometimes suspect a majority of travelers abroad on the trails know their location only to within several miles and that if an exceptionally dense mist were to settle on the land for several days the backcountry mortality rate would approach that of the Black Death.

Even the hiker who intends never to stray—on purpose—from well-beaten paths must learn the basics of orientation (determining present position in relation to surroundings) and navigation (getting from one known point to another); getting from one unknown point to another is called "being lost" and requires no elaboration beyond that in Chapter 6.

Any honest veteran will admit that more than once he has been, if not lost, terribly confused, and has felt at least early symptoms of the overpowering unreason, the panic, caused by total disorientation. Once or twice is enough; the mark of the veteran is that whenever he walks a few minutes without knowing exactly where he is, legs automatically halt, suspicious eyes rove. And if a sure sense of direction does not come quickly he pauses for orientation. The following brief outline is the merest introduction to the most elementary techniques of a complex science-art.

The first step is to *orient the map,* most easily done by lining up known landmarks with their symbols on the sheet. This failing, as in unfamiliar country, the compass is brought out: Spread the map flat and lay the compass on the sheet with dial north aligned with the true north arrow of the map (almost invariably true north is the top of the map). Rotate map and compass as a unit until the needle points the correct number of degrees east or west of dial north, in accordance with local declination. Compass and map are now oriented.

The next step is to *orient the hiker.* If he *knows the precise point* of his present location (river crossing, trail junction, mountain summit), any visible feature (peak, pass, valley) can be identified by placing a stick (or other straightedge) on the map touching the known point, aiming the stick at the visible feature, and examining the map to see what features are intersected by the stick. Similarly, if the hiker wants to find the position of an invisible feature (hidden by trees or fog), he places the stick on the map to intersect his known point and the invisible feature, which then lies in the direction indicated by the stick.

Orientation is more complicated when the hiker *knows only he is somewhere on a certain line* (trail, river, ridge). He must be able to identify at least one distant feature—say, Bald Mountain. A simple procedure, not as craftsmanlike as the methods of the masters, is to place the compass on the map with the compass center exactly atop the symbol for Bald Mountain, orient map and compass as a unit, place the stick on the compass center and point it at Bald Mountain. The intersection of the stick with the known line (trail, river, ridge) is the present location—*approximately.* A second distant feature is desirable for verification. Comparison of the surroundings with the map determines if the results are reasonable.

When a hiker *knows only he is in a certain area* (perhaps on one of several possible trails, rivers, or ridges) at least two distant features must be identified and the technique is beyond the elementary.

And if no distant features are visible, as in fog or deep forest? Or none can be positively identified? Time then for advanced navigation methods beyond the scope of this book. Either that or sit down and wait for the search party, as discussed in Chapter 6.

STAYING ON COURSE

The beginner may say, "I don't need to bother about all this route-finding stuff because I'm always going to stick to trails." Well and good—if he can. But sticking to the trail, and finding it in the first place, isn't invariably a cinch.

For openers, in multiple-use public lands of the United States and the entirety of Canada outside National Parks the trailheads often lie amid a maze of logging roads, either completely unsigned or, in some National Forests, marked only by cryptic numbers meaningless without the proper Forest Service map. Stops may be necessary at junctions to consult the map and guidebook, which perhaps are obsolete because of new roads built and old ones abandoned. At length finding the presumed start of the wanted trail a party may see naught but a chaos of logging slash, or perhaps several paths heading in different directions, and no signs. Again map and compass may be required even before leaving the road, and possibly short scouting trips.

Once his boots are pounding a broad, well-maintained, heavily-used trail usually the hiker must only avoid walking with eyes steadily on the path underfoot and failing to see a junction and hours later having to ask a stranger, "Pardon me, but do you know where I am?" Similarly, ground-watchers have been known to walk off the end of a switchback and without a pause plunge bravely forward into brush.

Many otherwise distinct trails require frequent reference to the map because they lack signs at junctions, or have signs so mauled by bears, chewed by porcupines, or shot up and chopped by idiots to be past deciphering. At any dubious junction the party should assemble, particularly if the rearguard members are inexperienced or are notorious, given two choices, for instinctively taking the wrong one.

Traveling old, little-used trails is more akin to cross-country roaming than trail-following. On some the tread periodically vanishes in blowdowns, meadows, marshes, and rocks, on others frequently divides and redivides into myriad tracks beaten by deer, elk, goats, sheep, or cattle. There may be blazes on trees—but also "lost-man blazes" made by falling trees and rocks (and lost hikers). There may be cairns or ribbons—helpful if placed by people who knew where they were going. Often a hiker can steer through the maze by figuring

I KNOW THE BOOK SEZ... "KEEP THE PARTY CLOSE TOGETHER" BUT THIS IS — RIDICULOUS

where he would have built the trail if it had been his job. The second and third in line should pay as much attention to routefinding as the leader, who in forest may not see a blaze or sawn log off to one side and on a fogswept ridge fail to note diverging branches of the crest.

When a path disappears and does not immediately resume the party should *stop*. The temptation is to forge straight ahead, hoping to pick up the way eventually, but if the trail turns sharply in the missing section every forward step leads farther into nowhere. With the party halted and assembled, two or three members (more just muddle matters) should fan out and scout for tread, blazes, sawn logs, and the like, staying in communication so any of them can sound the recall; the scout who goes beyond intelligible voice range perhaps enjoys his solo exploration but may return to fuming companions.

Several rules are important when traveling sketchy trails and wandering away from trails, particularly in poor weather. *Keep the party together,* every member in sight or sound of others at all times.

Maintain constant orientation, at every step observing close and distant landmarks, periodically relating them to the map.

Since half the fun is getting home, prepare for the return by noting prominent boulders and trees, cliffs and creeks. *Look over the shoulder* frequently to see landmarks as they will appear on the return. If terrain is complicated or visibility limited, mark the route at critical points with toilet paper or crepe paper draped on trees or shrubs. Plastic ribbons are more durable but *should not be used unless faith-*

fully removed later on; toilet paper disintegrates in the first rain and crepe paper in the second but plastic is a semipermanent and most obnoxious addition to the landscape.

A final rule: a good leader should take it upon himself to train less-experienced party members in routefinding—especially wives and children who otherwise may never progress past heel-watching.

Enough. Already the discussion has far exceeded proper limits of the novice.

But everybody is a beginner sometime and the only way to master wilderness navigation is doing it. By maintaining constant orientation, probing cautiously, invariably keeping open the line of safe retreat, inexperienced hikers can venture some distance into uncertainty without unreasonable risk. Yet always should be remembered how unpleasant it is, and potentially fatal, to be lost in wildlands.

17:

WHEN THE WAY GROWS ROUGH

THE elements of walking and camping are properly mastered on well-marked, well-manicured trails; indeed, the majority of hikers, to minimize danger and nastiness, choose never to stray from the comparative friendliness of turnpike terrain. They feel no need to prove their bravery and fortitude, which they do every workday driving freeways and breathing city air, and are happy to forego high adventure in exchange for peaceful enjoyment of forests and waterfalls and flower gardens.

Others, though, having put a few hundred miles on their boots, are called so loud and clear by wildness, are compelled so urgently by an inner force stronger than reason, they climb above trails into brush, up rocks and snows, to tall summits. Such restless souls must look elsewhere than these pages for instruction; the Appendix suggests places to start, particularly *Mountaineering: The Freedom of the Hills*.

Between the choices of easy-trail hiker and wilderness mountaineer is the subject of this chapter—a middle way that departs the beaten track but stops well short of "technical climbing."

Actually, no hiker is so puristic he will not occasionally abandon the security of tread to wander gently through a meadow valley, up a broad ridge, over an open desert, along a wave-washed beach. But the more ambitious, studying maps, see how little wildland is traversed by trails—they wonder about all those other valleys and ridges, peaks and basins, streams and lakes. Thus they graduate from trail-pounder to cross-country rambler and find adventure at its best.

Without ever leaving trails a hiker may be challenged to something more than hands-in-pockets walking. In maritime mountain ranges of the Northwest even turnpikes are completely snow-free only a few weeks of summer; ability to cross a lingering snow patch safely can make the difference between continuing to the planned destination or turning back disappointed. Similarly, trails frequently come to river banks and quit, no bridge or footlog leading to a resumption of tread on the far side; the hiker must either ford or go home. And a good many paths, including some very popular ones, have been built solely by boots and hooves and nary a stick of dynamite and are interrupted by short sections of rock that require use of hands as well as feet.

Let it be sternly stressed that rough country is not for everybody and surely not for the beginner; when the next step can be taken only at the risk of becoming a statistic in the annual report of the local mountain rescue organization, the mandatory decision is: *don't take it, turn back.*

Further, the act of reading this chapter does not give automatic certification as a fully-educated wildland rover; for that one should seek personal tutoring from veterans, best done by joining an outdoor club.

However, by adding a few items of equipment to his outfit and learning a few simple techniques a hiker who has served his trail apprenticeship can greatly increase his safe hiking range. These tools and techniques will not be described here in detail, but rather introduced, their potential suggested, and the interested reader referred elsewhere for more information.

ICE AX AND ROPE

A hiker may feel presumptuous even to think about carrying ice ax and rope, traditional symbols of the climber, yet through their use he frequently can pass otherwise dangerous obstacles with no more risk than walking a broad trail. So what if somebody does accuse him of dressing up for a masquerade? It's his trip, his fun, his neck.

ICE AX

The ax at work is discussed in following sections; here, several remarks about the instrument itself.

The ice ax is a dangerous weapon; one was used to assassinate Leon Trotsky in his Mexico City hideout and others have accidentally wounded and killed climbers on many a mountain. Fresh from the shop the pick and spike are dagger-like and the adze razor-like, this for high alpine needs; the hiker's first action after purchase should be to dull everything on a grinding wheel. Even then the ax retains considerable potential for damage and always should be handled with care not to inflict injury on companions or self.

The various refinements of fancy models have no utility for the hiker, who can do very well with the simplest and least expensive. The shaft should be just long enough that with carrying arm hanging loose, hand gripping ax head, the spike firmly contacts the ground; however, length isn't too critical and several inches this way or that make no appreciable difference.

If a hiker is sensitive to the sneering and gawking occasioned by an ice ax miles from the nearest snow—even though, as noted below, the value is not limited to snow and indeed is very great on slippery driftwood of an ocean beach—he may prefer a steel-tipped cane that does much (but not all) the work of an ax and with less threat from errant metal.

The alpenstock still cherished by a scattering of oldtimers serves some of the same purposes, as does a bamboo staff or a sturdy stick picked up in the forest and discarded when no longer wanted.

ROPE

A snow patch, a steep bit of rock, a footlog, a cliff of slick grass, may bother some members of the party not at all but call upon others to step near or over the line of mortal peril. The weeping and the whining, the silent fear frozen into a face, must never be ignored by the strong, the brave, the sure-footed. By tying a rope to the frightened and thus endangered child, wife, or weary friend they often can remove the risk of tragedy from what is, after all, supposedly a pleasure trip. The cost? A few extra minutes—nothing compared to the time spent on a rescue, a funeral.

Even if the risk is merely imagined, the terror is real, and except in small, infrequent, controlled doses the average hiker gets no fun from terror.

Unlike the climbing rope the "hiking rope" is intended strictly for short stretches where the only falls possible would develop relatively minor forces. A good choice is 60 feet of 5/16-inch nylon weighing 1¾ pounds, light enough to be carried without excessive complaint. The breaking strength is around 2800 pounds, which may sound like overkill, but keeping in mind that a knot reduces the effective strength by as much as half, and that a 150-pound person in a free fall of 10 feet gains a kinetic energy of 1500 foot-pounds, really is about the safe minimum.

Totally lacking any notion of how climbers tie into a rope and establish belays a hiker can fumble up some way to attach the rope securely to the waist of a companion and find a solid stance for safeguarding his passage. Obviously the job can be done better with knowledge of knot-tying and rope-handling; for hiking (but not climbing) purposes enough can be learned from books—see the Appendix.

WALKING ROUGH GROUND

When the route leaves trail for untracked forest, steep meadow, talus or scree or moraine, rock slabs, brush, marsh, or snow, the hiker accustomed to having decisions made for him by established tread tends to stop after each and every step to plan the next; the pace slows to a creep and the sun goes down with the desired camp still hours away.

The essential difference between trail-tramping and cross-country rambling is the hiker must constantly be looking and thinking ahead, or *hiking with the eyes,* a three-part process: periodically he halts momentarily to survey the area and choose the broad line of approach; while moving he scans the terrain a dozen yards in front to pick the easiest going; simultaneously he examines the ground of his next several steps. With practice the long-, medium-, and close-range studies fall into an automatic routine and the pace is almost as fast and rhythmic as on a trail.

To reveal a secret about the ice ax: even a climber uses it maybe 1 percent of the time for chopping steps in ice, perhaps 9 percent for security on snow, and 90 percent purely as a walking stick. Old climbers are accused of carrying axes on trails and beaches out of snobbery, so they will not be mistaken for mere hikers, but in truth, take away the old climber's ax and he walks off-balance, pawing the air with his empty ax hand, falling down a lot.

On any steep and/or slippery terrain, not just snow but also wet heather, mud, moraines and talus, stream beds, footlogs, brush, and driftwood, the ice ax (or cane, staff, or stick) *provides a third leg.* If a foot slips weight can be shifted to the ax while recovery is made. To put it another way, the ax is an arm extension that allows use of one or both hands in maintaining stability.

CROSSING STREAMS

A trail is plainly shown on the map, clearly signed at the parking lot, and obviously maintained regularly. Does this not mean the land-managing agency—U.S. Forest Service, National Park Service, or whatever—officially certifies every step of the way is certain and safe?

No. Those blue lines on the map remain always the same but not the streams they symbolize. Maps, guidebooks, rangers cannot pro-

vide money-back guarantees that any particular blue line, though usually a peaceful dribble easily stepped across on boulders, may not become, however briefly, a hell-roaring torrent. During a recent several-year period more hikers were killed in the North Cascades by drowning—swept away while fording or after slipping from footlogs —than by falls from cliffs, falling rock, avalanches, hypothermia, and all other wildland hazards combined—and most were on "turnpikes."

The first lesson about stream crossings: a passage simple last week and simple next week may be fatal today. Whenever a solid bridge is lacking—and in back country bridges often are the exception rather than the rule—the trail may be absolutely blocked for hours or days.

In the absence of a bridge perhaps there is a footlog. Is it wide, dry, and level? Splendid. Or is it narrow, steeply tilted, slippery with spray? Beware. A helping hand may be enough to steady a small child or nervous friend; a rope tied to the waist of the insecure body and anchored from the bank will not prevent a fall but may permit a rescue. The wisest decision may be to give up the trip and try again later in the summer, when the log is not water-drenched, the flood has diminished and the consequences of a tumble are not so drastic, or the trail crew has arrived and felled a bigger tree.

With footlog lacking at the trail crossing and none to be found by

searching upstream and down, the trip is not necessarily deadended. Quite broad and deep waters can be waded safely if not excessively rapid and cold—but probably not by the beginner who has yet to learn what "excessively" means. Gently-flowing, relatively-warm streams of lowlands and deserts are no problem when shallow; even when deep often they are easily swum, rafting the pack on an air mattress. But mountain torrents are something else and any depth greater than a foot requires thought. Swift water only knee-deep may boil above the waist, half-floating the body; unweighted feet cannot grip the bed and with the shift of a boulder underfoot the hiker suddenly becomes a swimmer—except swimming is impossible in turbulent foam composed equally of water and air. Drowning and battering aside, a person's life-expectancy submerged in snowmelt is a matter of minutes.

Fording big, rough rivers is as complex and hazardous as ascending cliffs and traversing glaciers and is far beyond the proper ambitions of the novice. However, by starting with little creeks, gradually moving to larger ones, studying and practicing, he can in time handle rather substantial waters. To begin the education following are several rules not universally applicable but often helpful:

Generally cross not at the narrowest point, where kinetic energy is concentrated, but at the widest. Up to a point, choose the slow and deep water in preference to the shallow and fast. On occasion, pitch camp by the stream and cross in morning; snow-fed rivers are usually lower after a cool night than at the end of a scorching day; similarly, the flash flood from a cloudburst ordinarily subsides in hours.

Before any crossing not completely worry-free (tricky footlogs as well as fords) release the waist strap of the pack so the load can be turned loose instantly; better to splash around later trying to retrieve the pack than be dragged under by its weight.

Wear short pants or in the right company no pants. If the bed is soft sand or rounded boulders and the water not too cold, barefoot wading is delightful; however, wear boots when rocks are sharp, footing treacherous, or water so icy bare feet might lose sensation. Wet feet on the succeeding trail can be avoided by taking off socks, wading in boots alone, and on the far bank dumping out water and donning the dry socks. Boots can be kept completely dry by wading in heavy socks, adequate for intermediate situations, or in tennis shoes carried for the purpose.

In rapids face upstream and move sideways, using the ice ax—or stout stick—as a third leg. Move each foot separately and place it securely, remembering the sometimes tendency of boulders to depart downstream at the slightest excuse.

The point has been belabored sufficiently that a party in doubt must give up the attempt, turn back. However, a ford unquestionably safe for a large adult may surpass the unaided capacity of a smaller one or a little child. In such case the strong can accompany the weak on the crossing to provide support.

Rigging a handline generally is a mistake since the give of the rope is certain betrayal in time of real need. When more than convoy-type security is wanted the hiking rope is better tied to the forder's waist, an anchor on shore ensuring against his being swept away—all the way away, that is, the pendulum swing to shore remaining to be endured.

ROCK SCRAMBLING

Another scary subject is raised—to be quickly dropped, and without revealing the magic formula by which any trail-tramper can step

into a telephone booth and emerge moments later as a human fly. For the sake of family and friends, rangers and rescue groups, and his own tender flesh and brittle bones a hiker must quit, go back, seek another route or switch to another destination when confronted by steep rock from which a fall would be damaging. Let him keep in mind that the body, with hands and eyes at the upper end, blind and clumsy feet at the lower, is much better designed for going up cliffs than down; a common cause of scrambling tragedies is the daring novice managing to get high on a wall, finding he cannot proceed upward, and then

finding he cannot descend what he has climbed; weariness, panic, and gravity do the rest.

However, many trails never improved by blasting powder and many off-trail routes include brief sections of rock that seem dangerous but really are not, or at least no more so than merging from an on-ramp into freeway traffic. With practice, and always with caution, a hiker can negotiate short rock steps in ease and security by observing the fundamentals of what mountaineers call "balance climbing."

Keep body weight directly over the feet by standing erect. Legs do the work, just as in ordinary hiking. Hands are not for pulling the body up but for gripping holds that serve as anchors in case a foot slips. Leaning into the slope in quest of false security causes body weight to thrust the feet sideways, slipping off holds or breaking them out.

Support the body always by three points. At every moment be connected to the slope by two hands and a foot or two feet and a hand. Thus, if a hold fails, two points of connection to the slope remain.

Test holds. Before trusting a foothold with the body weight, or a handhold as an anchor, make sure it is firmly attached to the mountain.

Move smoothly. Smooth transference of body weight puts minimum stress on holds. A rhythmic pace (the rest step described in Chapter 1) maintains a reserve of strength for surprises and is conducive to the proper mental composure. A jerky pace breaks holds, sets lungs to gasping and heart to pounding, and leads to doubt and thence to fear and panic.

Climb with the eyes. Constantly look ahead to spot the easiest line of progress, to study holds and plan the next sequence of moves, and to avoid climbing into traps.

To repeat with emphasis, these expressions of common sense do not amount to a mystical incantation, are nothing but words on a piece of paper until they become reflexive in mind and muscle through practice.

Inevitably some hikers scramble better than others. In a party of mixed experience and ability the hiking rope can eliminate terror and tears from short stretches of steep rock (or heather or mud)—a strong and confident scrambler belays from the top, the inexperienced or weary or tiny companion is protected from a fall by the rope tied around his waist and perhaps on occasion (especially in the case of a small child) given a helpful pull to get up a section of thin holds. For reasons stated earlier, the rope should *not* be used as a handline.

Fewer hikers are endangered, injured, and killed by falling from mountains than by being fallen upon, and the most frequent menace is not natural disintegration. Never, ever, should a hiker roll boulders down a slope or throw them into an abyss for the thrill of it—how is he to know who may be below? Never, ever, should a hiker scramble carelessly, blithely loosing barrages. If despite caution he dislodges a rock and there is the slightest possibility people are below, he must immediately sound the alarm by shouting "ROCK! ROCK! ROCK!" In steep terrain with a considerable human population, on trails and off, the hiker must at all times be alert for attacks from above, watching and listening, and when appropriate, shouting, cursing, threatening.

SNOW TRAVEL

Snow is full of tricks. In winter and spring it avalanches. Undermined by streams it conceals pits to trap the unwary. When steep it provides speedy toboggan runs ending bloodily in boulders, trees, cliffs. Being cold and wet it is an ideal agent for hypothermia. All and all, broadcasting an invitation to "Come have fun in the snow!" would be tantamount to mass murder. The novice who reads the few words here, rushes to a mountain shop to buy ax and rope, and attempts a full-scale invasion of the white wilderness is on the way to becoming a statistic. Though books noted in the Appendix offer more information, most emphatically the subject should be studied under the tutelage of experienced companions, as through joining an outdoor club.

The rewards are worth the effort. By mastering certain basic techniques a hiker can enormously enlarge his realm of safe wan-

dering, add months to his high-country hiking season, feel the exhilaration of walking on top of brush instead of fighting through it, and pretty much get away from the madding crowds.

As the beginner will be taught in any course of instruction, the most important tools of snow travel actually are the boots, used to kick platforms, and the most important technique is standing erect so boots are not thrust sideways by body weight, breaking out the platforms or slipping off them. The ice ax, however, serving as a cane—a third leg—is the tool that gives the stability and thus the confidence necessary to stand erect and that provides an anchor when a foot skids, stopping most slides before they start and further reinforcing confidence—and on snow having confidence is more than half the battle.

Alpenstock, cane, staff, or stick also can act as a third leg. The ice ax, though, has a further value in putting on the brakes once a slide has begun. *Self-arrest,* where a person digs ax pick into slope, presses chest against shaft to give the pick purchase, and spreads legs and digs in toes, will not be elaborated here. Suffice to say the technique must be learned by anyone intending to do much snow hiking—and cannot be learned from books but only by intensive practice under expert instruction.

The hiking rope has uses on snow when some members of the party are experienced and sure-footed and others are not. For example, a father with a background in climbing usually can safely convoy a small child over a snowpatch hand in hand. But if he needs both hands for ice ax control lest he himself slip, he does better to tie the rope to his waist and that of the kid. And if he has any doubts about being able to arrest a joint slide, the mother should stand on safe ground, belaying the child with the rope, while the father does convoy duty. (Or mother and father may exchange the roles specified.)

ROUGH ROADS TO FREEDOM

There are hazards in snow travel, rock-scrambling, river-fording, off-trail wandering generally, rough-country exploring particularly. Many dangers are more apparent than real and vanish like goblins in the light of experience. While gaining the experience a hiker discovers unsuspected dangers and how to avoid some, and develops the wisdom and humility to turn back when faced by the others. With patience and caution and imagination he can, if he so wishes, escape the confines of trails, become a cross-country rambler, and to a very considerable extent enjoy what mountaineers call "the freedom of the hills."

18:	**SUFFER THE LITTLE CHILDREN**

WE USED to go hiking all the time, but then we had the kids."

"We'd like to take the kids hiking with us, but they're too young."

"We'd like to start hiking, and will when the kids are bigger."

Such sentiments often are expressed by parents: experienced back-packers who consider wildlands too brutal for young innocents, or else that coping with children on the trail is too complicated; beginning hikers who still find the back country somewhat spooky; car-campers who want to venture away from roads but don't quite dare.

Let it be said at the outset that no editorial position is taken on the proper way to run a family. If the father wants to go hiking with friends and leave wife and kids home, and they don't mind, well and good. Parents with rotten kids may find occasional vacations from them essential to preservation of sanity—the rotten kids, parked with grandparents, may enjoy the vacation from rotten parents. In no holy book is it written that a family always must go everywhere together; indeed, if the wife abhors hiking the marriage is not enhanced by compelling her to undergo agony—which any competent wife invari-ably can force her husband to share.

No—this is not a homily on family living. The sole intent is to suggest to beginning hikers, and experienced hikers who are begin-

310

ners as parents, how they may take the children along with fun and games for all.

Certainly many parents so desire. Commonly they wish to raise their offspring in their own life pattern. And much of the pleasure of parenthood is watching young ones discover the wide, wide world. Finally, on long backpacks often a mother can be found off in the woods, weeping, and when asked what's wrong wails "I miss my baby!"

And what about the children's desires? At a certain age when momma leaves them overnight they fear she has abandoned them forever. Somewhat older, they protest the bitter injustice of their folks going off without them to wonderful secret places, they agitate for Children's Lib, full membership in the family, share and share alike.

No brief is made here for the wisdom or necessity of being totally child-centered; people do not give up all their rights, become third-class citizens, in changing status from "man and woman" to "daddy and momma." However, if they *want* to take the kids hiking, they *can*.

Almost invariably worries are exaggerated. Children are amazingly tough little beasts, usually better able than city-pampered adults to withstand trail rigors. (Except bugs, which eat tender-skinned youngsters alive, requiring either special protection or avoidance of horridly buggy areas and seasons.) Moreover, ordinarily they are accustomed to a totalitarian regime, to being forced into unfamiliar situations (after all, nearly everything in the world is unfamiliar to them), and stoically put up with a lot of guff. (Not so in extreme cases of the "permissive parent," but brats are a couple other books.) If introduced to trails early they probably will grow up to be loyal citizens of the wild country—and better people for it and better friends of the Earth (editorial opinion).

For many families the question of leaving kids home is academic. No free babysitters, such as grandparents, are available, and no money for a hired babysitter; either the kids go along or nobody goes—or only the father, which is grossly unfair if the mother is a devout wild-lander. (The fair alternative, if the father is capable of babysitting, is for parents to take turns staying home.)

Hiking and backpacking with children is a special subdivision of the sport, but not so complicated as some parents make it. The proper gear solves most problems, as already discussed—boots in Chapter 8, packs in Chapter 10, and sleeping bags in Chapter 11. That, of course, brings up another problem which looms especially large in a large family—the cost of equipping children while growing, and growing, and *out*growing. To re-emphasize a point previously made, the budget can quickly be busted unless recourse is made to thrift shops and hand-me-downs among several families of friends.

One bit more about equipment. Poorly-fitting boots and badly-adjusted packs give a child just cause for complaint and he can turn any such inadequacy of gear into evidence of a plot to destroy him. Protests therefore must be heeded. For example, hurt feet require instant attention, applying moleskin at the first redness lest a real blister develop and momma and daddy be haled into Children's Court as unfit parents.

So much for prelude. Each family must invent its own formula, but following pages offer a mixed bag of hopefully-helpful hints drawn from the memories of real-life backpacking families—mainly my own and several others we know well, leavened with observations of the behavior of strangers encountered on the trail and comments by a number of parents and experienced ex-kids.

TAKING IT EASY

The capacity of the average child to endure hardship is incredible. The prime examples are derived from family annals of "Little League" parents who recite with competitive pride that Junior carried a 12-pound pack 10 miles when only 4, conquered Tiger Tooth Peak at 7, and climbed all the 14,000-foot mountains of the nation before puberty. Aside from being a pain in the neck to other parents to whom they brag, the pace-forcers take a risk; Junior may grow up to be a famous mountain climber but there is a 50-50 chance that once old enough to escape the lash he'll turn in his boots and pack on a surfboard.

However, Junior's exploits demonstrate that children can perform prodigies of exertion beyond the belief of overprotective parents, and normally with no physical harm. (Needless to say, strength and hardiness vary widely; doubts should be resolved by consulting the family doctor.)

Nevertheless, a child, just as an adult, gains most pleasure operating below maximum potential. Maybe he *can* cover 6 miles in a day but hate it, yet enjoy 3 miles. Trips with kids generally, therefore, should be shorter than for adults alone, and the pace slower. How much shorter? How much slower? The only way for a family to find out is on the trails; the rule is, take it easy at first, and as muscles and ambitions grow, still keep the effort not only within the *physical* limits but the *fun* limits.

APPLIED CHILD PSYCHOLOGY

Why is it a child can dash full tilt around a playground for hours, yet collapse on the trail in minutes, whimpering and complaining? Every child is a natural malingerer—it's the only defense against adult tyranny—but the deeper explanation is motivation. The kid is impelled in the playground marathon by a constant succession of im-

mediate goals—racing Patty to the swing, chasing Ira up the monkey bars, Indian-wrestling Tommy, teeter-tottering with Peggy—meaningful goals, kids' goals.

But trail goals are adult goals, incomprehensible or impossibly remote. Describing wonders of the day's destination—the creek to play in, the boulders to climb, the special pudding for dessert—may stir interest, but when not instantly attained the whining questions arise,

313

"Are we almost there? Why aren't we there? Why do we have to go there?" What use telling a little child camp is only an hour away—when he doesn't know what an hour is? Seeing eternal suffering ahead, no fun, he despairs and collapses. At which point momma may cry, "You poor dear!" and daddy may find a smug lump perched on his shoulders. Even very tiny kids quickly become adroit at pulling this fraud.

To keep the poor dears happy and off daddy's back, parents must become equally crafty, and the secret lies in thinking as kids do—from minute to minute, step to step—and seeking or arranging a con-

stant sequence of goals, forgetting the rules for covering ground efficiently. The family group may walk 10 or 15 minutes and rest 15 or 20. Or take a dozen steps and pause, a dozen steps more and pause again. This latter pace, of course, is cruelly painful to heavily-burdened adults. The father therefore may pile most of the gear on his back and stagger steadily to camp, leaving lightly-loaded mother to dawdle with the babe. Otherwise, say spokeswomen for Mothers' Lib, the father should alternate in the dawdling duty.

The stops and pauses are occasioned less by needs for rest than by happening upon things that make satisfying kids' goals. Water is an unfailing delight; at an age when gorgeous panoramas mean nothing a child never tires of tossing pebbles in a pond, floating sticks down a stream, building castles in a sand bar, mucking around in a mud puddle. Perhaps he spots a beetle and is fascinated by watching it creep; parents should then join the watching—perhaps suddenly to remember how once they too loved beetles and ants and ladybugs. And so with flowers and frogs, mushrooms and spider webs, a festoon of moss and a chittering chipmunk. (But drop the pack if the session promises to be long!)

Be alert to point out a hawk circling high in the sky, a towering cloud that looks like a dog—a knight—a witch—Aunt Prunella. Teach the mysteries and solemnities of the wildland—that the trail lies on the slopes of a volcano and all these rocks were once hot as fire, that the valley below once was full of ice. Answer questions— "Will the volcano blow up while we're here, Daddy? Will the glacier come back and cover us up tonight?"

When nature fails to offer continuity of motivation, stage an impromptu party by bringing from the pack a piece of candy, a favorite toy; chewing a chunk of toffee while playing with cars in trail dust is a worthy goal.

Devices of this sort suffice on leisurely trips. However, with darkness or storm approaching, or for other reasons, sometimes it is necessary to keep a kid purely and steadily walking. Adults then must dip into another bag of tricks to relieve boredom while maintaining motion.

Perhaps promise a party at the very next creek or viewpoint, with animal crackers and root beer, and thus gain 10 or so minutes of constant advance. In the interim, a bit of trail candy usually is good for a few more steps.

Try games. Announce the family is a train and have locomotive father and caboose mother and freight-car and mail-car children make appropriate locomotive and caboose and etcetera sounds. (But let kids call their own game—one time a little boy who always before had loved to play train continued glum; that particular day he didn't want to be part of the family train yet became perfectly happy when permitted to be a Pepsi Cola truck.)

Tell stories from folk literature, the family past. Or start a story and have each hiker add an episode in turn. Or extract a story by ask-

ing a series of questions—one time a boy walked most of a day without complaint while describing the dinosaurs he was going to invite to his birthday, and those he was not, and the foods he would serve and the games they would play.

Try singing. One time a father was at the bottom of a nettle patch, awaiting his wife and 3-year-old daughter, and was alarmed to hear the girl scream as she was attacked by vicious bushes, and was alarmed further when strange sounds arose from the greenery—until he recognized the child's voice, and the mother's, raised in song: "I'm Popeye the Sailor Man, *toot toot*!"

In such ways do parents try to outwit their offspring. But the wily child fights back. One time a father and mother patiently cajoled their 3-year-old daughter 3 miles upward from a camp beside the Stehekin River nearly to Cascade Pass, and turned back in the snow when the girl had a tantrum, apparently from approaching exhaustion. On the descent the poor babe tottered, stumbled, fell, and daddy carried her the last mile, fearing for the health of the comatose little darling. And immediately on reaching camp Sleeping Beauty awoke and for hours on into darkness splashed in a river pool, gathered pretty rocks and beautiful sticks, and when the put-upon parents at last sought to stuff her in a sleeping bag, complained "I'm not tired!"

Similarly, parents often have felt pangs of conscience about pushing the family to a highland camp—and once there the destroyed children have miraculously revived and spent hours running up a snowbank and sliding down. (Snow, incidentally, is even better than mud; any camp with a snowbank makes a perfect holiday.)

So goes the psychological warfare between kids and folks, the struggle between long-range goals of adults and short-range goals of children. When the conflict is conducted in a spirit of love and compromise both sides win, everybody has fun. In later years the trails and camps may well be remembered as the best of times—the moments when the family was closest.

Obviously, "taking it easy" means one thing with infants and another with rugged teenyboppers, and obviously each family and its trail adventures are unique. However, the following chronological discussion of hiking with children from babyhood through adolescence, though based on the experience of a few families, suggests the possibilities.

BABIES

A babe in arms can be taken on roadside picnics and car camps and with proper protection from sun and wind and mosquitoes be perfectly comfortable. To be sure, an infant derives little if any pleasure from the outing but the parents do, and in the process gain confidence for more ambitious ventures.

At 3 months or so they can stow the baby in a child-carrier pack (see Chapter 10) and on suitably mild days go for short or long walks, hauling the appropriate paraphernalia of diapers and bottles. Babies generally enjoy the lulling bounce and spend most of the time sleeping; in fact, if colicky they sleep better on the trail than in a crib. Care is of course required to bundle the baby warmly, shade eyes from glaring sun, protect delicate skin from sunburn and insects. Somewhere around 6 months a child starts to take a positive interest in wildland attractions, dabbling fingers in sand, picking up pebbles, watching ants.

When does backpacking begin? So far as the baby is concerned, from 3 or so months on he can be just as happy in a back-country camp as at home. The problem is the parents—or more specifically, parents with their first child, still worried about breaking it. The initial trials should be relatively short so that if something goes wrong —a sudden storm or one of those alarming high fevers infants develop for no apparent reason and without warning—a quick retreat can be made to car and home. Though an adult party usually considers a camp only a mile or two from the road hardly worth the trouble of backpacking, this much distance is enough to reduce the population density to a fraction of that in automobile campgrounds, and on such short trips parents learn how much special gear is needed —bottles, dried milk or formula, strained foods, teething biscuits, baby aspirin, many changes of clothing, and the like.

(Note: up to about 12 months a baby's respiratory system cannot adjust readily to major changes in elevation; for example, if his home is at sealevel, during extended stays at camps above 7000 feet or so, as in the High Sierra and Wind River Range, he may fuss continuously.)

Actually, a child is easier to carry at 1-1½ and younger than later on, weighing and wiggling less and—being always on the back—not presenting the problems a toddler does on muddy or rocky trails. However, with one parent hauling the babe and thus not much else, the other must pack most of the gear, and this limits the length of a hike.

Still, after a few overnights the family may be ready for deeper probes into wilderness—5 or 7 miles—and longer trips—several days or a week, with a basecamp chosen for its immediate attractions and the variety of possible day hikes and close enough to the car for the father to fetch more food and diapers in mid-trip.

Thus far the discussion has assumed an only child. In a larger family with children widely spaced, backpacking a baby can be much easier, the older siblings helping. But two children only a year or two apart (or in the extreme case, twins) may be entirely too formidable on the trail until both are well past babyhood; parents probably had best give up extended backpacks the first 2 or 3 years and (lacking complacent grandparents) take turns babysitting.

TODDLERS

The awkward age for backpacking is roughly 2 to 4, when a child usually is too much of a load to be carried any great distance yet can't walk very fast or far. Also he has developed definite notions of how the world should be operated, has a loud wail and not the slightest sympathy with adult goals. Frequently his attachment to momma is so firm that more than momentary separation is simply not tolerated,

making it hard for daddy to be an effective babysitter or to share dawdling duty on the trail.

Hiking with a toddler demands the utmost patience. A pace of ½ mile an hour may be too swift and a trip longer than 4 miles too rigorous. Probably he must be carried part of the time, but aside from the fact parents may find the weight more than they can bear comfortably, the lump typically grows bored and wants to get down and walk—or rather stumble. A warning about piggyback rides: they eliminate the child-carrier pack and are thought great fun by little darlings but place such pressure on daddy's neck muscles and nerves as literally to cause temporary paralysis. If extended hauling is planned a child-carrier is essential.

Paradoxically, parents may find it necessary to plan shorter trips (and certainly slower) with the toddler than with the infant. As compensation, none of the special gear is required and packs thus are lighter. They are, that is, if momma doesn't lose her head piling up shirts and pants, skirts and shoes, sweaters and mufflers and pajamas. If momma doesn't know it daddy must sternly inform her: the toddler is no longer a baby and needs as much clothing as an adult but no more—with the sole major exception of one or two complete changes for when he falls in a creek, and moments later a second. Oversolicitous, overloading mommas are a major cause of back trouble among daddies.

Many toddlers, though long since potty-trained, continue to be inveterate bed-wetters. Parents may try such devices as withholding liquids past suppertime and routing the kid out periodically in the night but nothing works. The best solution is *not* to have the bed-wetter sleep in momma's bag but in his own bag filled with polyester, which dries quicker than down and unlike down insulates even when wet.

For all the difficulties of the toddler age it is a most exciting family era: fresh young imaginations are stimulated by the richness around them—and their visions can at least be glimpsed by jaded elders.

One time a 2½-year-old boy spent a whole afternoon sitting all by himself on a grassy tussock a few feet from the shore of a meadow pond, dabbling a stick in the water, totally absorbed, and when asked what he was doing said, "Sailing my boat." To what fantastic seas did he voyage?

And this is the age when trail country puts to shame the playgrounds built by recreation experts. A fallen log wedged between two trees becomes the most exciting teeter-totter ever; on being torn away to go home the kids ask, "Can we come back again? When? Next week?" Boulders become forts, snowfields toboggan slides, shallow alpine tarns the most-fun swimming and wading pools. Beautiful stones are gathered by the pound and hours spent combing bushes for mountain goat wool.

If, at this age, parents do not insist on too long, too tough trips, do not force incomprehensible adult destinations such as mountain summits and fishing-type lakes but learn to accept and enjoy the goals of kids, chances are another generation will be converted for life to the wildland way.

SELF-PROPELLED PACKS

Seen on the trail: a mother suffering under a huge load, a father collapsing under an enormous load, and their large, loutish kids running about pack-free and happy. Something has gone terribly wrong in this family. The loving daddy doubtless is the same guy who piggybacks his darlings up to the moment they make the high school football team.

Also seen on the trail: a small mountain of gear mysteriously in

motion, two legs protruding from the bottom—a self-propelled pack. Tender-hearted adults cry out in horror, drooling louts sneer, but in this family something has gone right.

At a certain age the child must pay the price. He outgrows momma's sleeping bag and needs his own. Though he doesn't require as many changes of clothing as when he fell in every creek, his body is bigger and clothes heavier. And he eats more, at least as much as an adult. Unless he starts sharing the burden the family backpacking becomes too painful for parents to endure.

What is that certain age? No absolute rule can be stated; obviously the size and sturdiness of the child are factors as well as parental attitude. It is important, however, not to wait too long, but rather to ease the kid into responsibilities gradually—by being saddled when too young to know what's happening he grows up with the stone and can't remember when it wasn't part of life.

Actually the average toddler, especially if he has older siblings, feels that to lack a pack is to be denied full membership in the family and demands one long before his folks think he's ready. In this case parents should be utterly permissive. Thus, at 3 or 4 the kid starts with a little rucksack containing perhaps a sweater and a toy. Inevitably the rucksack is taken over by a parent or sibling before the end of any long walk, but the precedent is established.

At 4 or 5 a child can proceed beyond tokenism. One time a girl of

this age was given strong motivation by being assigned the family's entire candy supply for a whole week and marched as proudly as if she were carrying Fort Knox; to be sure, the honor was yielded to an adult for the final miles of tough days.

At around 5 or 8 the self-propelled pack appears, the child carrying sleeping bag, clothing, and perhaps some food, no longer in a rucksack but a packframe-bag; again, part or all the load often is transferred to bigger backs before camp.

Year by year carrying capacity increases. But parents must not be misled by the youngster's apparently unlimited energy into overloading his growing, still-soft bones, lest in later years he suffer backpacker's backache.

At around 9 or 12 the child carries all his own gear plus a fair share of the food and parents begin to dream about hiking with steadily lighter packs. However, along about this age independence is declared and momma and daddy experience new tribulations.

For one, youngsters want to walk faster than the family bunch and discover the country by themselves. The freedom should be encouraged within limits, such as ordering kids to stick strictly to the trail and wait up at forks; stay close to the folks in confusing terrain; give a blast on the emergency whistle if lost or confused; don't fall into big rivers, over long cliffs, or otherwise get killed.

For another, children grow bored with parents and seek more exciting intertribal relationships. Inviting a pal on a hike adds a new dimension of fun for toddlers; with moody young teens the presence of a confidante may save the trip. Ideally, compatible families with compatible children (and above all compatible mothers, to avoid bloody debates on the proper way to raise kids) should be sought. But when two or more compatible families march into the wilds with their 2-20 compatible children they must maximize discipline in order not to render an entire valley uninhabitable to others. Particular attention must be given to sanitation, since the ordinary human takes a dozen years to learn the manners a cat does while still a kitten.

A few years more and no matter how closely momma clutches her baby he or she is gone with friends on his or her own adventures, perhaps to rejoin the old folks on family reunions. The pity is that just as daddy thought he had it made, a packmule or two at last thoroughly seasoned, they leave him in the lurch.

Well, there are always the grandchildren.

19:   ON INTO WINTER

MOST hikers confine their trail trips to summer, and for novices it's just as well, since wildlands then are friendliest and basics of walking and camping can be learned with least discomfort and danger.

Others, who love to see leaves budding in sudden warmth to the green exuberance of youth and turning in frost to the yellow-and-red glory of death, roam also in spring and fall; they gain not only different feelings but greater solitude. (Except during hunting season, when gun-shy pedestrians had best stick to National Parks or stay home.)

Relatively few think of winter as a time for hiking, yet the traditionally dark and dreary months can be, perhaps briefly, spectacularly bright and shining, and when somber and melancholy speak to the poet and philosopher perhaps more profoundly than the months of steady-glaring sun. Moreover, in winter the domain of wilderness expands enormously—if temporarily—beyond summer boundaries.

The following brief discussion does not amount to even the sketchiest of manuals on winter travel, but this book cannot conclude without at least suggesting to the beginner the opportunities that await once he broadens his horizons from a "hiking season" to the "hiking year."

BELOW SNOWLINE

In many parts of America—including the entire South and the Pacific Coast west of the mountains—snow is unknown or infrequent in lowlands and foothills and trails are open most if not all the winter.

Mainlanders are starting to realize that a few hours away by air lie the volcano slopes and subtropical forests of Hawaii, a hiking paradise every month of the year and magical over Christmas vacation.

Ocean beaches are never more exciting than in winter, and though the word is getting around, the January population of wave-swept sands still is a small fraction of that in July.

Winter is the height of the season in some Southwest deserts, and locals are meeting increasing numbers of strangers drawn from far away by the magnificence. Similarly, the semi-desert of the Columbia Plateau often offers delightful walks over rolling ridges and up secret canyons dusted by sun-bright snow while windward slopes of the Cascades, a couple hours away by car, are drenched by rain.

Winter hiking at sealevel

Not to be overlooked are low-elevation valleys extending deep into wild mountains and in a normal winter snow-free (and snowmobile-free) all but several weeks. This is the lonesome time there; even the roads, deserted by picnickers of summer and hunters of fall, offer quiet walks. Despite the camper-truck and vacation-trailer revolution of the past decade most auto campgrounds are comparatively empty and rarely does a walker feel crowded on the trails.

There are good reasons. In the latitude of Washington State at the winter solstice the sun is technically up just a bit more than 8 hours and is so low in the south that during cloudy weather the entire short day is twilight; on backpacks the camp evenings are almost as much of the trip as actual travel and tent fever may rage. More clothing and other equipment are required to stay warm and dry—safe from hypothermia. From beaches to mountains the storms are legendary for their grandeur and ferocity.

All in all, the beginner is wisest to sharpen skills in summer, then try spring and fall. But he should not forget winter.

Out in the grand white

OUT IN THE GRAND WHITE

As winter white expands and contracts, so most hikers retreat and advance. However, more and more of those who value lonesomeness are penetrating the snow frontier, whether on lightly-decorated hills near home or in high mountains where the deeply-buried landscape is totally transformed.

To be sure, North America currently is suffering a plague of snow-mobiles and though the proper medicine is obvious apparently some time must pass before the patient consents to be cured. Meanwhile, terrain too rough for machines or off-limits through administrative ruling or by law (as in the case of National Wilderness Areas) remains a land of surpassing white peace.

Again there are reasons. Snow country is blizzard country, ava-lanche country, hypothermia country. Yet with the right equipment and technique any hiker of average strength and determination can experience the vast quiet (of spirit, that is; winds may be loud, very loud).

BOOTING

The most elementary method of snow travel is booting, identical to trail-walking except for the surface differences, which range from minor to considerable.

A foot of early-winter fluff or slush impedes passage only slightly.

Into the winter woods at low elevations

An impenetrable midwinter crust permits a good pace—until it disintegrates and becomes bottomless in sunshine, warm wind, or rain. On a well-consolidated late-spring snowpack feet may sink to the ankles in cool morning—to the shins in hot afternoon.

When legs plunge knee-deep, as they jolly often do after a fresh snowfall, the death of a crust, or the creation by sun, wind, or rain of a snow swamp, the hiker progresses by "post-holing," a technique needing no explanation and deserving no recommendation; a strong party alternating leads may find ½ mile an hour an heroic pace.

Much snow-booting is so easy a hiker wonders, once he's tried it, why he ever shied away from the white. Even in the extremity of midwinter post-holing, though the effort demanded to get ¼ mile from the plowed highway perhaps exceeds that of 4 miles on bare trail, the reward may well be 16 times greater, may transport one into faery. In such ranges as the Cascades, fanatic post-holers begin their travels of high valleys and ridges in April, 2-3 months earlier than conservatives who wait for trails to turn from white to brown. Fanaticism pays.

SNOWSHOEING

When a hiker sinks to the knee, the hip, the waist, the chest, booting is definitely inferior to webbing. A half-century ago snowshoes rather abruptly gave way to skis in the favor of American recreationists and for decades were virtually extinct. Then, with the general increase in every variety of winter outdoor activity, reflecting the need of urban people to seek the solace of nature not merely in summer but in all seasons, webs made a comeback, were improved in design, and now are more popular than ever.

Snowshoeing is a go-anywhere sport, at the most advanced becoming winter mountaineering. The main attraction, however, is simplic-

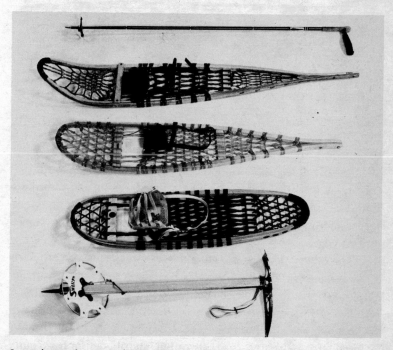

Several popular snowshoe styles. For balance, snowshoers ordinarily use either a ski pole or an ice ax with "basket" attached

ity. The only significant addition to summer gear is a pair of snowshoes costing about $50 (rentals available at many mountain shops) and probably one or two ski poles.

No extended training is necessary; with experience a hiker learns refinements but his very first day he can strap on the shoes and go for miles and after a few trial runs is ready to hoist pack on back and penetrate deep into winter wildlands.

For discussions of equipment and technique see the Appendix.

CROSS-COUNTRY SKIING

Until several years ago the original form of skiing, cross-country touring, had been so overwhelmed in America by downhill running

Equipment for cross-country skiing: pole, Nordic ski and boot, spare tip, blowtorch (for waxing), waxing kit, scraper. Ordinary hiking gear completes the outfit

as to be little more than a memory. Even the few who kept the spark alive mainly used Alpine equipment which had evolved for tow-hill conditions, was ill-suited to touring in mixed terrain, and caused discouraging problems. Then, in the late 1960s, the old Nordic skis returned to America in force and the cross-country revolution (or reaction) began.

Cross-country skiing is a quite different sport from that of the resorts, lacking the day-long succession of high-speed thrills and/or ballet-like patterns, and of course the effortless ascents and the mass socializing. In compensation? Its own delicate grace, the infinity of virgin white, and quiet, and wildness.

In addition, with no lift tickets to buy and the entire basic outfit of Nordic skis, boots, waxing kit, and incidentals costing only some

$100 or so, cross-country can be enjoyed by those who have been priced off the tow-hills.

Finally, the technique, though not so elementary as snowshoeing, is far less complex than downhill running. Under expert tutelage a novice can learn enough on his first outing to tour many miles. In contrast to snowshoers, who do well to make 2 miles an hour and 10 miles a day, cross-country skiers of just average strength and competence often slide along at 4 miles an hour on the flat, much faster on slopes, and in proper terrain consider 20 miles merely an average day.

Incidentally, cross-country is a great family sport. Kids can be equipped at relatively small expense and almost invariably they take to it eagerly and gleefully, often having much more fun and presenting fewer problems than when trail hiking.

For texts on equipment and technique see the Appendix.

CAMPING

Booters, snowshoers, cross-country skiers all may wish to enlarge their knowledge of winter to include nights as well as days. Since

pure water is all around, by use of a lightweight backpacker's snow shovel camp can be made anywhere, excavating a flat bed, digging or molding tables and chairs and windbreaks—and in spring the architecture melts, leaving no evidence of the stay, no damage to underlying plants. With the equipment described in earlier chapters snow camping can be as comfortable as on bare ground, and in many areas of American nowadays offers the only guaranteed opportunity to get absolutely away from mobs.

AN EARTH FOR ALL SEASONS

Many hikers hibernate in winter, doing the work of the world so they may vacation in summer with a clear conscience. But it's too bad for a person who loves the trail country to know it in only one season, to miss the full experience of nature from birth to maturity to wearying unto death—the complete cycle of life.

Some wildlanders do not accept the analogy of winter as death. For them, being of a classical temper as opposed to flower-loving romantics, winter is the uncluttered season, the season of purest wilderness, the best time of year.

20:

THE NEW ETHIC

AND now a brief word from our sponsor—namely, the Earth.

The purpose of preceding chapters is to help the beginning hiker enjoy opportunities presented by trail country. But hear this, beginners and veterans alike: no one has a right to the opportunities unless he accepts the accompanying responsibilities.

When man's numbers were few and his strength small he took an underdog's pride in extending the frontiers of civilization; history books are full of stories boasting how he came, saw, conquered. Now there are no true frontiers left this side of Mars but the conqueror complex persists and man the overdog still brags about slashing highways through jungles and tundra, damming rivers into tame ponds, tearing down mountains and trucking them to the smelter, cutting trees a thousand years old and slicing them into lumber and pulp.

Certainly man must use the resources of Earth to live. But the time has passed when he should commit any act of destruction—no matter how necessary it may be judged—with boastful pride, without deep regret. (Not dedication services but funeral ceremonies are appropriate when a river-killing dam is completed.) And surely if he approaches nature with reverence he finds many "necessary" projects really are not, having been planned by rut-bound timeservers who

335

keep doing what they've always done because they don't know how to do anything else, designed by engineers who do what they're paid to do and keep their mouths shut because there is no place else to get a job, and pushed by pork-barrel politicians, Chamber of Commerce

boosters, and newspaper editorialists purely in the Manifest Destiny belief that what *can* be done *must* be done. (Why build bombs if we can't now and then at least blow up Amchitka?)

Business and industry exploit nature, extracting raw materials to feed the machines of civilization. Forgetting for the moment the recreationist as consumer of the products of those machines, he also exploits nature in the course of escaping that civilization.

However, there is a difference between panzer-style, blitzkrieg recreationists and light walkers who take only photographs, leave only footprints. Some of the ways a hiker can and must reduce his impact have been discussed earlier: carrying out garbage—using wood fires sparingly and carefully if at all—not cutting boughs—sleeping on bare dirt rather than flowers or heather—avoiding water pollution. From these sample precautions and the attitude they reflect, others can be deduced.

In remote wildlands, infrequently visited, many old freedoms may yet be exercised with good conscience. But in popular hiking areas

the life systems are literally being loved to death. Though the weight of 10,000 boots does not compare to that of a single bulldozer, or the noise of a valleyful of shrieking children to that of a military jet breaking the sound barrier, still, where population pressure is heavy, new and stricter regulations are becoming essential.

Fishermen long have been accustomed to game protectors issuing citations for illegal fishing, the goal being to save the fish and thus the sport. Hikers now griping at being cited for illegal camping must ask which is better: for every hiker to enjoy a flower garden by looking, or for a few freedom-lovers to sleep on it and make another patch of bare dirt? From necessity, plans are in preparation to close certain places even to day hiking for the years required to let ecosystems recover from generations of abuse.

Surely it is obvious that since the time has arrived for such drastic measures in some areas that in many others any heavier recreational use of the land than hiking is intolerable. Machines are banned from National Wilderness Areas and trails in National Parks but most of the world is theirs; eventually, to strike a balance, all the quiet-destroyers, land-wreckers—the trailbike, the snowmobile, the all-terrain-vehicle, the swamp buggy, the hovercraft, the dune buggy, the jeep—must be banned from all trails, all beaches, all off-road expanses of desert and prairie and tundra. Similarly, back-country landings by airplanes and helicopters must end and overflights of wildlands and parklands become less rather than more common. And motorboats, which own virtually all the waterways of America, must yield some of their domain to craft propelled by oars, paddles, and sails.

Something there is in nature that does not like a machine. Something there is in every machine-riding man that cannot let nature be.

What about that old friend of man, the horse (and mule, and burro)? A single horse may punish the soil and plants more than any hundred hikers and thus the use of pack and riding animals is being limited in some areas, banned in others. For an unknown number of years to come there will be room in wildlands for horsemen who handle stock discreetly; there is no room now for those who stake their beasts in lakes, streams, and gardens, carry chainsaws and double-bitted axes the better to hack at the landscape, and dump heaps of garbage.

And what of that other old friend, the dog? Pets are barred from National Park trails lest they disturb wildlife. Sad to say, even where not officially forbidden their presence is sometimes questionable; one family's beloved companion may be, to a family camped nearby, a yapping, vicious mutt.

And what of that old symbol of the wilderness man, the gun? The carrying of guns on hiking trips must absolutely, without exception, be condemned. Guns are not needed for self-defense, the common excuse; in reality they are used solely for "plinking." Aside from the toll of birds, marmots, rockchucks, chipmunks, and trail signs, gunshots are as ruinous to the wilderness mood of quieter travelers as the racket of a trailbike or helicopter. Guns are banned from National Parks; they should be banned from National Wilderness Areas and every popular trail system. If this be sedition, make the most of it, all you pistol-packing plinkers out there: the only weapon any hiker should carry is a pocket knife.

In the end only radical steps taken by the entire society, not alone by harassed rangers and the pressure groups which work with and on them, will halt the overcrowding and crushing of back country by recreationists. Zero population growth is essential for the salvation of wilderness as well as civilization itself, and for the sake of both must be not a distant vision but a goal to be achieved within the lifetime of some who now read these pages. A considerable body of expert opinion goes farther, says the present quality of human life cannot be sustained, much less improved, unless the quantity is sharply reduced, and to cite one nation as example, says the population of the United States must eventually be lowered to that of 1920.

In the interim hikers must accept increasing restrictions on their freedom: use of wildlands inevitably will be rationed by the granting of permits obtained by advance application; land managers, having determined the "carrying capacity" of a certain ecosystem is X number of people, will ask the $X+1$ applicant to choose another destination. Land managers are as distressed as hikers at the prospect. But what good to let 1000 hikers into a once-gorgeous meadow, if they arrive to find only bootprints in the mud? Better that 100 people see a living meadow and the 900 wait their turn.

Bitter medicine, all this, especially for the respectful hiker who walks quietly, camps on dirt, cooks on a stove, carries out garbage, doesn't pick flowers or plink chipmunks or smash mushrooms or carry away souvenirs and thus hurts the land a twentieth as much as an arrogant woodcrafter, a hundredth as much as a motorcycle hoodlum. The self-interest of every hiker who wishes to continue as long as possible to walk his favorite trails demands that he travel with the utmost delicacy, and demands further that he abandon qualms about being a busybody and develop the habit of calmly but firmly lecturing strangers observed violating the laws of nature and man, that he rejoice in the name of "fink" and cooperate fully with rangers in apprehending and prosecuting eco-criminals.

Ecology, the study of life systems and the inter-relationships of all their components, should be the hiker's passion, not merely to enrich his pleasure but so he may understand the functioning of individ-

340

ual ecosystems and how to fit into them as unobtrusively as possible.

The hiker should be a birdwatcher and animal-watcher and bug-watcher. He should be curious about rocks and minerals and note the slow process by which soil is created. And gain a feel for the dynamic balance of a river, of a glacier, and how they carve valleys. And grow intimate with trees and flowers, mosses and lichens, fungi and molds. And learn the meaning of a progression of clouds, a change in winds, and the relationship of the atmosphere to the mantle of living green and underlying rocks. And at night he should look out to the moon and stars and deeply comprehend this is the only Earth we ever will have.

There is more to learn. The few remaining bits and pieces of wilderness cannot be preserved unless the whole Earth is preserved. The last half of the 20th century and the first half of the 21st will be known in history books of the future (if any) as the Crisis Era, when man's ingenuity and appetite and pure, plundering, crushing, numbers drove him dangerously out of balance with his sustaining life-systems. In recent years man's awareness of the peril to the Earth and thus himself has grown, but not so rapidly as the momentum of destruction.

Consider the example of the trailbike, virtually nonexistent a dozen years ago and in this short time blighting most of America not already blighted by the automobile. But the trailbike is a no-see-um alongside the Earth-wreckers insanely feeding an insane civilization —from which come the sanity-seeking, light-walking hikers who love the land, but being in the main relatively affluent feel free to treat aluminum and poly and nylon and paper and gasoline and butane as if they were cheap, never thinking of the poisoned rivers and oceans and skies and the depleted and non-renewable ore bodies and fossil-fuel reserves.

It is not enough to walk trails lightly. To save the wilderness each hiker must work for zero population growth, minimum energy consumption, complete recycling of resources, and follow the old New England adage:

> Eat it up.
> Wear it out.

Make it do.

Do without.

To conclude by repeating, no one has a right to the trails unless he accepts personal responsibility for their preservation.

An individual can do much alone by writing letters to newspapers and public officials, but to gain maximum leverage in a democracy which operates through pressure groups must add his voice and dollars to one or more organizations with programs in conservation, preservation, environmentalism, ecology, and the like. There now are thousands of these in America and more by the month and hardly a community in the land lacks action groups easily found and joined by agitated citizens. But in addition to local or regional matters each person should connect himself to more basic issues by joining such an organization as the Sierra Club, founded by John Muir and national in scope (Mills Tower, San Francisco, California 94104), or Friends of the Earth, founded by David Brower, national and international in its activities and publisher of the eco-newspaper, *Not Man Apart* (529 Commercial St., San Francisco, California 94111).

A hiker and backpacker must be a giver as well as a taker, a saver as well as a user, if he is to be a full, responsible citizen of the wild country, the trail country, the Earth.

APPENDIX: SOME RECOMMENDED READING

UNTIL becoming involved in this book my knowledge of the purely hiking (as distinguished from climbing and mountaineering) literature was limited pretty much to the 1938 edition of the *Boy Scout Handbook* and occasional magazine articles. Having completed a first draft, for which the only research was in the minds of men and women and children I knew personally and a stack of mountain shop catalogs 5½ inches thick, I thought it might be well to see what the other fellows had been up to and dug into a 13½-inch pile of materials suggested by this person or that.

By 1975, when time came for a thorough revision, I'd accumulated a yard and a half of new books and magazine articles.

The following rambling notes are decidedly uncomprehensive, covering naught by the 13½ inches plus a foot or so of specialized works I knew already, plus the new yard and a half. No attempt has been made to provide anything resembling a full bibliography, which would run to better than a mile, but merely to suggest sources of information on subjects I've not treated.

344

For further reading the hiker should check mountain shops, whose book sections are not 100 percent garbage-free but usually are stocked with a degree of discrimination. (And also a degree of prejudice, fine works often ignored because of owners' pet peeves.) A large general bookstore typically carries a wider selection, displaying everything published, excellent or execrable, and letting the public choose. Caveat emptor.

MAGAZINES

Aside from whatever else they may offer, magazines are useful for keeping up with the latest developments in equipment, both through articles and ads.

Most climbing and hiking clubs publish journals or magazines of local, regional, or in a few cases, national interest; for a close view of any given province of American trail country a person does well to read the publications of its habitual travelers.

Of the independent walking-oriented magazines with national circulation the oldest (since 1954) is *Summit* (Big Bear Lake, California 92315). Newer on the scene are *Backpacker* (28 West 44th Street, New York City 10036), *Wilderness Camping* (1654 Central Avenue, Albany, New York 12205), and *Mountain Gazette* (2025 York Street, Denver, Colorado 80205). All focus totally or considerably on hiking; some mix in more or less about climbing, which is the sole concern of several other current magazines.

BOOKS—GENERAL

Until a couple of decades ago a beginning hiker seeking helpful hints found that his only resources were volumes in the woodcrafter tradition, as best exemplified by Horace Kephart's *Camping and Woodcraft* (Macmillan, New York, 1921), the classic manual on how to shape up the landscape in the way of the pioneer. A novice may wish to browse the historically fascinating woodcrafter literature; understanding how hard the old-timers had to work with crude equipment to be comfortable gives perspective on today's pampered hiking. Despite the maxim that "woodcraft is dead," during a recent visit to a large Seattle bookstore I found 50 books on the subject, including some that were brand-new. Amazing!

The first genuinely modern book on hiking, and the first derived from Western experience (the Sierra almost exclusively) was *Going Light With Backpack and Burro,* edited by David Brower (Sierra Club, San Francisco, 1951). The paperback version, *Sierra Club Wilderness Handbook* (Ballantine-Sierra, New York, 1971) is patchily updated.

Mountaineering: The Freedom of the Hills, by the Climbing Committee of The Mountaineers (The Mountaineers, Seattle, first edition 1960, third edition 1974), was the first comprehensive description of American mountaineering and also the first modern treatment of rough-country backpacking; it remains valuable to hikers as well as climbers.

In the 1960s arrived *Backpacking,* by R. C. Rethmel (Burgess, Minneapolis, fifth edition 1974) and *The Complete Walker,* by Colin Fletcher (Knopf, New York, second edition 1974). Though both books originally drew mainly from experience in the Southwest and/or the Sierra, the new editions have broadened horizons. Both have earned continuing status as bestsellers.

Then, in 1972, the Great Explosion. Unbeknownst to me and REI, as we were approaching press with this book a multitude of other manuscripts were in progress. On my last bookstore inspection I found 25 books devoted to the fundamentals of backpacking. I despair at even listing them all; anyway, each year there will be more and more. Of those I've read or skimmed, a half-dozen strike me as first-rate, contributing fresh insights useful to a novice. Another half-dozen are decent enough but say nothing new, are uninspired rehashes. A dozen are so full of stuff and nonsense they should be treated as penitentiary offenses.

5: BUGS AND BEASTS AND SERPENTS

The Complete Walker discusses rattlesnakes at length, crediting as a major source *Rattlesnakes: Their Habits, Life Histories, and Influence on Mankind,* by Laurence M. Klauber (University of California, Berkeley, 1956).

Medicine for Mountaineering (see below) is definitive on treatment for snakebite.

6: DANGER!

Outdoor Living: Problems, Solutions, Guidelines, edited by Eugene H. Fear, assisted by John Simac and Everett Lasher (Tacoma Mountain Rescue Council, Tacoma, 1970) is the finest survival manual for backpackers I've seen, encyclopedic in its coverage of hazards in every realm of hiking terrain from snow to deserts. Quite similar is *Surviving the Unexpected Wilderness Emergency,* by Gene Fear (Survival Education Association, Tacoma, 1974).

Accidents in North American Mountaineering (American Alpine Club, New York, published annually) includes hiking accidents in mountainous terrain; knowing how other people have gotten into trouble can help a hiker stay out of it.

7: ASSEMBLING THE OUTFIT

If no satisfactory outdoor suppliers are located convenient to a hiker's home, the best way to find one is to buy several copies of hiking/climbing magazines, look for ads of mountain shops, and write for their catalogs.

Lightweight Camping Equipment and How to Make It, by Gerry Cunningham and Margaret Hansson (Colorado Outdoor Sports, Denver) guides the handy hiker seeking to save money by doing it himself.

14: FOOD

More has been written about food than all other aspects of backpacking combined. Most of the books listed above have an enormous lot to say. In addition there are a score or more booklets and books devoted specifically and entirely to wildland cookery.

The several *Stalking* books by Euell Gibbon (David McKay, New York, 1962 and 1964) are delightful story-style introductions to enlivening the diet with wild foods. The edible plants native to various parts of America are described in a number of regional booklets; see local bookstores and mountain shops.

Hikers who object to chemicalized foods may patronize the health-food stores found in most communities, taking due care not to be victimized by the superstitious mumbo-jumbo and pure ripoffs which are the stock-in-trade of some. A few mountain shops now feature "natural food" departments; doubtless more will in future.

15: ESSENTIALS

Mountaineering First Aid, by Dick Mitchell (The Mountaineers, Seattle, 1972) describes contents and use of the first aid kit and treatment of common injuries, ailments, and miseries.

Medicine for Mountaineering, by James A. Wilkerson and others (The Mountaineers, Seattle, 1967) is a detailed "doctor book" written by physicians with experience in many mountain ranges of the world and covering not only first but second aid.

16: ROUTEFINDING

Be Expert with Map and Compass, by Bjorn Kjellstrom (American Orienteering Service, La Porte, Indiana, revised edition 1967) starts from scratch and proceeds to methods as advanced as the average hiker ever is likely to need.

Scores of guidebooks describe American trail country. Some mountain shops attempt to stock guides for the entire nation but most concentrate on their immediate region; the fullest selection for any given area thus is found in a local shop.

17: WHEN THE WAY GROWS ROUGH

Freedom of the Hills is the basic text for the cross-country rambler, the recommended reference for use of ice ax and "hiking rope" and for travel on rock and snow and other rough terrain.

19: ON INTO WINTER

Two comprehensive treatments of snowshoes and related gear and the technique of webbing and winter travel are *Snowshoeing,* by Gene Prater (The Mountaineers, Seattle, 1975) and *The Snowshoe Book,* by William Osgood and Leslie Hurley (The Stephen Greene Press, Brattleboro, Vermont, 1971).

Three books are essential for the cross-country skier: *The New Cross-Country Ski Book,* by John Caldwell (Stephen Greene, Brattleboro, Vermont, 1971); *Nordic Touring and Cross-Country Skiing,* by Michael Brady (Dreyers Fortag, Oslo, Norway, 1971); and *Ski Waxing* by Michael Brady and Lorns O. Skjemstad (distributed by Eiger Mountain Sports, 1971). A fourth is fun: *The Cross-Country Ski, Cook, Look, and Pleasure Book,* by Hal Painter (Wilderness Press, Berkeley, 1973).

Freedom of the Hills has thorough chapters on snowcraft and avalanches.

ABC of Avalanches, by Ed LaChapelle (Colorado Outdoor Sports, Denver, revised edition 1969) is a pocket summary by the outstanding American expert and should be carried on every snow trip.

20: THE NEW ETHIC

The books, magazines, newspapers, journals, and newsletters on ecology, the environment, conservation, and preservation number in the thousands. If for no other reason than to receive their publications the hiker should join the Sierra Club, Audubon Society, Wilderness Society, National Parks Association, Canadian Nature Federation, and/or other conservation groups.

Alone in its field as a national/international newspaper is *Not Man Apart,* published by Friends of the Earth, 529 Commercial Street, San Francisco, California 94111.

For books on rocks and minerals, geomorphology, flowers, trees, mosses, ferns, birds, fish, animals and their tracks, insects and arachnids, weather, and stars, visit bookstores and mountain shops.

HARVEY MANNING, wildland backpacker since the 1930's, is the editor of *Mountaineering: The Freedom of the Hills* and the author of *The Wild Cascades: Forgotten Parkland, The North Cascades National Park,* and six other books on hiking, climbing, and conservation. He is editor of *The Wild Cascades,* magazine of the North Cascades Conservation Council, and Northwest editor of *Not Man Apart,* international eco-newspaper of the Friends of the Earth.

KEITH GUNNAR, freelance photographer, has hiked and climbed from Alaska to Peru, New Zealand to the Alps, and throughout the American West. His work has been published in several books and numerous magazines.

BOB CRAM, freelance commercial artist, is well-known among climbers for his lively contribution to *Mountaineering: The Freedom of the Hills* and among skiers for his cartoons in books and magazines and as host of a long-running Northwest television program.

VINTAGE POLITICAL SCIENCE
AND SOCIAL CRITICISM